THE
WORTH
OF
WAR

ALSO BY BENJAMIN GINSBERG

The Value of Violence

THE
WORTH
OF
WAR

BENJAMIN GINSBERG

Prometheus Books

59 John Glenn Drive
Amherst, New York 14228

Published 2014 by Prometheus Books

Cover design by Jacqueline Nasso Cooke

Inquiries should be addressed to
Prometheus Books
59 John Glenn Drive
Amherst, New York 14228
VOICE: 716–691–0133
FAX: 716–691–0137
WWW.PROMETHEUSBOOKS.COM

18 17 16 15 14   5 4 3 2 1

Library of Congress Cataloging-in-Publication Data

Ginsberg, Benjamin.
    The worth of war / Benjamin Ginsberg.
        pages cm
    Includes bibliographical references and index.
    ISBN 978-1-61614-950-5 (hardback) — ISBN 978-1-61614-951-2 (ebook)
    1. War—Economic aspects. 2. War and society. 3. Economic development.
I. Title.

HC79.D4G534 2014
303.6'6—dc23
                                                                        2014012136

Printed in the United States of America

For Sandy

CONTENTS

INTRODUCTION

WAR, PEACE, AND PROGRESS

Peace and progress are often seen as being fundamentally related to one another. The conventional view of this relationship is that human progress is dependent upon domestic and international peace. From this perspective, eras of tranquility are, unfortunately, interrupted by retrogressive periods of conflict and warfare from which civilization must recover in order to resume its onward march. In his famous nineteenth-century work, *Progress and Poverty*, the political economist Henry George summarized this idea, saying, "If we compare society to a boat, we see its progress is not based on the total exertion of the crew. Rather, it depends only on exertion devoted to propelling it. The total is reduced by any force expended on bailing, or fighting among themselves, or pulling in different directions."[1] Similarly, in his well-known essay, *War and Progress*, historian John U. Neff sought to show that war was an impediment to and interruption of mankind's economic and moral development. Neff asserts, for example, that Europe's "general prosperity" at the close of the Middle Ages came to a rapid end because of "fighting" that "grew fiercer and more contentious" in the sixteenth century.[2]

This perspective, unfortunately, seems to ignore the fact that many of the world's great centers of science, technology, culture, and civilization were also great military and imperial powers, and were frequently engaged in armed conflicts with their neighbors. We might consider such examples as the Egyptian, Chinese, and Roman empires, ancient Athens, the British empire, and the contemporary United States. Each of these hegemonic powers developed a high culture, a dynamic economy, became a center of scientific learning, and engaged in many wars.

With the current exception of the United States, of course, none of these regimes exists today. One might ask, however, for how long these regimes would have existed if not for their military prowess—or if they would have been created at all. The United States would certainly never have come into being. It was the product of an exceedingly bloody revolution and a successful French attack on British forces in North America. Moreover, according to historian Geoffrey Perret, the continuing existence of the United States has been marked by more wars than have been fought by any other state on the face of the earth.[3]

The unpleasant fact is that although war is terrible and brutal, we should not assume that all its consequences are abhorrent. For better or worse, the world that we know, including its national borders, modes of thought, technologies, and forms of governance were shaped by war. In all likelihood, this world will eventually be unmade by war. A Roman maxim held that, *purgamenta hujus mundi sunt tria, pestis, bellum, et frateria.* The world is purified by three means: by plague, by war, and by monastic seclusion. I confess to being somewhat dubious about the value of monastic seclusion, but war and plague can certainly be important.[4]

War is a powerful instrument of social and political change. War can destroy established states and societies and pave the way for new ones. To be sure, not all change is progress, but all progress requires change. Indeed, rather than serve as retrogressive interruptions, war and preparation for war have been great drivers of human progress. As we shall see, war is a powerful antidote to primitive or irrational thinking, war promotes technological progress, war promotes economic development, and, perhaps surprisingly, war tends to mitigate the cruelty inherent in the process of government.

While watching his troops repulse a Union attack during the 1862 Battle of Fredericksburg, General Robert E. Lee is said to have remarked to his subordinate, General James Longstreet, "It is well that war is so terrible, otherwise we should grow too fond of it." War is terrible and we should not grow fond of it. Yet, our terror of war also should not prevent us from giving some consideration to its role and place in human societies.

As we shall see below, war selects for and promotes certain features of societies that are generally held to represent progressive modes of thought and action. These include rationalism, technological and economic development, and less harsh modes of government. One might imagine other ways of defining progress. Perhaps we should refrain from valorizing a Western model of progress. But it is the same model that seems to be preferred by most of those with more pacifist inclinations. They simply aver that peace is the critical ingredient for progress along more or less these same dimensions.[5]

Before I am accused of committing the sin of Social Darwinism (recently rediscovered by President Obama), let me freely confess to having some such tendencies.[6] Indeed, at the risk of being excommunicated from the faculty club and consigned to a cell in Purgatory alongside the late Herbert Spencer, I will confess to being guilty of both Social Darwinism and Lamarckism. That is, consistent with the neo-Lamarckian view articulated by the evolutionary economist Richard R. Nelson, I take the position that innovations often come about from conscious, and intelligent, efforts to find better ways of doing something.[7] Second, with apologies to President Obama, I take the neo-Darwinist position that competition among groups will over time reveal whether new practices or old ways of doing things are more efficient and effective. Third, again following the neo-Lamarckian model, I believe that more efficient and effective innovations and practices can be taught to or imitated by others in the broader society.

Where I perhaps take matters a step further than most Darwinians and Lamarckians are willing to admit, at least in polite academic company, is on the subject of war. For Social Darwinians and, to some extent, neo-Lamarckians, competition is the necessary catalyst that drives social innovation. Better ways of doing things become evident only when compared to or entered into competition with worse ways of doing things. The problem is that societies, more often than not, seek to restrain potentially useful competition by adopting various sorts of protectionist policies. Some work to protect the power of a privileged leadership clique or social class against potential competitors; some use legislation to protect established merchants and manufacturers from foreign and domestic rivals; some offer job security for workers who might be threatened by more efficient labor; some assert that various principles of social justice and equality should trump unrestrained social or market competition. "Established" religions are, in some nations, protected from the efforts of rival faiths to recruit adherents. While many of these claims may have merit, policies based upon such principles restrain competition and block innovation. As a result, inefficient firms, inept governments, and corrupt religious establishments have little reason to change their ways.

It is at this point in the discussion that war makes its admittedly ugly appearance. Despite humanity's claims that it is diligently seeking ways to prevent war, armed conflict seems quite ubiquitous. Even periods when the incidence of war appears to diminish are reliably followed by periods of intense conflict. Armed conflict, unlike more peaceful economic or social competition, cannot simply be legislated out of existence. War, moreover, is the most severe form of competition. It can, indeed, pose an existential threat to a society, placing it under extreme pressure to disregard the protectionist claims of established groups and interests. As we shall see below, many states have felt compelled to adopt new technologies as well as political and economic practices because not to have done so would have left them at a military disadvantage and might, in fact, have threatened their continued existence. Even cherished traditions and beliefs can be subject to re-examination and revision in wartime. States that limited voting rights to men and viewed women as intellectually unfit to take part in politics, for example, rethought their priorities when the pressures of war compelled them to seek the support of women. Whatever philosophical positions had justified the original state of affairs were discarded in the face of brutal armed struggle.

Of course, even in the teeth of war, some societies are resistant to change and remain unable or unwilling to identify or copy better ways of doing things. This may be one reason that most of the states, societies, and peoples that emerged at one time or another over the past several millennia no longer exist.

As we shall see, one important realm in which war is unlikely to produce progress is that of political freedom. War is, of course, sometimes necessary to break the chains of an oppressed or enslaved people. Americans should be the last to overlook this fact. In a broader sense, however, war has corrosive effects upon political freedom within those states prone to engage in frequent hostilities. War, as the late Charles Tilly often reminded us, tends to enhance state power. War makes states, building administrative capabilities and turning republics into empires. What even Tilly did not fully explore is that, once enlarged, state power can be turned inward in what amounts to a perverse process of beating swords into very malign plowshares. Americans are, unfortunately, currently witnessing this phenomenon first hand.

In writing this book I benefitted from discussions with Matthew Crenson, Stephen David, Robert Kargon, and David Satter. I was happy to have another opportunity to work with an excellent editor, Stephen Mitchell and, as always, my wonderful agent, Claire Gerus. And, for their efforts on the book's behalf, I thank Ian Birnbaum, Jade Zora Scibilia, Laura Shelley, Melissa Raé Shofner, and Catherine Roberts-Abel.

CHAPTER 1

WAR AS AN AGENT OF RATIONALITY

Organized warfare is among the most common and persistent of human activities.[1] Yet, war is usually said to be irrational, even a manifestation of collective insanity. In his eloquent 1967 "Beyond Vietnam" speech at Riverside Church in New York, for example, Dr. Martin Luther King Jr. declared, "Somehow this madness [of war] must cease." War is brutal but it would, nevertheless, be incorrect to say that war generally exemplifies or fosters irrational thinking. Quite the contrary. As terrible as it is, war and the possibility of war exert considerable pressure upon societies to think and plan logically in order to protect their security interests and, sometimes, their very existence. War, as Thucydides remarked, is a harsh teacher. Those societies unable or unwilling to engage in logical thinking and planning are not likely to survive what might be called the audit of war. Over time, moreover, war not only promotes rational thought in the security sphere but produces a spillover effect into other realms, as well. The fields of planning and engineering, for example, as well as bureaucratic forms of organization, all have military roots. Indeed, far from representing or promoting irrational thinking, war tests the validity of assumptions, penalizes errors in judgment and, above all, severely punishes those who engage in actions based upon fanciful or magical thinking.

Consider the example of the Lakota "Ghost Shirt." During the 1880s, some members of the Lakota Sioux came to practice a version of the "Ghost Dance" ritual they believed would restore the power and prominence of Native Americans and halt the spread of white settlements. Associated with this ritual was the wearing of Ghost Shirts, apparently inspired by Mormon Temple garments, that were supposed to possess magical properties, including the ability to stop bullets. A battle between a band of Lakota and a contingent of heavily armed US cavalry troopers culminated in the infamous Wounded Knee Massacre of 1890, the last battle of America's so-called Indian Wars. Whatever else they may have demonstrated, the carbines of the cavalry rather conclusively proved that religious rituals and Ghost Shirts offered no protection from bullets. In this example, war definitively refuted a form of magical thinking that had been gaining adherents among Native American tribes for a number of years. Absent the harsh audit of war, the magic of the Ghost Dance apparently had been attractive and plausible to tens of thousands of individuals. After the Wounded Knee battle, Ghost Dancing and magical Ghost Shirts fell from favor, having failed a rather significant reality test.

Delusory thinking may, as in the foregoing example, derive from religious sources, but it is certainly not limited to religious roots. Political leaders and policy makers, to say nothing of ordinary citizens, have also been known to engage in what might be seen as mundane forms of magical thinking. These are characterized by a rigid adherence to beliefs and preconceptions without evidence or even despite strong evidence to the contrary, a propensity to evaluate information through the lens of belief rather than the converse, a tendency to act upon the basis of accepted dogmas rather than objective facts, and an effort to achieve impossible goals. These secular or mundane forms of magical thought are often expressed as blind faith in leaders, stubborn adherence to ideologies, and fervid loyalty to institutions and institutional norms. Such beliefs are effectively ensorcelled and can be extremely resistant to rational examination. A minor but well-known example of this sort of magical thinking is the case of partisanship in the United States. Even America's rather shopworn Democratic and Republican parties seem to have many zealous adherents. Quite a few of these partisan loyalists are more likely to evaluate information through the lens or perceptual screen of their own party identification than to reevaluate their party affiliation on the basis of events and facts.[2] Reflexive partisan loyalty is said to lead some Americans to vote against their own objective economic or other interests.[3]

THE SECULAR SOURCES OF POLITICAL MAGIC

Humans are quite capable of many forms of foolish and fantastic thinking. Superstitions, for example, are widespread among Americans. Some take seriously the idea of demons and witches. Many claim to perceive causal forces in accidental events, impute supernatural or charismatic agency to mundane phenomena, and are convinced they apprehend mystical patterns in random occurrences. Some psychologists have argued that this tendency is hardwired into the human brain.[4] Many, if not most, superstitions are harmless. A few moments of prayer can provide comfort and catharsis. A lucky charm or amulet can offer comfort to a frightened person.

Unfortunately, in addition to harmless personal superstitions, millions of individuals are also willing to accept the various fantasies often devised by political elites to justify their own efforts to secure or retain power. Political life is filled with both secular and religious dogmas that seem dubious, even nonsensical, when viewed from the outside but make perfect sense when understood as creeds espoused by some ruling group to justify its grip on power. Such belief systems could be said to possess political but not objective validity.

Political leaders know that many ordinary individuals can easily become enthralled by high-minded if vacuous ideals, religious ideas, communal or national loyalties, or, for that matter, racial and ethnic hatreds. Elites, often cynically, see in such ideas powerful tools for mobilizing and maintaining popular followings. Thus, even elites whose own piety or patriotic commitments, for example, are weak may find reason to publicly preach religion and nationalism. In the United States, in recent years, many Republicans have publicly courted the support of religious conservatives while privately calling them "goofy" or "the nuts."[5] So often in politics, principles serve as vehicles for interests.

Take, for example the Incan practice of ancestor worship. The Incas believed that their apparently dead rulers were actually immortal. The carefully preserved mummies of these rulers, moreover, retained property rights. Because of this belief a substantial fraction of the empire's lands and labor were devoted to the production of goods for the benefit of long-deceased and mummified rulers who were displayed on ceremonial occasions.[6] Viewed from the outside, this belief seems rather foolish, if not macabre. The royal mummies, despite their occasional public outings, were quite dead. For one group in the empire, however, a strong and widespread belief in the continuing life, and especially the property rights, of the royal mummies was quite rational. Ancestor worship was assiduously promoted by portions of the higher Incan aristocracy, the *panaqa*, who served as the caretakers of the royal mummies and the guardians of their earthly interests. This position meant that members of the panaqa were the actual beneficiaries of the property rights nominally belonging to the royal mummies. Members of the panaqa also helped to articulate the advice and counsel of the mummies when important imperial decisions were to be made and the royal mummies seemed to have difficulty speaking for themselves. In short, for the panaqa, ancestor worship was as much a political and economic interest as a religious principle. Some members of the Incan aristocracy apparently did not actually believe in the immortality of the royal mummies.[7] For most, nevertheless, defending this belief system was both a political and moral imperative.

Despite their lack of objective validity, ideas that serve the interests of important elites and are promoted by them can acquire social momentum, diffuse through a society and become ensorcelled to the point that their instrumental origins are nearly forgotten. Thus, in eleventh-century Europe, the idea of a crusade to free the Holy Land arguably originated from political struggles within the Church and between the Church and secular rulers who had begun to challenge its authority.[8] Over the next two centuries, though, the idea of crusading captured the imaginations of members of the nobility as well as commoners, becoming a religious responsibility as well as a political stratagem. In a similar vein, the Spanish Inquisition was initially as much a political as a religious enterprise launched by Ferdinand and Isabella to enhance royal power and to cement the fragile unity of the newly established Spanish state.[9] Over the next century, however, the Inquisition took on a life of its own, engulfing Spanish society in several waves of denunciations and investigations in what appeared to be a never-ending effort to define, identify, and root out religious heresy.

MAGIC AND THE AUDIT OF WAR

In folklore, magical beings could not tolerate the touch of iron swords. Similarly, societies that have become prone to magical thinking are likely to be caught short in the audit of war. Unless vigorously challenged, widespread magical thinking and more mundane forms of fantasy can persist for decades—if not centuries. But war, sometimes even preparation for war, subjects unexamined beliefs and dogmas to a severe stress test. Will the incantations of the priests ensure a nation's success? On the battlefield, as Napoleon observed, God usually tends to support the side possessing the best artillery. Is a hallowed bureaucratic routine such as the "Navy Way" really the best way? The events of December 7, 1941, suggested that faith in the Navy Way of that era, at least, might have been misplaced. Will a socialist economy produce material and weapons likely to "bury" capitalism, as Soviet Premier Nikita Khrushchev once declared? The disappearance of the Union of Soviet Socialist Republics from the world map during its arms race with the United States suggests that this belief was not well founded.

Even the harsh audit of war is not a perfect device for separating fact from fable, but it comes close. Perhaps more than any other social force, war has the power to test and refute ensorcelled beliefs. In war, the punishment for irrational thinking and action can be extremely harsh—defeat and death. In war, those societies that tend to base their actions upon one or another form of fantasy, whether religious or secular in origin, are apt to find themselves in what Trotsky liked to call the "dustbin of history." Rationality does not guarantee victory, particularly against equally astute foes, but lunacy is usually a sure pathway to defeat.

It is important to note that there is a difference between magical thinking and erroneous thinking. States may certainly go to war on the basis of errors and miscalculations and will almost certainly make mistakes during wars. Ordinary errors and miscalculations, though, are subject to corrections based upon observed facts. Sometimes, albeit not always, these corrections come in time to save the day. The Soviet leadership, for example, was fairly certain that the Germans would not attack in 1941 and quite confident that an attack, if it came, would be repulsed at the border by the Soviet Army. When both these ideas proved disastrously false, Stalin and his lieutenants revised their thinking and planning, evacuated Soviet military industry to the Urals, and began to assemble new armies to replace the ones that had been shattered by the *Wehrmacht*. Magical thinking, on the other hand, is often not amenable to reconsideration based on new facts and information. Instead, facts are likely to be interpreted through the lens of belief. As we shall see below, while the Russians revised their strategy, throughout the war German leaders continued to view the world through the lens of Nazi ideology, a form of magical thinking that proved to be ruinous.

War tends to unmask and refute magical thinking. States that are not rational actors, to use the vocabulary of contemporary strategic theory, are likely to engage in war without carefully weighing their chances of success or the potential costs and benefits of their actions. Such conduct is often a product of the political rather than objective validity of their ideas. Engaging in warfare may make sense in terms of some set of internal considerations even though it is objectively foolish. The result of such conduct is often quite disastrous. Whatever their reasons for launching wars, irrational actors are also apt to engage in wartime practices that reduce their chance of victory.

Consider the example of the aforementioned Incas. The fact that deceased former rulers retained the rights to a large portion of their royal estates meant that the agricultural land and income available to the living current ruler of the Inca empire were reduced. Efforts, moreover, to limit the property rights of the royal mummies were fiercely resisted by the panaqa. The solution to this problem, from the imperial perspective, was the continual annexation of new lands that would produce income for the current emperor rather than the royal mummies. Of course, with the eventual death of the emperor a portion of these new lands, too, would belong to a mummy, leaving the next emperor with the same problem and the same solution—the conquest of new territories. During the fifteenth century, the Inca empire expanded substantially as successive rulers launched wars of annexation against surrounding polities.[10]

Though initially successful, after several decades this imperial policy of conquest and annexation undermined the Inca state. By the end of the fifteenth century, the empire had come to occupy most of the arable land in the region, including the Central Andean coast and highlands. Further expansion meant penetrating the Amazonian rain forests east of the Andes Mountains. These forests were inhabited by fierce, primitive tribes who, along with the tropical heat and diseases, took an enormous toll on Incan armies sent to secure the region. Such land as could be occupied, moreover, proved difficult to cultivate and impossible to administer from the Inca capital of Cuzco. The cost of subduing and garrisoning these lands was far greater than the revenue they produced for the royal treasury, leading to a fiscal crisis for the crown. The military demands of garrisoning the new territories, moreover, depleted Incan strength in other portions of the realm, opening the way for many revolts among subject peoples. In these ways, the program of military expansion, launched because of a peculiar religious belief, proved ruinous.

In the early sixteenth century, the newly installed emperor Huáscar attempted to solve the problem of the royal mummies once and for all by stripping deceased rulers of their property rights. Huáscar declared that the mummies should be buried and their lands taken over by the state. This decree was, of course, deeply resented by the panaqa, which had much to lose from the elimination of the property rights of the dead rulers. Accusing Huáscar of blasphemy and heresy, some members of the panaqa launched a revolt and sought to replace the emperor with his half-brother, Atahuallpa, who controlled the Incan army in Ecuador. The resulting civil war lasted three years and was won by Atahuallpa, but, before he could be crowned, Francisco Pizarro and his band of 168 adventurers arrived. Pizarro was able to exploit the continuing political and ethnic divisions in the already-shattered empire to bring it under Spanish control. Over the next decade, the Spaniards hunted and destroyed the royal mummies, which they saw as symbols of Incan resistance to Spanish rule.

Thus, decades of warfare prompted by a species of magical thinking undermined the empire of the Incas and left it vulnerable to conquest by a handful of conquistadors. The empire's endless wars may have made sense on the basis of purely internal political and religious considerations, but it was objectively foolish.

During roughly the same period of time, the Aztec empire located far to the north of the Inca domain was also engaged in endless warfare prompted by magical thinking. In the fifteenth century, the Aztecs expanded from the island of Tenochtitlan in Lake Texcoco to the control of a large empire centered in what is now the southern portion of Mexico. Like that of the Incas, Aztec imperial expansion was driven by magical thinking. The Aztecs believed that they were the chosen people of the sun, and that it was their duty to keep the sun alive by providing him with human blood—in particular, the blood of captured warriors, "the precious liquid," that would strengthen the sun and save the universe from destruction.[11] The source of this liquid, needed by the priests in large quantities, was the sacrifice of living victims, generally prisoners captured in war. Since major ceremonies required the sacrifice of thousands, even tens of thousands of persons, Aztec armies were compelled to engage in constant warfare and expansion of the borders of the empire to capture the requisite numbers of enemy warriors.

As in the case of the Incas, these beliefs had a certain internal political validity, legitimating the power and unity of the state and its noble and priestly classes while enhancing the loyalty of the common people. The higher classes also shared in the booty brought back, along with captives, by victorious Aztec armies. The blood of the captives fed the sun while their possessions fed the empire's economy. By the sixteenth century, though, the empire's expansion had slowed as it reached its geographical and logistical limits. Military campaigns fought at the empire's far southern and northern borders were enormously expensive and produced few captives and little booty. Conquests in these distant regions, moreover, were too far from the imperial capital to be sustained administratively or logistically.

At the beginning of the sixteenth century, Emperor Moctezuma II called a halt to futile efforts to expand the empire's borders and directed his armies, instead, to attack and seize sacrificial captives from the several large, quasi-independent kingdoms within the borders of the empire that had resisted incorporation into the Aztec realm. These enclaves included the mountainous region of Guerrero, the populous Mixtex states of Totopec, and several others. These kingdoms mounted the same sort of fierce resistance to the Aztecs that had blocked their incorporation in the first place and gave the empire little booty and few sacrificial captives for its efforts. Several Aztec armies were routed while seeking to conquer the strongly defended enclaves. These signs of Aztec military weakness, in turn, encouraged revolts among tributary states within the empire that had good reason to hate the Aztecs. When Cortés arrived in 1519 with his conquistadors, more tributary states revolted and several joined the Spaniards, providing Cortés with tens of thousands of fighters to help his band of Spaniards overthrow the huge Aztec empire.

As in the case of the Incas, decades of warfare inspired by magical thinking left the Aztecs vulnerable to conquest by a small group of European adventurers. The Incas fought to acquire more land to feed their royal mummies while the Aztecs fought to seize captives whose blood would strengthen the sun. In each case, these beliefs served internal political purposes. However, by leading to endless warfare, overexpansion, and the enmity of all their neighbors, magical thinking failed the audit of war. The available data moreover seems to suggest that the sun has survived despite no longer being nourished by the blood of sacrificed captives.

WAR AND SECULAR MAGIC: THE CASE OF NAZI GERMANY

A more contemporary state whose military defeat can be traced to its leaders' magical thinking is Nazi Germany. Germany's leaders led the nation into war in 1939 for a mix of reasons, including both Nazi ideology and the more traditional motives of *Realpolitik* that drove Germany into the First World War. In 1939, it was by no means a foregone conclusion that war would lead to the eventual destruction of the German state. Quite the contrary. Germany possessed a superb army, easily overran Western Europe and, in 1941, seemed poised to destroy the Soviet Union, which would have meant German domination of the European continent. That Germany did not win the war is due in no small measure to its leaders' insistence on engaging in magical, in this case *ideological* thinking, that could not survive the audit of war.

Wilhelmine Germany had been among Europe's great powers, and it required the combined military might of Great Britain, France, Russia, and the United States to defeat Germany in the First World War. Germany, too, had been a center of literature and high culture, science, and even administrative capability. In almost every respect, Wilhelmine Germany had been among the most advanced states on earth. The collapse of the German economy and the German state between the wars, however, undermined traditional elites and created an opportunity for groups from what normally would have been dismissed as Germany's lunatic fringe—the German equivalent of America's various paramilitary groups—to come to power. The Nazi party, led by Adolph Hitler, was one of several right-wing paramilitary movements that attempted to appeal to unemployed, working, and lower-middle class Germans through propaganda, political organization, and violent confrontation during the last days of the Weimar Republic.

The centerpiece of Nazi ideology was a system of nonsensical racial classifications that placed Germans and other members of the so-called "Aryan race" at the top and others below them in descending order of racial quality. The Slavic peoples of Eastern Europe, including Poles, Russians, and Ukrainians, were near the bottom and labeled *Untermenschen* (subhumans). Jews, of course fell at the very bottom of the Nazi racial hierarchy. The Slavs were to serve as a source of slave labor and the Jews, as Nazi ideology evolved, were to be exterminated.

Racist appeals, along with violence, helped the Nazis to seize power in the 1930s.[12] Racism and anti-Semitism were simple themes that offered ready solutions and scapegoats for Germany's complex problems. The ferocity of Nazi violence, moreover, had a certain allure for desperate and angry workers.[13] Once Hitler was elected chancellor of Germany in 1933, racism, in particular anti-Semitism, played a major role in the Nazi party's ability to consolidate its control of the German state. For this purpose, codification of the Nazis' racial ideology proved important The 1935 Nuremberg Laws established strict racial categories. Anyone with at least three Jewish grandparents was defined as a Jew. Later, those defined as Jews were excluded from the civil service, stripped of most of their property, expelled from schools, and subjected to numerous other disabilities. An individual with two Jewish grandparents was defined as a *Mischling* (person of mixed blood) of the first degree while an individual with one Jewish grandparent was defined as a Mischling of the second degree. Depending upon their precise classification, Mischlinge were subject to various indignities, but not treated as badly as Jews.

This system of racial classifications and the subjection of the Jews to various forms of discrimination helped tie major institutions of Germany's government and society to the new regime. The classification, exclusion, transportation, and, eventually, murder of Jews required the help of a host of government bureaucracies, as well as accountants, lawyers, judges, engineers, and so forth. As they took part, agencies and their employees were gradually drawn into the orbit of, and subordinated to, the Nazi regime that defined their new missions and priorities and rewarded and punished conduct.[14] In a similar way, racial laws linked various institutions of German society to the regime. Churches were a source of birth records and so became involved in the system of racial classifications. Non-Jewish banks and businesses profited from the confiscation of Jewish properties. Those who took the positions from which Jews were expelled in the universities, professions, and civil service had reason to become supporters of the regime, and so forth.

Racial codes also became instruments through which the Nazis subdued the social stratum from which their chief political foes were drawn, namely, Germany's urban bourgeoisie. After World War I and the collapse of the Hohenzollern monarchy, the urban bourgeoisie became Germany's new ruling stratum. Along with gentile members of their social class, Jews came to occupy positions of leadership in the liberal Weimar Republic. Before World War I, Jews constituted barely 1 percent of the German populace. But, in a pattern not so different from that of the contemporary United States, Jews were well integrated into the urban bourgeoisie and played important roles in the financial, cultural, and political institutions controlled by the bourgeoisie—banks, universities, the media, and so forth, while having little or no presence in other sectors of German society. The Weimar Republic's various foes sought to discredit the government by pointing to the prominence of Jews among the regime's supporters. Rightists declared that the regime was dominated by Jews and their puppets working against the true interests of the German people and derisively called Weimar a *Judenrepublik*.

The Nazi accession to power had represented a defeat not only for the Jews but for the liberal bourgeoisie more generally. The entire social stratum with which Jews were allied and through whom Jews had risen to positions of prominence had been overthrown. Once they had taken control of the government, the Nazis proceeded to use this stratum's association with Jews to cow the liberal bourgeoisie into utter submission. In particular, the Nazi system of racial laws and classifications made hundreds of thousands of non-Jewish members of the German bourgeoisie directly vulnerable to the Nazi regime's system of sanctions. Germans and Jews had intermarried for generations. An enormous number of middle- and upper-middle-class Germans had sufficient Jewish ancestry to be disqualified from desirable positions in the government and private sector or to be considered Mischlinge and therefore subject to a number of disabilities.[15]

The eagerness of such Germans to upgrade their status led to the creation of a new occupation, that of *Sippenforscher*, or genealogical researcher specializing in helping individuals prove their Aryan descent. Fortunate Mischlinge might be able to secure reclassifications, or "liberations," enhancing their career opportunities while diminishing the possibility that the government would one day decide to consider them Jews. Moreover, Millions of middle-class Germans with no discernible Jewish ancestry had past or present social, business, professional, or romantic relationships with Jews that could bring them to the attention of the authorities. Such individuals lived in fear that they might be denounced to the Gestapo by their enemies, hostile neighbors, or business rivals for such associations. In this way, a formerly powerful social stratum was unnerved and subdued as its Jewish allies were extruded from German society.

In sum, for the Nazis a bizarre system of racial classifications, no less a form of magical thinking than the beliefs of the Incas and Aztecs, became a powerful instrument of governance. It helped Hitler and his followers extend their control over the state and the society and undermine the influence of their most formidable political rivals. Despite its lunacy, Nazi racism possessed a form of internal political validity. Nazi ideology, however, soon failed the external audit of war as decisively as had the magical beliefs of the Incas and Aztecs four centuries earlier.

In 1939, of course, Germany embarked upon a military campaign to conquer Europe. Initially, German armies were spectacularly successful. In a few short months, the Wehrmacht defeated and occupied Poland, France, Belgium, Norway, and Denmark and drove the British from the European mainland. In 1941, Germany launched a massive attack upon the Soviet Union. In the first months of fighting, German advances were spectacular and German forces occupied much of European Russia. In 1942, however, Soviet resistance stiffened. By 1943, Soviet armies, equipped with new weaponry as well as American lend–lease supplies, turned the tide of battle. The Germans began a long retreat ending in Germany's surrender in 1945.

Among the major factors leading to Germany's defeat was its leadership's commitment to Nazi racial ideology. This form of magical thinking greatly weakened Germany's military capabilities in at least three ways. First, throughout the war, Germany devoted substantial resources that were badly needed by its military forces in the furtherance of racial policies, particularly the campaign against the Jews. The Germans built some ten thousand concentration camps to imprison and murder Jews and other putative racial enemies. Despite the fact that German military manpower was stretched to its extreme limits, more than 100,000 soldiers and military police officers, as well as tens of thousands of civilian officials, were assigned to the task of rounding up, incarcerating, and killing Jews.[16] Similarly, trains, trucks, and supplies badly needed by the military were used, instead, to facilitate the transport and murder of Jews. Even as the German army was being driven back by the Soviets, trucks and trains transporting Jews to death camps were given priority over military transports. Like the Aztecs preoccupied with the blood of their captives, the Germans assigned a lower priority to their military effort than to their magical rituals.

A second way in which Nazi ideology had a disastrous impact upon the German military effort was the German treatment of Slavs. German racial ideology defined Slavs as Untermenschen who would be worked to death to make room for future German colonists. Germany's military plan for the Russian campaign, however, assumed that the army would be able to acquire food and other supplies from Russian and Ukrainian peasant farmers. Local requisition had been the practice of German armies since Frederick the Great.[17] Initially, of course, these materials would simply be confiscated, but some cooperation from the peasantry would be useful if the army was to be supplied over a longer term.

When German forces first crossed the Soviet border, the Wehrmacht was greeted as an army of liberation by millions of peasants who long had been abused under Soviet rule. In addition, large numbers of Soviet soldiers, themselves drawn from the Russian and Ukrainian peasantry, were only too happy to surrender to the Germans at the first opportunity, thinking that so civilized a nation as Germany would offer them better treatment than they received from their own commissars and officers. Soon, however, the Germans disabused peasants and soldiers of these hopeful notions by showing that Soviet cruelty paled by comparison to that of the Nazis. Germany's generally brutal treatment of the Russian, Ukrainian, and other peasants in the occupied portions of the Western Soviet Union, along with its savage treatment of Soviet prisoners, quickly turned the initial welcome into intense hatred of the Germans, particularly among ethnic Russians. An oft-repeated joke among peasants began with the question, "What did Hitler accomplish in one year that Stalin was unable to achieve in two decades?" The answer was, "He made us like Soviet rule."[18] Some German military officers understood the importance of eliciting the cooperation of the peasants rather than antagonizing them. One Wehrmacht officer reportedly sought to explain this principle to a Nazi deputy governor in the Ukraine. The support of the Ukrainian peasants was useful, this officer explained, and, at any rate, 40 million Ukrainians could not simply be exterminated. The Nazi official rebuffed the soldier, declaring, "It is our business."[19]

German brutality soon provoked resistance in the form of peasant cooperation with Stalin's scorched-earth policy to deprive the Germans of food, and the formation of numerous partisan groups that continually hammered at Germany's long and vulnerable rail and supply lines. Some Ukrainians, whose hatred of the Soviet Union was intense, continued to cooperate with the Germans. Russian peasants, however, resisted, and many Ukrainians fought against both the Russians and the Germans. Ultimately, shortages of food and supplies were among the major factors leading to the German defeat.[20] As to Soviet soldiers, surrender rates had been high in the early months of the war. However, as troops began to learn of the inhuman manner in which the Germans treated Soviet prisoners, surrender rates diminished sharply, and even groups of soldiers cut off from their units would continue fighting rather than lay down their guns and turn themselves over to the Germans. Here too, Nazi ideology prevented the development of a rational policy designed to encourage Soviet soldiers to surrender.

Then, of course, there is the matter of the atomic bomb. Late nineteenth- and early twentieth-century Germany became a world leader in the natural sciences thanks in no small part to the work of its Jewish scientists. The most famous of these were, of course, such physicists as Albert Einstein, James Franck, Max Born, Hans Bethe, and a host of others—many of whom had struggled against professional and academic restrictions prior to Weimar—who helped to make Germany the unquestioned world leader in the field of physics at the beginning of the twentieth century. In the 1930s, however, these and many other scientists were forced to leave Germany. One of the Nazi party's early anti-Jewish enactments was the 1933 Law for the Restoration of the Civil Service. Among other things, this measure and its subsequent amendments, followed by the Law Against the Overcrowding of German Schools and Institutes of Higher Learning, was designed to drive Jews from the universities. Thousands of Jewish professors lost their posts and many, particularly the most eminent, soon sought positions abroad. What ensued was an enormous transfer of intellectual capital from Germany and its allies, such as Hungary, to the United States, and, to a lesser extent, Great Britain. Soon, scientific research and teaching in Germany lost its pre-war momentum with a loss of some 3,000 teachers and researchers and a 65 percent decline in the number of students in physics and mathematics.[21] Asked by the German education minister if his department had suffered because of the departure of the Jews, the head of the mathematics faculty at the University of Gottingen replied, "Suffered? It no longer exists.[22] Of special importance were the great German–Jewish and Hungarian–Jewish physicists who stood at the forefront of this realm of science in the early twentieth century. The departure of these individuals from Germany was, perhaps, the greatest transfer of human capital in a short period of time in the history of the world.

The list of emigrants includes the greatest names in physics as well as chemistry and other natural sciences, including 33 present of future Nobel Prize winners: Hans Bethe, Felix Bloch, Konrad Bloch, Max Born, Ernst Chain, Peter Debye, Max Delbruck, Albert Einstein, Enrico Fermi, James Franck, Denis Gabor, Fritz Haber, Gustav Hertz, Gerhard Hertzberg, Victor Hess, Bernard Katz, Hans Krebs, Rita Levi-Montalcini, Fritz Lipmann, Otto Loewi, Salvador Luria, Otto Meyerhoff, Wolfgang Pauli, Max Perutz, Josef Rotblat, Erwin Schrödinger, Emilio Segrè, Jack Steinberger, Otto Stern, Georg Von Hevesy, Eugene Wigner, and Richard Willstatter. Other scientific luminaries included Leo Szilard, Edward Teller, Stanislaw Ulam, and John Von Neumann.[23] Some of these scientific refugees fled to Great Britain, where the newly formed Academic Assistance Council helped them find positions.[24] Most, however, found their way to the United States where university positions were found for them by the Emergency Committee in Aid of Displaced German Scholars, a private organization funded mainly by the Rockefeller Foundation.[25]

A major result of the transfer of scientific talent from Germany to America was, of course, that it was the United States, not Nazi Germany, that developed the atomic bomb. In 1939, Szilard and Einstein, in consultation with fellow Jewish refugees Edward Teller and Eugene Wigner, sent a letter to President Roosevelt in which they described the possibility that a new type of weapon of unprecedented power could be built, based upon the principle of nuclear fission. Such a weapon, they said, might potentially destroy an entire city with one blast. Moreover, the letter went on to say, there was reason to believe that Germany had already begun work on a nuclear bomb. Roosevelt received the Einstein–Szilard letter a few days after the German invasion of Poland and was sufficiently concerned to authorize the creation of an advisory committee, which, in turn, funded the first stages of work on what would become an atomic bomb. Over the ensuing years, for the Jewish scientists, both native-born and refugee, who joined the project, the defeat of Nazi Germany was an overriding objective. "After the fall of France," Hans Bethe wrote, "I was desperate to do something—to make some contribution to the war effort."[26] And

Oppenheimer wrote, "I had a continuing, smoldering fury about the treatment of Jews in Germany."[27]

It turned out the fear of a German atomic bomb was misplaced. Absent the Jewish physicists, such a project had few advocates in a Germany, whose leaders had other obsessions. The Nazis said that nuclear theory smacked of "Jewish science," which was to be supplanted by a purer "Aryan science." The leaders of this Aryan science included two once-eminent but now superannuated German physicists, Johannes Stark and Phillip Lenard, who apparently were unable to make much sense of such newfangled notions as relativity and quantum theory, which they dismissed as *Judenphysik* and "kabbalistic" in origin. At the same time, Germany's leading Gentile nuclear physicist, Werner Heisenberg, was accused of being a "white Jew" and very nearly arrested for his ideas and Jewish associations.[28]

Thus, in these three ways, Nazi ideology greatly undermined the German war effort. For ideological reasons, substantial resources were diverted from the war effort to a campaign of murder. For ideological reasons, the potential cooperation of the Soviet peasantry was rejected and its enmity ensured. And, for ideological reasons, Germany's potential to build an atomic bomb was thrown away. It was Nazism and not *Judenphysik* that turned out to be a magical form of thought and proved unable to survive the remorseless audit of war.

THE GENERAL CURRICULUM OF WARFARE

At the level of the participant, war seems to encourage superstitious beliefs. Roman soldiers prayed and sacrificed to the gods before battle. Nervous soldiers going to war often carry lucky charms and amulets to calm their fears. Even as famous and intrepid a warrior as the late admiral William F. Halsey harbored the common belief that thirteen is an unlucky number. Assigned to command Task Force 13, Halsey angrily changed the flotilla's numerical designation to sixteen and accused the navy's high command of attempting to "jinx" him.[29]

At the societal level, however, those groups that frequently engage in warfare, particularly against opponents who pose a serious threat to their survival, tend to learn a number of basic lessons. This educational process has both Lamarckian and Darwinian components. That is, war confronts societies with harsh realities that they must master. Those threatened by powerful foes and unwilling or unable to learn these lessons are not likely to survive. The survivors are likely to be those who have learned to be smarter about the realities of war. The first lesson societies must learn from war is what might be called a rationalist or realist perspective. The essence of this perspective is succinctly stated in Thucydides' account of the discussion between the Athenians and the Melians during the Peloponnesian wars.[30] In 416 BCE Athens invaded the island of Melos and presented the Melians with an ultimatum. They could surrender or be destroyed by the powerful Athenian army. In their response, the Melians appeal to justice and declare that the gods will surely support their just cause. The Athenians, having had a good deal of experience of war, explain that neither justice nor the intervention of the gods will help a weaker army defeat a stronger foe. The Melians refuse to surrender, appeal to the gods, and are destroyed. Of course, some years later, the Athenians were reminded of the wisdom of their advice when they were, in turn, defeated by the Spartans. The rationalist perspective derived from the experience of war is evident in the works of the great early theorists of war and statecraft. These include Sun Tzu, Kautilya, Vegetius, and, later, Machiavelli and Clausewitz, as well as the writings of more contemporary authorities. These theorists of war generally wrote in times and places that had experienced a good deal of armed conflict and sought to elaborate the lessons learned from that experience. For example, Sun Tzu, himself a high-ranking military leader, wrote during China's Warring States period, probably in the fourth or fifth century BCE, and presents military theories and axioms derived from China's two millennia of warfare. Writing in India during roughly the same period, Kautilya played a central role in the decades of military struggle leading to the destruction of the Nanda empire and the rise of the Maurya empire during the fourth century BCE. Not too many centuries later, the work of the Roman, Vegetius, reflects lessons culled from nearly a millennium of Roman military experience. While each of these theorists represents a particular time and place, a number of commonalities seem to arise suggesting what might be called a general curriculum of war learned, or at least studied by, most militarily experienced societies.

The basic perspective of the general curriculum is realism. Like the Athenians, societies with martial experience learn to think realistically about war or, like the Melians, court destruction. Thus, Sun Tzu points out that in the realm of warfare it is important to consider facts rather than to consult the heavens.[31] The Romans watched with contempt as their barbarian foes painted their bodies and asked their gods to guarantee victory. Roman commanders showed respect for the gods but relied mainly upon superior military force to bring success in battle.[32] In a similar vein, Machiavelli famously dismisses "unarmed prophets" as doomed to failure. In other words, victory is won by military prowess, not ideology.[33] Clausewitz avers that war should be undertaken only as an instrument of policy and only to achieve concrete goals.[34] Following from the general perspective of realism are several main principles of warfare. Each of these, as we shall see, is the philosophical equivalent of a dual-use technology. Societies that learn these principles in the military sphere are inclined to make peaceful use of them as well.

Of course, even once they are learned, rational principles may be forgotten or ignored when a society succumbs to a wave of religious or ideological fervor that sweeps away reason. This is where Lamarckism falls short. Lessons learned can be forgotten The Germans knew a great deal about war and statecraft but, as we saw, even German Realpolitik could be overwhelmed by Nazism. Realistic thinking can eventually reassert itself though as in the German case, the cost of post-graduate studies in political realism can be quite steep.

Planning

The first element of the martial curriculum is planning. Societies that regularly engaged in war learned, as Sun Tzu said, not to trust sooth-sayers or look to the heavens for portents but turned, instead, to rational planning to predict and, perhaps, to control the future. In the broadest sense, military planning refers to the formulation of what is sometimes called "grand strategy," that is, planning the ways in which resources should be coordinated and directed toward the general security goals of a society.[35] In the Second World War, for example, Allied grand strategy called for the defeat of Germany as the primary American and British goal, with Japan and the Pacific as a secondary matter. In addi-tion, Allied grand strategy affirmed at such meetings as the Yalta con-ference included planning for the post-war era.

Successful ancient empires and military powers also developed grand strategies. Grand strategies are seldom conceived quickly and are often the product of decades of thought, planning, and execution. Rome, for example, pursued a long-term strategy that historian Arthur Ferrill calls, "preclusive security."[36] Beginning during the reign of the Emperor Hadrian in the second century CE, this carefully crafted strategy entailed the construction of walls and fortresses at the perim-eters of the Empire. These perimeter defenses were connected by an elaborate system of roads and sea transport so that troops and supplies might quickly be moved to a threatened frontier from other areas. The Emperor Constantine abandoned this strategy in favor of the less expensive expedient of maintaining one central, mobile army. Con-stantine's shift in strategies may have left the Empire more vulnerable to attack.[37] China's "Great Wall," a 5,000 mile long series of fortifica-tions built in stages between the seventh and third centuries BCE is another example of a preclusive security strategy.

Below the level of grand strategy is strategic planning for particular wars, the design of appropriate tactics to implement that strategy, the organization of military forces, and the construction of the logistical systems needed to equip, transport, and supply those forces. Such plans can themselves be very complex. Prior to the First World War, the German general staff raised planning to a high art. The Schlieffen Plan, which detailed Germany's strategy for attacking France in World War I, was hundreds of pages long, providing detailed prescriptions for the mobilization, movement, and supply of millions of German troops. The Germans spent nine years devising the initial plan and several more years adding modifications. Military historians argue about whether Germany's defeat in World War I reflected shortcomings in the plan or the army's failure to properly execute the plan. In the years between the wars, the United States, for its part, developed a number of color-coded contingency plans for wars with possible and not-so-possible foes. War Plan Black was a plan for war with Germany and War Plan Orange was a plan for war with Japan. War Plan Crimson, improbably enough, dealt with war with Canada. While Orange and portions of Black actually were used, Canadian readers should be happy to learn that Crimson was never put into effect.

Successful ancient empires also engaged in extensive planning for their military campaigns. Sun Tzu discussed the importance of planning in the first of the thirteen chapters of *The Art of War* and said, "The general who loses a battle makes but few calculations beforehand. Thus do many calculations lead to victory, and few calculations to defeat: how much more no calculation at all! It is by attention to this point that I can see who is likely to win or lose."[38] Several centuries later, Machiavelli wrote, "Men who have any great undertaking in mind must first make all necessary preparations for it, so that, when an opportunity arises, they may be ready to put it in execution according to their design."[39] A wise prince, said Machiavelli, needs to know, "how to find the enemy, take up quarters, lead armies, plan battles and lay siege to towns."[40]

Planning for war, of course, also includes economic planning. This principle has been understood since ancient times. Kautilya, for example, urged rulers to carefully examine their likely sources of revenue before going to war.[41] Over time, a nation's military might is tied to its economic capabilities and level of economic development.[42]

One reason that Khrushchev's boast that he would bury the West rang hollow was that Soviet industrial capabilities were quite inferior to those of the United States and its allies. The difference in economic capacity proved telling when its futile effort to compete in an all-out arms race with the Americans in the 1980s led to the collapse of the Soviet State.

Economic capacity does not translate directly into military power. Productive potential must be harnessed and plans made for its conversion to military uses. Failure to make adequate economic plans for war can be as damaging as failure to make appropriate military plans. In the United States, preparation for World War II, for example, included the creation of an elaborate network of private defense contractors and subcontractors to build the weapons that America would need to prosecute the war.

A similar network remains the backbone of American military production today. Secretary of War Henry Stimson reportedly declared that in a capitalist society, if you wanted to go to war you needed to hire the industrialists. The Soviet Union by contrast established an enormous group of state-owned military industries to build weapons for the same war. Unfortunately, these were mainly located in the Western USSR where factories were quite vulnerable to German attack. After the German invasion, though, the USSR was able to disassemble and transport several thousand industrial plants to the distant Ural Mountains where they produced huge numbers of tanks, fighter planes, and artillery pieces for the remainder of the war. The Germans, for their part, felt assured by faith in Nazi racial ideology of an easy victory over the Slavic Untermenschen and the "mongrel" Americans. Accordingly, Germany did not put its economy on a full military footing until late in 1943.[43] By this time, it was far too late for the Germans to produce sufficient quantities of military equipment to vie with the enormous productive capabilities of the Russians and Americans.

Organization

Closely related to planning is organization. A key difference between a military force and a mass of armed individuals, however fierce and heavily armed, is organization. Small numbers of well-organized and disciplined Roman troops usually had no difficulty defeating much larger numbers of barbarian tribesmen.[44] Military forces are arrayed in groupings designed to maximize their effectiveness as well as the ability of officers to oversee and direct their troops. Military theorists and commanders spend a good deal of time considering the most effective organization of their forces. Kautilya, for example, taught that an army should be divided into four corps: the infantry, the cavalry, the chariot corps, and the elephant corps. Each required its own commander and each occupied a different place in the army's order of battle. The elephants, for example, were to march in front in order to crush the enemy's foot soldiers.

Relatively few armies employ elephants today, but organization continues to be a major preoccupation of military strategists. Generally speaking, military organization is hierarchical, with high-ranking officers commanding large bodies of troops organized into subdivisions commanded by lower-ranking officers. Each subdivision is assigned a specific task and may have specialized training or equipment for that task. In the US military, an army consisting of several hundred thousand troops is commanded by a general. The army is divided in corps; corps are divided into divisions, and divisions are, in turn, divided into brigades of roughly 3,000 soldiers commanded by a brigadier general. Brigades are divided into regiments (commanded by colonels), which are further subdivided into companies, then platoons, then squads commanded by sergeants. Naval and air forces have their own organizational charts, and all are tied together through complex systems of command, control and coordination.

Though all military organizational is hierarchical, successful armies usually invest subordinate officers with a considerable quantity of actual authority so that their troops will respect them as authentic leaders rather than view them as mere servants of higher commanders. Discretion also allows subordinate officers to take advantage of opportunities or deal with crises immediately instead of relying on higher authority that is usually far removed from the battlefield. The Roman legions trained centurions to exercise a good deal of discretion. The German Wehrmacht, under the rubric of *Auftragstaktic*, or "mission-oriented command," gave its noncommissioned officers a great deal of authority.[45] And, in the US Marine Corps, sergeants are given wide latitude to lead their troops in combat.

Recruitment, Training, and Discipline

A third element of the general martial curriculum is the recruitment, training, and discipline of military forces. Among primitive peoples, all members of the tribe or group were expected to fight to protect or expand the group's territory, population, and food supply.[46] With the development of states and the emergence of the military as a recognized occupational group, rulers recruited military forces in a variety of different ways depending upon costs, needs, the skills deemed necessary for successful military efforts, the likely loyalty of the troops, and a host of other factors. The proper characteristics of soldiers and officers has been among the central concerns of military theorists, princes, and, more recently, presidents. Kautilya said the best troops were professionals, recruited from among, "natives of the country, dependent upon the king, sharing his interests, constantly trained."[47] Other types of forces were inferior to these in terms of effectiveness and reliability.

Vegetius, for his part, was concerned with the physical and other standards that should be met by military recruits asserting that legionaries should be at least five feet ten inches tall and with a broad chest and muscular shoulders. He also favored recruits from the country rather than the city and suggested that individuals who had pursued "masculine" trades—smiths, carpenters, butchers, and huntsmen—were to be preferred.[48] Writing in the late imperial period, Vegetius also recommended a return to what he believed to have been the successful training methods used by the legions in an earlier era. These included years of drill, exercise, swimming lessons, and extensive training in the use of the chief weapons of the era: the sword, bow, sling, and javelin. Machiavelli agreed with this recommendation, saying that soldiers should train by running, wrestling, leaping, carrying heavy arms, using weapons, and swimming.[49]

In early modern Europe, changes in the international system and technology made the recruitment of troops a pressing issue. During the medieval period, kings had relied upon the feudal host, composed of nobles and their retainers. The nobles, usually organized as a heavy cavalry, were responsible for their own training and equipment. Commoners, brought into battle by their lords, were armed with light infantry weapons, including bows, and usually had little training. The introduction of new weapons and tactics in the fifteenth century sharply diminished the military effectiveness of heavy cavalry and compelled princes to give a good deal of thought to the recruitment and training of troops. Some princes relied upon private military contractors to provide trained troops when needed. The problem with mercenary forces was, of courses, the issue of loyalty. Mercenary troops, often not members of the same nationality group as their employer, were not inclined to risk their lives and might, for a fee, be induced to change sides during the war. Machiavelli was one of many who advocated the recruitment and training of native forces and abjured the use of mercenaries. He called the latter, "useless and dangerous."

In recent decades, most discussions have focused on the relative merits of professional armies composed mainly of volunteers versus armies composed mainly of conscripted "citizen soldiers." For much of its history, the United States relied primarily upon citizen militias and conscripts. Since 1972, the United States has built a professional military composed mainly, albeit not exclusively, of American citizens hired to fill military positions. These individuals receive several months of general military training as well as additional weeks or months of specialized training. Officers may receive several years of training in combat operations, planning, logistics, and, in some cases, engineering.

However recruited and trained, troops must be ranked and graded by aptitude and performance and they must be disciplined. That is, they must obey instructions even when asked to perform tasks that may involve great danger to themselves. Some authorities advocate harsh methods of discipline while others advocate exhortation and indoctrination to win the loyalty of the troops. Machiavelli was an advocate of harsh discipline. "But it is not sufficient just to give out good orders for this purpose, if their observance is not enforced with the utmost severity; for there is no case whatsoever in which the most exact and implicit obedience is as necessary as in the government of an army." Machiavelli continues with an approving description of an extraordinarily harsh method of execution used by the commander of a legion to punish disobedience.[50] Kautilya, on the other hand, believed that soldiers should be taught loyalty and exhorted to obey orders bravely. "Bards and praise-singers shall describe the heaven that awaits the brave and the hell that shall be the lot of cowards. They shall extol the clan, group, family, deeds, and conduct of the warriors."[51] Of course, most armies rely upon a mix of exhortation and punishment. During the Second World War, for example, Soviet troops received a steady diet of propaganda, exhortation, and political indoctrination. At the same time, special NKVD (security service) "blocking units" were positioned behind the front lines to shoot shirkers and deserters.

Without training and discipline, it is very difficult to induce soldiers to engage in violence. Most individuals, including soldiers, are not especially violent, nor are they particularly adept at the use of violence.[52] Most suffer from fear, uncertainty, and remorse when they become involved in a violent confrontation.[53] As Sociologist Randall Collins concludes from his studies of fights and disturbances, most hostile confrontations between two or more individuals are characterized by "bluster and gesture" that do not lead to actual violence.[54] Collins attributes this outcome to what he terms "confrontational tension and fear." That is, faced with the possibility of engaging in or becoming the targets of violence, most individuals experience a high level of tension and often an overwhelming sense of trepidation which leads all sides to prefer face-saving—or even humiliating—ways of backing down and avoiding violence. In the case of military combat, according to Colonel David Grossman, a surprisingly high percentage of troops fail to use their weapons against the enemy.[55] A famous study conducted by S. L. A. Marshall, the US Army's chief combat historian during World War II, concluded that only about 15 percent of the army's front line troops had actually fired their guns in combat. Even face-to-face with enemy forces, the majority of soldiers took no hostile action whatsoever.[56] Studies of other armies and other wars seem to bear out Marshall's findings.

Armies seek to overcome this fear of confrontation with indoctrination and training that help to inure their troops to the fear of violence. One example is the case of contemporary modes of US military training. Beginning in the Vietnam War, as Grossman reports, the US military introduced major changes in its training methods designed to increase the number of soldiers who actually fired their weapons in combat. These changes include training that simulates actual combat situations, so that soldiers will be conditioned to reflexively fire their weapons. Rather than teach soldiers to shoot at stationary targets, soldiers today in such programs as Marine Corps Basic Warrior Training are conditioned to fire reflexively and instantly at olive-drab, human-shaped targets that pop up randomly and unexpectedly on the training field. If the target is hit, it falls, providing instantaneous positive feedback. Soldiers are rewarded for successfully "engaging" (a euphemism for killing) their targets and penalized for failing to do so.

The result of weeks of operant conditioning on the training field is that in actual combat soldiers react automatically as though they are still shooting at training targets. In the US and other armies using such training methods, 90–95 percent of the soldiers fire their weapons, in contrast to the 15–20 percent who fired in earlier periods of history.[57] During the 1982 Falklands War, for example, British troops trained via conditioning faced much larger Argentinian forces trained using traditional methods. The result was an unequal contest in which almost all the British troops fired their weapons while most of the Argentinians did not. One British veteran said he "thought of the enemy as nothing more or less than Figure II (man-shaped) targets."[58] Their high rate of fire is one reason American military forces have been so effective in recent decades. Indeed, in Iraq and Afghanistan, US casualties were mainly caused by improvised explosive devices (IEDs) or "booby traps" rather than exchanges of rifle fire—from which American troops almost invariably emerge victorious.

Armies have also discovered that leadership is a critical factor in providing the discipline that will induce individuals to engage in violence. Like the subjects in Stanley Milgram's famous experiments on obedience, soldiers are more likely to fight when given orders by a respected authority figure who is physically present to observe and encourage them. In the absence of authoritative leadership, soldiers will often find reason to avoid violent confrontations with their foes. Take, for example, the accounts compiled by Grossman of the *ad hoc* truces that sometimes developed between British and German soldiers facing one another during World War I. Out of sight of their officers, these nominal opponents might leave their trenches, play soccer with one another, and exchange Christmas gifts, only to resume combat when officers intervened. In the Roman legions, centurions wielding distinctive staffs stood behind every group of eighty legionaries, watching and encouraging them, and making certain that they would endeavor to kill their opponents.

Engineering

The origin of the term "engineer" is an individual who designs, builds, and operates military equipment. More generally, engineering could be defined as thinking rationally about the physical world and devising techniques for the construction and manipulation of physical objects. The armies of the Roman, Chinese, and other ancient empires employed many complex forms of military hardware, The Romans, for example, made use of a variety of catapults, many adapted from Greek designs, including the "polybolos," a catapult with the capacity to fire bolts repeatedly without the need to reload. It was, in effect, the ancient equivalent of a modern machine gun. Roman military engineers also built forts, roads for the rapid deployment of forces, and carefully fortified camps for Roman forces on the march. Every legion included engineering officers responsible for the production of fortifications and siege equipment, and every Roman soldier carried a spade in addition to his weapons. Though the actual weapons carried by individual Roman soldiers were not much better than those wielded by their opponents, the Romans produced enormous quantities of swords, knives, spears, pikes, and other instruments. The Roman advantage in the realm of light infantry weapons was quantity more than quality.

The construction of fortifications was the highest art of military engineering through ancient times—until the modern era, when then increasing power of munitions made most fixed fortifications vulnerable to artillery and aerial attack. Improvements in artillery were brought about in the sixteenth century by the application of chemical and metallurgical discoveries to the design of weapons and gunpowder. During the same period, Galileo studied the trajectory of projectiles and discovered that such trajectories were parabolic. Niccolò Tartaglia experimented on the relationship between the angle of fire and the range of a projectile, ascertaining that a forty-five degree angle produced the maximum range.[59] A result of these developments was that during the sixteenth and seventeenth centuries, the powerful siege guns first introduced by the French rendered most medieval fortifications obsolete.[60] European military engineers responded with new fortress designs that were able to withstand battering by artillery. The best known of these individuals was Sébastien Vauban, who became Europe's leading authority on both the construction of fortifications and the design of methods for the capture of these selfsame fortifications.

By the end of the seventeenth century, the growing importance of military engineering and military technology led European governments to invest resources in these pursuits. The Royal Society of London was chartered in 1662, and the French *Academie Royale des Sciences* began in 1668. Both focused on military science and engineering, including ballistics, gunpowder, naval navigation, and military cartography.[61] Military engineering gradually became a major factor governing the outcomes of battles, campaigns, and wars.[62] Today, of course, the military forces of every major power vie with one another to design and produce weapons systems capable of projecting military might on land, at sea, in the air, in space, and in cyberspace.

Supply and Logistics

Napoleon is reputed to have observed that an army marches on its stomach. Maintaining military forces, particularly on the march or in combat, can require large quantities of transport, food, fuel, weapons, spare parts, ammunition, and other supplies. Since ancient times, military strategists have pointed to the issue of supplies and logistics as central problems of warfare. Sun Tzu advised generals to, "Bring war material with you from home, but forage on the enemy."[63] "A wise general," he continued, "makes a point of foraging on the enemy. One cartload of the enemy's provisions is equivalent to twenty of one's own."[64]

In the ancient world and even in early modern times, armies seldom possessed enough supplies and materiel to remain in the field for more than a brief period, and battles seldom lasted longer than a day or two. Most, though not all, armies were small by modern-day standards since large armies could seldom be supplied and sustained for very long. Recall that William the Conqueror commanded a force that totaled only 7,000 soldiers at the Battle of Hastings. Many troops had already left William's army because of a shortage of supplies.

Typically, if the outcome of a battle was not decided quickly, the combatants were forced to return to their homes, perhaps hoping to renew hostilities at some future date when they might be able to rebuild their stores of supplies and arms. Only the greatest of the ancient empires—Egypt, China, Persia, Rome—had the capacity to provision sizeable armies for weeks or months in the field. Even these forces relied upon their ability to purchase or, more often, to seize supplies and provisions from towns and settlements along their route of march.

Alexander the Great, for example, was able to keep his army on the march by planning his line of advance to take advantage of the presence of cities from which supplies could be extorted.[65] Centuries later, Genghis Khan's Mongol armies excelled in the realm of logistics, often bringing enormous herds and flocks with them as they moved forward. The Mongols also organized huge camel caravans to carry supplies to their soldiers. Superior logistics was one of the keys to Mongol military prowess.[66] Nevertheless, Mongol armies in the field could by no means be fully provisioned from their home bases and depended upon their ability to capture food and other supplies along their route of conquest.

Indeed, theft from local granaries had always been an essential component of military tactics, and remained so until the twentieth century. Armies led by such generals as Napoleon, Wallenstein, Gustavus Adolphus, Robert E. Lee, and, to some extent, even Moltke and Guderian depended upon food and supplies requisitioned, scavenged, and stolen from the country through which they passed. It was the problem of feeding soldiers in a poor and inhospitable land that led the ancient Greeks to develop and master their characteristic tactic of quick and decisive shock battle. Wars involving contending armies of Greek hoplite foot soldiers were typically resolved in an hour or so of combat.[67]

Only with the development and elaboration of their logistical "tails" could armies be substantially enlarged and freed from the need to end wars quickly or to find local supplies along their route of march. Part of the solution to this problem, of course, entailed the use of new modes of transportation such as railroads and, later, motor transport and aircraft, which increased the range and speed of movement of military forces and made it possible to bring large quantities of supplies to distant armies for long periods of time. The military potential of railroads, for instance, was initially suggested by the German economist Friedrich List in the 1830s and quickly demonstrated by the Russians, Austrians, and French in the 1840s.[68]

But rail transport technology alone did not change the character of warfare. It was the organization of bureaucratic entities able to make use of the rails that freed armies from their historic dependence upon local supplies and made it possible for them to fight for years in hostile lands. In the 1860s, for example, the Prussian Army constructed an elaborate organization to take advantage of the possibilities manifested by the railroad system. By 1870, each Prussian Army corps was served by a "train battalion," with 40 officers, 84 doctors, and 670 wagons, which carried the corps' provisions, food, ammunition, baggage, medical supplies, and a field bakery.[69] These helped to bring about the success of the Prussian military effort against France.

During the American Civil War, logistics, ordnance, and military engineering were raised to high arts, especially in the Union Army under the leadership of Quartermaster General Montgomery Meigs, who supervised railroad construction and military contracting and procurement. General Ulysses S. Grant also took a special interest in these matters.[70] When on the offensive, the Confederate Army adhered to the traditional tactic of seeking to capture food and other supplies along the route of march. The need to scavenge limited their mobility and the length of time Confederate forces could remain in the field, especially if their route of advance was blocked by northern troops. The Union Army, on the other hand, was the first in history to be fully supplied in battle over long distances and for long periods of time by railroad.[71] The Union Army also developed a substantial quartermaster's department and detailed men from each line regiment to handle supply problems. By the end of the war, the Union Army's administrative and logistical tail had reached a nearly modern length and helped to bring about the North's victory in what became a long war of attrition, in which supplies counted as much as fighting spirit and generalship.[72]

At the conclusion of the Civil War, the armies were demobilized and their wartime capabilities soon lost. Six decades later, when the United States entered World War I, it had little or no capacity to equip or supply a large army for a protracted fight. To address this problem, the Wilson administration established the War Industries Board (WIB) to convert the nation's economy to war production. The WIB was mainly a failure, and the American Expeditionary Force (AEF) was compelled to purchase virtually all of its equipment and supplies from the British and French. During the course of the war, the AEF bought from the French nearly 5,000 artillery pieces, 10,000 machine guns, 40,000 automatic rifles, millions of rounds of various sorts of ammunition, and more than 4,000 aircraft.[73] Perhaps overlooking the fact that no American horse soldiers had been dispatched to Europe, the WIB did see to it that more than 300,000 gas masks for horses would be shipped to the AEF.

At the beginning of World War II, the United States was better prepared. Between the wars, a joint board of army and navy war planners established a Joint Planning Committee, which engaged in strategic contingency planning for possible future wars against Japan and Germany. In addition, the 1920 National Defense Act had made the secretary of war responsible for military procurement and supply policies. Successive secretaries issued orders detailing these functions and creating new agencies, such as the munitions board, a procurement division, a planning branch within the office of the assistant secretary of war, and the Army Industrial College (AIC) to ensure that the US military would possess an adequate capacity for planning, procurement, and logistics in the event of a future war. Aircraft production was stepped up in 1939, and between 1940 and 1941, military budgets had been sharply increased, conscription had been instituted, and work begun on aircraft carriers, tanks, and artillery in preparation for a war the Roosevelt administration thought almost inevitable.

The AIC, which included students and instructors from all services, was designed to train officers in all aspects of manpower mobilization, military procurement, supply of combat forces, logistics, and industrial organization for wartime needs, as well as to provide planning in these realms.[74] By 1939, graduates of the AIC occupied important positions on the munitions board and in the planning branch, where they helped to manage military mobilization and industrial procurement. In addition, the individual services developed tactics, equipment, and organization designed to carry military forces and their equipment to distant battle fields and supply them for long periods of time. The Marine Corps, for example, developed tactics of amphibious warfare designed to land heavily armed troops on distant and hostile beaches along with logistical plans and personnel sufficient to supply those troops for years of fighting in regions where the time-honored military tactic of living off the land was not an option. The vaunted German Army, as we saw above, was hampered by not having developed a similar logistical plan.

In the decades since World War II, of course, the United States has been at war on almost a continual basis. The nation has fought large engagements in Korea, Indo-China, and the Middle East, as well as numerous smaller conflicts throughout the world. For better or worse, America's prodigious military effort has been made possible by the enormous bureaucracies constructed to arm, feed, supply, and transport American troops to distant battlefields where they may spend months or years in combat.

Command

The final element of the general military curriculum is the question of what characteristics are needed in those persons who command armies. Sun Tzu said that a commander must possess wisdom, sincerity, benevolence, courage, and strictness. "These five heads should be familiar to every general: he who knows them will be victorious; he who knows them not will fail."[75] Machiavelli was suspicious of professional soldiers and favored generals who were "civic-minded" and happy to return to civilian life at the conclusion of a campaign.[76] Machiavelli thought, further, that in addition to martial skill and experience, his ability to command depended upon his "courage and good conduct," and his understanding that to lead troops he must "pay well and punish soundly."[77] And, of course, Machiavelli famously averred that a leader must combine the courage of a lion and the cunning of a fox.[78] Clausewitz, who greatly admired Machiavelli, thought a general must be imbued with a "lucid intellect" and "great moral courage."[79]

Some famous military leaders seem, of course, to have possessed these qualities and to have made it their business to personally direct battles and to inspire the troops by their personal presence on the battlefield—sometimes at the head of the front-line forces. Alexander the Great, for example, personally rode at the head of the elite Macedonian Companion Cavalry at Issus and Gaugamela. This sort of personal, charismatic leadership, however, has severe limitations. If the charismatic leader happened to be killed or incapacitated, the entire army could be thrown into disarray. For example, the death of Richard III during the Battle of Bosworth Field in 1485 led his army to quickly disintegrate and flee from their less numerous Tudor foes. Premodern military encounters, moreover, generally took place on relatively small battlefields where the presence of the leader could be felt by all the troops. Modern battles can, of course, be fought across hundreds of square miles of land and sea where no one general, however charismatic and energetic, can make his presence felt by the forces at his command.

Successful armies usually lessen their dependence upon the charismatic commander by developing cadres of lower-ranking leaders who can be suffused throughout the organization. The Roman legions, for example, depended heavily upon their centurions, a group of several thousand highly trained career soldiers who are the ancestors of today's NCOs. Centurions could be transferred from legion to legion as needed and generally served in the army for life. If a centurion was himself killed or incapacitated, another would take his place. In essence, the Romans supplanted the individual charismatic leader with a bureaucratic organization. This bureaucratization of leadership gave the Roman legions a distinctive advantage over opponents led into battle by some individual king or chief. According to Roman legend, a consul's son was executed for breaking ranks and slaying the enemy leader in single combat, a severe breach of discipline.[80] Even today, bureaucratically organized armies are seldom thwarted by the death of a senior officer while forces that depend upon individual charismatic commanders—say, an Osama bin Laden—can be thrown into disarray by their leader's demise.

CIVILIAN APPLICATIONS: SWORDS INTO PLOWSHARES

Charles Tilly observed that war made states. In other words, societies regularly threatened by war were able to survive if and only if they succeeded in establishing powerful armies, systems of taxation to support those armies, economic infrastructures and financial systems to generate sufficient revenues to provide the needed taxes, and a large cadre of trained administrators to operate the entire system.[81] Building states required large-scale rationalization of authority. Like successful armies, successful states could only be built upon the foundation of bureaucratic systems of command. Bureaucracies developed from war. Once built, they expanded the scope of their operations to handle purely civilian tasks as well. Those societies unable or unwilling to build administrative institutions through which to facilitate waging war generally failed to survive, and had no need to study the remaining elements of the martial curriculum.

War also required societies to learn the rudiments of fiscal policy. Armies and war are expensive. And, very often, the expense cannot be deferred. A state threatened with attack must secure the funds to pay for armaments, fortifications, supplies, and troops. Once in the field, troops must be supplied and paid or they are likely to desert or mutiny. War is a harsh creditor as well as a harsh teacher. Over time, rulers have resorted to a variety of expedients to pay for their military efforts. In medieval and early modern Europe, the most common were outright expropriation and tax farming. The latter policy entailed selling some group the right to collect taxes from an area in exchange for current funds. In England, both policies often revolved around exploitation of the Jews. During the thirty-five-year reign of Henry II (1154–1189), Jews received royal privileges and protection in exchange for the useful commercial and fiscal services they provided to the Crown. During this period, Jewish merchants, a tiny fraction of England's population, paid approximately one-seventh of all the taxes collected in the kingdom. At the same time, Jewish financiers, most notably Aaron of Lincoln, as well as consortia headed by Moses of Bristol, Brun of London, and others, were essential to the Crown's finances. These financiers earned money through the loans they made to members of the nobility and others needing cash. They then advanced funds to the Crown for its day-to-day expenditures and received, in turn, royal notes secured by anticipated tax revenues. Thus, they performed functions similar to those undertaken by commercial banks and such institutions as the US Treasury today. Without the Jewish financiers, the Crown would soon have found itself in financial difficulties. With the help of the Jews, England under Henry was quite prosperous.

Henry's successors continued to depend upon the Jews for taxes and to fund the Crown's debt. Indeed, during the reign of Richard I, the Crown created an institution that came to be known as the "Exchequer of the Jews" to govern transactions between the Crown and Jewish financiers and to safeguard the king's interests. While the Jews faced considerable popular and clerical anti-Semitism, made worse by their identification with the unpopular, however necessary, occupation of money lending, as well as the continued growth of a crusading spirit in the realm, their value to the Crown meant that the Jews could normally count upon the king's protection.

Richard, however, was followed on the throne by King John, who seems to have been unaware of the idea that one should not kill the goose that lays the golden egg. Desperate for revenues, John instituted a series of heavy new taxes and assessments against the Jews, held Jews in prison, demanding ransom from their coreligionists, and confiscated a good deal of Jewish property. These policies made it difficult for the Jews to pay their customary taxes or to support the royal debt on a regular basis.

To make matters worse, the outbreak of a civil war between the king and a number of his barons created great hardships for the Jews, who came under attack from both sides—but particularly from the king's foes. The barons saw the Jews as instruments of the Crown both because of the king's dependence upon Jewish financiers and the king's practice of acquiring debts that members of the nobility themselves owed to the Jews. Indeed, in the Magna Carta of 1215, the barons compelled King John to accept limits upon the capacity of the Jews to recover debts from the landed gentry. The king was also forced to agree to accept restrictions upon his own power to acquire and recover debts that members of the gentry originally owed to the Jews. The acquisition of such debts had been a significant—and hated—mechanism through which the Crown extracted resources and enhanced its power over the nobility.

The hardships of the civil war coupled with harsh royal fiscal policies led most of England's Jews to flee the country toward the end of John's reign. In the absence of the Jews, the finances of the kingdom suffered. With the death of John and the succession of the child-king Henry III in 1216, William Marshall and Hubert de Burgh, successive regents, set about repairing the realm's financial system. To this end, they appealed to the Jews to return. To reassure Jewish returnees of their welcome, the regents released Jews being held in prison, promised to protect the Jews from anti-Semitic violence, restored some of the property that had been confiscated, and even went so far as to strike the clauses referring to the Jews when the Magna Carta was reconfirmed after John's death. Many Jews did return, and the old fiscal regime was reestablished.

Unfortunately, however, when Henry III reached majority and began to rule on his own, the Crown's revenue needs for foreign campaigns, for participation in crusades, and for expensive construction projects led the king to reintroduce the harsh policies of his late father, seeking as much short-term revenue from the Jews as possible without considering the long-term fiscal consequences. Thus, Henry introduced a variety of confiscatory taxes, and, if a Jew was unable to pay, the Crown might order his arrest, the imprisonment if his entire family, and the confiscation of his property. These policies were continued by Henry's successor, Edward I, who extorted money from the Jewish community by imprisoning large numbers of Jews and demanding that they be ransomed by their coreligionists. Jews who could fled England again, and, as a last act in 1290, Edward expelled England's handful of remaining Jews and confiscated their property. The expulsion of the

Jews was followed by fiscal problems for the Crown and capital shortages in the country.

In due course, England, like other European states, began to develop fiscal systems that did not depend upon outright expropriation. We shall return to this matter in chapter 4. At the heart of these systems was what historian Samuel Finer has called the extraction–coercion cycle.[82] That is, early modern rulers created administrative agencies charged with identifying and enumerating all the state's inhabitants. Most, if not all, inhabitants were required to pay regular taxes. Collection of taxes was enforced by the military, which could now be paid on a regular basis. As revenues began to flow more regularly into the state's coffers, more troops could be recruited, trained, and equipped. This, in turn, meant that a higher level of extraction could be sustained which, in its turn, created the fiscal foundation from more soldiers. So long as rulers were careful not to kill the goose, or taxpayer, that laid the golden egg, large armies could be created, equipped, and paid on a regular basis.

Planning

Like attention to fiscal policy, the other lessons learned in the general curriculum of war have had important civilian applications. Societies that learned these lessons benefitted from them. Let us consider the case of planning. Planning began mainly as a military practice but evolved into a standard function in civilian agencies and private firms. Rather than consult soothsayers or fortune tellers as they once might have, government officials and the heads of large enterprises have learned to think rationally and to promulgate strategic plans that more or less parallel those of military organizations.

One important technique imported by civilian and private agencies from the military planning sphere is systems analysis. Systems analysis began as a method of comparing the costs, benefits, and risks of alternative military programs and plans.[83] Military planning required the study of large-scale systems, integrating many different types of components to produce a desired result. This same form of analysis proved extremely useful in the design of civilian systems. The lessons drawn from military planning, for example, regarding the interactions between human motivations, technology, economic forces, and so forth, applied also to the design of health care delivery systems and other civilian applications—sometimes with mixed success.

As it developed in the military sphere, planning, especially planning in the realm of grand strategy, became the domain of specialized planning institutes or "think tanks" that gathered experts and spent years analyzing strategic problems, often at the behest of government agencies. The first of these was Great Britain's Royal United Services Institute for Defense and Security Studies (RUSI), founded in 1831 by the Duke of Wellington. Since its founding, RUSI has studied broad questions of security policy, primarily at the behest of the British government.

In the United States, a number of institutions within the military engage in long-term or strategic planning. These include the Institute for National Strategic Studies, the Center for Naval Warfare Studies, and the Strategic Studies Institute. In addition, the US government has established a number of quasi-public, quasi-private Federally Funded Research and Development Centers (FFRDCs). These include the RAND Corporation, MITRE Corporation, and the Institute for Defense Analysis. Often making use of systems analytic techniques, these and other FFRDCs have brought military planning and research methods to bear on civilian problems. RAND began as a consultant to the US Air Force and continues to undertake defense-related analysis and planning. At the same time, however, RAND has conducted major studies of American health policy, labor markets, corporate governance, and welfare policy. In a similar vein, the MITRE Corporation, which was created to provide planning and systems analysis for the Defense Department, expanded the scope of its activities to include planning and engineering support for civilian agencies, including the Internal Revenue Service, the Administrative Office of the US Courts, and the Centers for Medicare and Medicaid Services.

The notion of using military-style strategic planning for civilian purposes is also evident in the concept of the policy institute or think tank. These are private institutions in the United States as well as a number of other nations that engage in policy research and planning with civilian as well as military applications. Often, the research is supported by government contracts. In Britain, the Centre for Strategic Research and Analysis undertakes both military and civilian planning for the British government. In the United States, similar functions are performed by Hoover Institution, the Council on Foreign Relations, the Brookings Institution, and a host of others. Similar think tanks are found throughout the world.

Recruitment, Training, and Discipline

Military methods of recruitment, training, and ranking or grading workers on the basis of their aptitudes and performance were imported directly from the military sphere to civilian life. Take, for example, the use of intelligence and aptitude testing or scores on achievement tests to help determine new workers' assignments. This common personnel management practice was introduced by the military during the First World War to assess the aptitudes and leadership potential of military recruits. Similar techniques were subsequently adopted by civilian agencies and firms in the civilian economy.

More generally, as Max Weber observed, military discipline was the model for factory and other forms of civilian production. "Military discipline," Weber said, "gives birth to all discipline."[84] By this Weber meant that modern modes of production, like military service, require workers to learn to tolerate processes and tasks they naturally find unpleasant, such as to arrive for duty at the specified time, take their assigned place, and precisely execute received orders regardless of their personal preferences and perspectives. Just as military discipline requires the soldier to subordinate his personal feelings, whether these are fear or excessive enthusiasm, the discipline of the workplace requires the worker to focus on "the job," that is, his or her place in the overall productive machinery of the firm, rather than pursue some other motive. The workplace analog of recruit training is personnel or human capital management, the group within a firm or agency responsible for the selection, training, and evaluation of workers with the goal of maximizing each worker's job performance. In the factory, as in the military force, says Weber, "the individual is shorn of his natural rhythms . . . in line with the demands of the work procedure."[85]

Engineering

As noted previously, the term *engineering* originally referred to the design and manufacture of military machines and equipment. The first engineers built fortresses, battering rams, and catapults, as well as bridges and roads to facilitate troop movement. In his multi-volume work *De Architectura*, the first century BCE Roman military engineer Marcus Vitruvius Pollio described the construction of a variety of Roman military engines such as siege engines and ballistae.[86] In his accounts of Roman engineering, though, Vitruvius also describes various structures and pieces of equipment built by military engineers that also had obvious civilian uses. These include hoists, cranes, and pulleys, as well as sundials and water clocks and the *aeolipile*, a primitive steam engine. Obviously, the skills developed by military engineers were easily transferrable to civilian projects. Vitruvius himself played an important role in the construction of Rome's aqueducts and was involved in the design of central heating systems for villas.

Until recent times, the same engineers built civilian and military works, but in the eighteenth century those engineers who focused primarily on civilian projects began to call themselves civil engineers to distinguish themselves from those whose interests were mainly military. Civil engineers build structures of various sorts, design transportation systems, water and sanitary systems, power grids, and communications systems. Nevertheless, the origins of engineering are military. Civil engineering might be seen as a spillover from the martial curriculum.

Logistics and Production

From military logistics, societies directly learn how to maximize the production and distribution of goods. Just as Roman roads carried both troops and commerce, so America's Eisenhower-era National Defense Highway Program was a dual-use project. This is most evident in the realm of mass production. The practice of assembly-line production using interchangeable parts, the basis of contemporary factory systems, derives directly from methods devised to maximize the production of military weapons and supplies. Perhaps one of the earliest examples of mass production in the bronze-triggered crossbow produced in China during the Warring States period. The military success of the Qin Empire in 221 BCE was due in no small measure to its ability to mass produce crossbows with which to arm his troops.[87] Several centuries later, the Venetian Arsenal, a state-owned shipyard and armory, mass-produced warships using prefabricated parts at the rate of one ship per day. In the nineteenth century, what came to be known as the American system of manufacture was introduced in America's Springfield and Harpers Ferry arsenals for the rapid production of guns—using interchangeable parts. Subsequently, of course, mass production with interchangeable parts became the basis for all factory production and, hence, the bedrock of civilian industrial economies.

THE LESSONS OF WAR

War is brutal and terrible and, as General Lee suggested, we should not grow fond of it. The fact that war is terrible, however, does not mean that nothing is to be learned from it. Indeed, societies have, over the centuries, learned a number of valuable lessons from war. Fundamentally, they learned to be realistic. They also learned how to rationalize authority, to plan, and to develop engineering and production skills. The cost of these lessons was high. Lessons learned were sometimes forgotten and had to be relearned. Nevertheless, the curriculum of war, perhaps more than any other text, brought about the development of a more modern world.

CHAPTER 2

WAR AND TECHNOLOGICAL PROGRESS

Just as it promotes rational thinking, war is an important factor in the incubation and diffusion of technology. Modern war, of course, relies heavily upon technology. The US military makes substantial use of computers, precision-guided munitions, remotely piloted aircraft, orbital satellites, and so forth. Today, the US Army is testing a robotic dog with the capacity to accompany troops and carry their supplies over rough terrain. The robot, whose official military name is "Legged Squad Support System" or LS3, responds to voice commands and will eventually be armed and able to engage opposing forces. The LS3 may resemble some device from a science fiction film, but military use of advanced technology is nothing new. Cutting-edge technology and war have always gone hand-in-hand. Though robotic dogs might have been beyond their capabilities, ancient Greek, Roman, and Chinese engineers also developed complex weapons, armor, siege equipment, and a host of other military tools that shocked and frightened their less sophisticated foes.

Some weapons may have no civilian use or immediate counterpart. The land mine, for example, designed to detonate if disturbed by pressure or vibration, is a simple and useful weapon with no obvious civilian application. But, of course, the same chemistry and materials science and production technology used to design and construct land mines is also used to synthesize chemicals, fabricate containers, and assemble a variety of pressure-sensitive switches used every day in the civilian world. Technology is technology. The same skills and techniques employed in the design and manufacture of weapons are also used to design and build bridges, televisions, automobiles, cell phones, and the other devices upon which civilization depends. Technology is inherently dual use.

Given the ubiquity and, one might say, life-and-death importance of warfare in human history, it is probably not surprising to discover that a good deal of human ingenuity has been devoted to the development and perfection of ever more potent instruments of destruction. As in the case of the land mine, many of these swords, despite biblical prophecy, cannot directly be turned into plowshares. War and preparation for war, nevertheless, have played a major role in the incubation and dissemination of civilian technologies. In a sense, perfecting the sword has also helped to perfect the plowshare and vice versa. There are three main conduits through which warfare can advance or disseminate civilian technology. These are conquest, imitation, and civil–military technology transfer.

CONQUEST

Military conquest is among the most common routes for the dissemination of technology. When, as has often occurred, societies with superior technologies conquer those with less technological ability, surviving members of the conquered society may be eventually absorbed into the technical culture of their victorious foes. They learn not only to wield more advanced weapons, but also become familiar with the tools, machines, and production technologies of their conquerors. In other cases, technologically more advanced societies have been conquered by their technological inferiors. In these instances, the conquerors have usually taken advantage of the opportunity to appropriate the technologies of those whom they defeated. In a ricochet effect, they sometimes use those technology to expand their conquests and increase the technological capabilities of still other societies.

An important example of technological dissemination through conquest is the case of the European subjugation and colonization of vast stretches of the world between the sixteenth and nineteenth centuries. This conquest was made possible by the Europeans' superior armaments which, in turn, reflected Europe's general technological advantage over those whom it defeated.

Of course, nothing guaranteed that it would be the Europeans who conquered the world. The Chinese might have seemed more likely candidates for this role. At the end of the fifteenth century, China possessed technology and weapons more advanced than those to be found in Europe. Ships commanded by Chinese Admiral Cheng Ho cruised the Indian Ocean and certainly had the potential to cross the Pacific. The Chinese might have found and conquered the New World.[1] In early modern Europe, however, complex patterns of competition between merchants and among princes meant that new technologies were generally likely to be viewed as a potential source of profit by the former and a potential advantage in Europe's unrelenting arms race by the latter.

Competition produced a virtuous cycle of ongoing improvement in both military and civilian technologies, with each helping to advance the other. Merchants, for example, supported the construction of larger and more sturdy ships, which in turn provided princes with better gun platforms for naval artillery, which in turn expanded the trade routes accessible to the merchants, and so on.

In fifteenth- and sixteenth-century China, by contrast, the mandarins who effectively ruled the empire saw both commerce and technology as socially disruptive forces. They believed that both needed to be tightly regulated to preserve the peace of the empire and their own power. This perspective was exemplified by the imperial decision of 1433 to end explorations of the Indian Ocean, followed by a 1436 decree prohibiting the construction of seagoing ships.[2] Hence, China entered a period of stagnation as Portuguese, Spanish, English, Dutch, and French vessels explored the world and employed their superior arms to subjugate the various indigenous peoples. Over time, though, European armaments and more general technology were absorbed by the surviving descendants of the various defeated groups, erasing much of Europe's technological and military advantage.

The Spanish adventurers who landed in Mexico and South America in the early sixteenth century encountered the enormous Aztec and Inca empires. For reasons discussed in the previous chapter, both empires had been badly weakened by civil war and revolution. In addition, the Spaniards unwittingly brought with them smallpox and other diseases that ravaged populations never previously exposed to them that, accordingly, lacked resistance. Nevertheless, a handful of Spaniards would not have been able to defeat and overthrow the Aztecs and Incas if they had not also possessed weapons far superior to those of their unfortunate adversaries.

At the 1532 Battle of Cajamarca, for example, superior weaponry along with military skill and guile allowed Francisco Pizarro and his force of 168 Spaniards to defeat a veteran Inca army of some 80,000 warriors, killing many thousands and capturing the emperor Atahuallpa. Not a single Spaniard was killed in the encounter. The armaments wielded by the Incas included wooden clubs and maces, slings, spears, bows, and stone or copper axes. For protection, Inca soldiers wore wooden helmets and carried wood and leather shields. Officers wore padded cotton tunics as a kind of body armor. Horses were unknown in the New World, so all Inca troops were on foot.

The Spaniards, for their part, wielded steel, double-edged, three-foot-long swords as well as steel daggers that easily cut through Inca helmets, shields, and quilted armor. In battle, moreover, the Spaniards wore steel armor that gave them considerable protection from Inca weapons. The Spaniards also possessed firearms, including arquebuses (an early musket design) and several small cannons. These firearms were useful, but even more important than firearms were the horses and lances of Spanish cavalrymen. Some sixty of Pizarro's soldiers were mounted and armed with long wooden lances tipped with iron or steel points. Riders and their horses wore armor and the cavalrymen, like the foot soldiers, carried steel swords for close combat. A rank of armored Spanish horsemen with lances fixed had little difficulty sweeping through large groups of Inca foot soldiers. On open ground, the Incas had no defense against cavalry.[3] Spanish foot soldiers, also armored and carrying steel swords, were well able to wreak havoc among the dazed survivors of the cavalry charge. Similar disparities in weaponry made it possible for Cortés and his force of 600 Spanish soldiers to overthrow the Aztec empire and for other conquistadors to wrest control of virtually all of South and Central America from native peoples.

Again, weapons were not the whole story. Native peoples were weakened by European diseases such as smallpox, typhus, and influenza. In the case of the Aztecs and Incas, imperial policies had led to civil wars and rebellions that seriously weakened both empires. Neither Pizarro nor Cortés would have prevailed if the enemies of the Incas and Aztecs had not contributed tens of thousands of warriors to fight alongside the Spaniards. Superior weaponry, though, was critical. Had the Spaniards not demonstrated the power of their weapons, potential native allies would have been reluctant to join them.

In North America, too, superior weapons paved the way for conquest and settlement by Europeans. Muskets and swords and, eventually repeating rifles and Gatling guns, overpowered native resistance. In the North American case, of course, indigenous people were gradually able to acquire and use European weapons to defend themselves. For reasons that will be discussed below, however, this proved to be of little use in checking the European invasion.

The superiority of European weapons relative to those wielded by the Incas, Aztecs, and other peoples of the Western Hemisphere reflected the larger technological gap between the Old and New Worlds. The cultures of the New World were somewhere between the stone and bronze ages in terms of technological development. Their European invaders had long mastered the production of iron, and were regularly combining carbon with iron to manufacture steel weapons and implements that were far superior to the brittle stone or soft bronze counterparts available to the peoples of the New World. It was European maritime technology, moreover, that made possible the long voyages that brought the conquistadores and later groups to the New World. These technologies included the lateen sail able to power large boats, the compass and astrolabe for navigation, and the hinged, stern-mounted "pintle and gudgeon" rudder that allowed large ships to be maneuvered even in heavy weather.

A second wave of European conquests, these beginning in the seventeenth century, depended less on steel and more on gunpowder. Firearms were introduced early in the fourteenth century in both Europe and China, and while the Chinese invented gunpowder, it was the Europeans who invented—or, at least, perfected—the gun.[4] The first gunpowder weapons were artillery pieces of various sorts which, by the mid-fifteenth century, were sufficiently powerful to knock down stone castle and town walls that had previously been considered impregnable. Initially, artillery pieces were made of bronze and were so expensive that only the largest and wealthiest states could afford them. By the mid-sixteenth century, though, European manufacturers had learned how to build cannons using iron rather than bronze, which significantly lowered the price and increased the availability of these weapons. The original cannons had been enormous, but rapid improvements in gunpowder, ammunition, and design led to canons that could be carried to the battlefield on horse-drawn carriages and quickly moved as needed to support infantry and cavalry.

While large guns came first, small firearms that could be used by individual soldiers were not far behind. The earliest effective hand weapon, the arquebus, was a muzzle-loaded long gun fired by a matchlock mechanism. The soldier loaded one or more pieces of metal shot into the gun's barrel, took aim, lit the match, and pulled the trigger to bring the match into a flash pan, which would ignite a predetermined quantity of gunpowder and fire the weapon. As this description suggests, the arquebus's rate of fire was slow, albeit faster than that of the crossbow. However, this weapon had many advantages relative to the longbows and crossbows it soon replaced. Bowmen required years of practice to develop any degree of accuracy, but very little skill or training was required to fire the arquebus successfully. Metal shot from the arquebus, moreover, could easily penetrate even the best armor at a fairly long range, and a soldier armed with an arquebus could carry enough ammunition and powder to fire his weapon repeatedly during an engagement.

By the 1530s, the Spaniards, who were among the first to make use of the arquebus in battle, developed a formation called the *tercio*, or Spanish square, to take advantage of the new weapon. Initially, the tercio consisted of between 1,500 and 3,000 infantrymen, some designated as pikemen and some as arquebusiers. A third group consisting of swordsmen became less important as the lethality of firearms gradually improved. The pikemen were arrayed in a hollow square. Their eighteen-foot-long pikes, tipped by four-foot-long iron or steel spearheads were designed to hold off cavalry charges and to mount shock attacks against opposing infantry.

This formation had been invented by the Swiss who, with infantry phalanxes armed with pikes and halberds—hooked weapons designed to drag horsemen from their saddles—had brought an end to the battlefield supremacy of the feudal cavalry.[5] In the Spanish tercio, the halberdiers were replaced by arquebusiers who could direct fire at opposing cavalry and infantry. The pikemen protected the arquebusiers from being overrun by cavalry charges and, in turn, launched shock attacks against enemy formations. At the same time, engineers were assigned to throw up field fortifications to shelter the tercio from its opponents' gunfire and shock attacks. Improvements in the design of armaments during the course of the sixteenth century led to the substitution of muskets for arquebuses. The musket, also a long gun, was more accurate and easier to load and hence able to maintain a more rapid and effective rate of fire than the arquebus. Muskets, in turn, put an end to the need for pikemen. Infantry armed with muskets, and supported by cavalry and artillery, became the mainstays of European battlefields after 1600.

Of course, the Europeans were not the only ones to make use of firearms during this period. Between the fourteenth and seventeenth centuries, the Ottoman, Safavid, and Mughal empires built or acquired cannons and muskets and established what some historians have called "gunpowder empires."[6] During this period and the ensuing three centuries, however, the Europeans maintained a substantial lead in the technology of warfare. This included the development of ship-borne heavy artillery that allowed European states to project enormous power across the maritime world. Equally important, the Europeans developed tactics and training designed to maximize the effectiveness of their firepower. Early in the seventeenth century, the Dutch prince, Maurice of Nassau, introduced tactics that made his forces quite maneuverable on the battlefield and drill and discipline that made them willing to maintain their formations while receiving fire from opposing forces. Subsequent military innovators such as Gustavus Adolphus of Sweden honed infantry tactics to perfection.[7]

Europe's lead in military technology widened sharply with the European industrial revolution of the eighteenth and early nineteenth centuries. The early technologies associated with the industrial revolution include the development of reliable and efficient steam engines that soon powered locomotives and ships; enormous improvements in the production of iron; the expanded use of efficient fuels—particularly coal; the development of various machine tools for cutting and shaping metal; the mechanization of production and agriculture; and new communications technologies—particularly the telegraph. These are only a few of the technological advances made in Europe and the United States during this period. As a result of the industrial revolution, rival European states were given the opportunity to harness new technologies to ever more powerful weapons. Cumbersome cannons were converted into breech-loading, rapid-fire artillery. Steam-powered steel warships carrying heavy guns ruled the seas. Infantrymen were equipped with mass-produced, breech-loading rifles to replace their more cumbersome muskets. With their weapons, their ships, and their tactics, European armies conquered the Americas, Africa, portions of Asia, and the Indian subcontinent. The only military forces that could reliably defeat European armies were other European armies employing similar forms of organization and technology.

As it conquered the world, Europe also disseminated its technologies, both military and civilian. In some regions, indigenous people were able to acquire European weapons and attempted to use them to repel the invaders. Native North Americans, as I mentioned earlier, acquired firearms and often became quite proficient in their use. The

North American Plains Indians learned the technique of combining the horse and the repeating rifle and by the late nineteenth century had become quite an effective light cavalry. By this time, however, European settlers had very nearly exterminated the indigenous people of North America, and there were too few survivors for a newfound mastery of European weapons to have any consequence. European technology was obviously disseminated to regions such as North America and Australia, where Europeans obliterated native societies, as well as to those regions such as South and Central America, where Europeans more or less permanently subjugated indigenous groups.

European technologies also spread to other parts of the globe that were controlled or even dominated, but not fully subjugated, by one or another European state. Here, not only the weapons but the technological base from which those weapons derived might be assimilated and ultimately employed to challenge European domination. Take the case of India. During the eighteenth and nineteenth centuries, as India came under British control, important elements of British technology were exported to and assimilated by India's own populace, eventually expanding manufacturing, agriculture, and commerce on the subcontinent. The most important British technology exports were in the realms of transport and communication. To cement their control over India and their capacity to move troops quickly wherever they might be needed, the British built thousands of miles of railroads, roads, and telegraph lines that promoted communication and transport throughout India. Like the ancient Roman roads, arteries built to move troops also promoted the flow of commerce.

Beginning in 1780, British engineers began a several-decades-long effort to expand and improve India's road network.[8] The original purpose of this effort was to facilitate the movement of troops and supplies in order to strengthen Britain's hold on India. These roads, however, particularly the improvement and expansion of India's ancient Grand Trunk Road, traversing 2,500 miles from India's eastern seaports through Calcutta and Delhi and ending in Kabul in modern-day Afghanistan, opened the way for horse-drawn (later, gasoline-powered) wheeled transport carrying mail and goods throughout India. Road-building greatly stimulated India's market economy and stimulated the production of local goods, as well as the distribution of imported products.

Similarly, beginning in the 1850s, the British began the construction of India's railway system, laying 120 miles of track between the West Bengal port city of Hooghly to the Raniganj coalfields.[9] This line was followed by hundreds of others, and some 24,000 mile of track laid during the nineteenth century alone, carrying millions of tons of freight and speeding both the transport of troops and goods throughout India. By the beginning of the First World War, India boasted the fifth-largest railway system in the world, the most extensive outside Europe and North America.[10] Initially, most of the locomotives and other rolling stock of the Indian railway system were manufactured in England. By the early 1900s, though, large workshops for the repair and assembly of railroad equipment had developed in Lahore and Rawalpindi. These workshops employed thousands of Indian workers who had an opportunity to learn the skills associated with building and maintaining locomotives and other railway equipment.[11]

The British introduced the telegraph to India and, by 1900, had installed tens of thousands of miles of telegraph lines and hundreds of receiving stations throughout the region. The telegraph, of course, had considerable military value, helping the British army to collect up-to-date information and direct troops where they were needed. But, of course, the telegraph also became an important commercial instrument, allowing Indian as well as European businessmen to conduct transactions rapidly across the entire subcontinent.

In addition to these systems of transport and communication, the British built factories, canals, and irrigation systems and brought many other elements of European technology to India. Of course, India already possessed a long tradition of scholarship in science and mathematics, and some existing technologies may have been extinguished under British rule. In general, however, Britain brought advanced technology to the subcontinent it conquered. Ironically, this created the technological base from which India eventually surpassed Britain as an industrial and scientific center. An important symbol of this shift came in 2008, when India's Tata Motors purchased Britain's venerable Jaguar and Land Rover motor companies and then spent hundreds of millions of dollars to bring these English vehicles up to Indian technological standards.

REVERSE TECHNOLOGY FLOWS: FROM THE CONQUERED TO THEIR CONQUERORS

Conquest leads not only to exports of technology from conquerors to those they subjugate; technology may flow in the other direction as well. This is especially likely to occur if a technologically more advanced society is conquered by a technologically less sophisticated foe. In the early twentieth century, to cite just one example, Germany was the world's leader in what today would be called aerospace engineering. During the closing years of the Second World War, the Germans fired V-1 and V-2 missiles at England. The V-1 was jet-powered, used an autopilot to control the missile's speed and altitude, and carried a 1,900-pound explosive warhead. The V-1 had a range of about 160 miles and flew at about 400 miles per hour, a speed which made it vulnerable to Allied aircraft and anti-aircraft guns. More than 9,000 of the missiles were fired at England and another 2,000 at targets on the European continent after the Allied invasion. The V-2 was an even more advanced weapon. It was the world's first ballistic missile and had a range of about 200 miles at a speed of more than 3,000 miles per hour, which made the weapon impossible to intercept. More than 3,000 V-2s were launched by the Germans. Their relatively small warheads, however, limited the damage they were able to produce. When the Allies defeated and occupied Germany, the Americans and Soviets acquired German aviation and rocket technology, along with German scientists, that became the basis for both nation's space and ballistic missile programs—as well as their development of jet aircraft.

One important example of conquered-to-conqueror technology transfer from the ancient world is the relationship between Greece and Rome, in which Rome's military conquest paved the way for an enormous flow of Greek technology into the Roman Empire. Rome's conquest of Greece over a period of about sixty-five years began with the so-called First Macedonian War (214–205 BCE). After the disastrous Roman defeat by the Carthaginians at Cannae in 216 BCE, Macedonian King Philip believed that the Romans would not be able to oppose his efforts to expand Macedonian power in Greece and the Aegean. Accordingly, he signed a treaty of alliance with the Carthaginian general Hannibal, in which the Macedonians agreed to support Carthage in its war against Rome in exchange for control over a number of Roman-held territories on the eastern shore of the Adriatic. Learning of this alliance, the Romans strengthened their forces in the Adriatic region and fought several small-scale battles designed mainly to prevent Philip from sending reinforcements to Hannibal, Rome's primary foe. The war ended inconclusively in 205 BCE, when the Macedonians concluded that Hannibal would be defeated and the Romans were happy to be able to shift their legions to more important military fronts to the West. During the war, the Romans were able to expand their influence and alliances in Greece and paved the way for the subsequent expansion of their power in the region.

An opportunity for such expansion came quickly. In 201 BCE, the Greek city-states of Rhodes and Pergamon asked the Romans for help against a Macedonian attack. The Romans, who by this time had defeated Carthage, had no particular territorial ambitions in Greece. Rome was, however, concerned about the rise of a rival power so close to its own territory and maritime interests. Thus, Rome wanted to prevent Philip from expanding Macedonian influence over neighboring city-states. This concern was heightened when Philip entered into an alliance with Antiochus III of the Seleucid Empire (the near-eastern portion of the empire that had been built by Alexander the Great.). An alliance between the Macedonians and Seleucids had the potential to conquer all of Greece and pose a threat to Roman domination of both the Mediterranean and Adriatic regions. In the Second Macedonian War, the Romans, aided by the Athenians and other Greeks who feared Philip—particularly the Aetolians—attacked Macedon and inflicted a decisive defeat on the Macedonians in the Battle of Cynoscephalae in 197 BCE. After this Roman victory, Philip was prohibited from threatening other Greek states, and the Romans acquired a good deal of territory in the modern-day Balkans.

Peace lasted only until 192 BCE. Despite the defeat of their allies the Macedonians, the Seleucids hoped to expand into Greece. Antiochus promised the Aetolians substantial territorial rewards if they would end their alliance with Rome and support his efforts instead. With the support of Aetolian forces and with Rome's most feared opponent, Hannibal, as a military advisor, a large Seleucid army entered Greece. The Romans, however, were determined now to allow the Seleucids to take control of the region and sent a large force to stop them. At the Battles of Thermopylae and Magnesia, the Seleucids were routed by the Roman legions and forced to cede to Rome the territory they had occupied in Greece.

Subsequently, Rome defeated Macedon two more times, first dividing the kingdom of Macedon into four nominally independent states controlled by Rome and then annexing Macedon altogether as the Roman province of Macedonia. Most Greek polities had been happy to see the Romans prevent Macedon and the Seleucid Empire from expanding their influence in the Greek world. Now, however, Rome seemed to pose an even greater threat than either of these Greek realms. Thus, in 146 BCE, a group of Greek city-states declared war on Rome and attempted to drive the Romans from Greece. After a short war, the Greeks were defeated and Rome annexed the entire region, dividing Greece into the new Roman provinces of Achaea and Epirus. Millennia of Greek independence had come to an end.

It is often observed that Rome conquered Greece militarily, but the reverse was true culturally. Greek culture was far older and more sophisticated than that of Rome, and the Romans, aware of this fact, eagerly absorbed—one might say swallowed—the culture of their new conquest. This was true in the realms of drama, poetry, literature, art, fashion, and, perhaps most important, technology. The Greeks had developed a number of important civilian and military technologies that the Romans appropriated, in many cases improving Greek designs. The Romans recognized their debt to the Greeks and often employed Greek engineers for important projects. The Greek engineer Apollodorus of Damascus, for example, was employed by the Emperor Trajan for the most complex and important imperial engineering projects. In 105 CE, Apollodorus built Trajan's bridge across the Danube, at that time one of the longest spans in Europe, to allow the legions to cross easily for Trajan's campaign in Dacia. Apollodorus also built Trajan's column in the Roman forum.

Beginning in about the sixth century BCE, the Greeks began to develop remarkable technologies that they employed for measurement, construction, transportation, irrigation, plumbing, ship building, and a host of other tasks. Among these "other tasks," of course, was war. The Greek city-states were almost continually at war with one another and with non-Greek foes. Technology provided the Greeks with a number of powerful weapons to use in battle. One of these weapons was the crossbow, a form of mechanical bow that fires a projectile with far greater penetrating power and accuracy, though a slower fire rate, than other bows. The fact that the bow is drawn mechanically rather than by hand allows it to be held at ready for an indefinite period of time and then fired when the target appears. Crossbows were developed in ancient China as well as ancient Greece, and perhaps also in other parts of the world. The Greek crossbow seems to date from about the fifth century BCE, when a hand-held device called the *gastraphetes* was employed by a Greek force against a Carthaginian army in Sicily. Over the next century or so, crossbows became larger and more diverse, with some large machines, operated by a crew like a modern artillery piece, designed to fire several arrows at a time.

By the third or fourth century BCE, the Greeks had introduced a more powerful mechanical arrow-firing device variously called the *katapeltikon* or *ballista*. In this device, the Greeks applied the principles of mathematics and physics they had begun to master. The device was built around a set of torsion springs usually made of animal sinew. These were mechanically wound to store energy which, when released, would propel a large arrow over a long distance with enormous penetrating power. During the third century BCE, both forms of arrow-shooting machines became standard elements in the arsenals of Greek armies. The principles of the ballista were adapted to build machines capable of hurling rocks as well as incendiary materials at enemy cities and fortifications.

Defenders used their own ballista and so forth to repel the attackers and, hence, the Greeks had devised both siege engines and field artillery. Philip II of Macedon and his son, Alexander the Great, employed large numbers of these early artillery pieces in their campaigns as well as large, mobile siege towers, tall structures from which attackers could fire projectiles over city walls.

The power of Greek weapons became very apparent to the Romans during the siege of Syracuse, which lasted from 214 to 212 BCE. Syracuse, a port city on the eastern coast of Sicily, had been a Roman ally. In 214 BCE, however, during the Second Punic War between Rome and Carthage, an anti-Roman faction came to power in Syracuse and sought an alliance with Carthage. Such an alliance would pose a serious problem for the Romans because a Carthaginian army and fleet based in Sicily could open another front against Rome, which already had more than it could do to ward off Hannibal's army in northern Italy. Accordingly, a Roman force was dispatched to capture Syracuse before the Carthaginians could reinforce the city. The Syracusean army was no match for the Romans, but the city was protected by high walls and by an array of weapons constructed under the supervision of Greece's most famous scientist and mathematician, Archimedes. Ballistae, designed by Archimedes and mounted on the city's walls, pounded the Roman fleet and troops with rocks and arrows. Archimedes, moreover, had devised a giant crane and hook—dubbed the "Claw of Archimedes"—that could reach down, pull Roman ships from the water and shake them to pieces or smash them on the rocks below. According to legend,

Archimedes also built a device involving a large array of bronze mirrors able to focus the rays of the sun on Roman ships and cause them to burst into flame. There is, however, some doubt that such a device was possible given the materials actually available to Archimedes. After a two-year siege, despite these remarkable weapons, the Romans were able to take the city—as much by stealth as by force.

As they took control of Greece, the Romans came into possession of many Greek weapons, often along with the engineers who had designed and operated them. The Romans had, indeed, hoped to capture Archimedes, but unfortunately the scientist was killed when Roman troops stormed the city. Many Greek weapons entered the Roman arsenal. The Romans, with the help of Greek engineers, often modified the weapons but seldom introduced radical new designs. Thus, the Romans took the Greek ballista and modified it to improve its accuracy and range and added a universal joint that allowed the ballista's aim to be altered without moving the weapon. Another Roman modification of the ballista was the *onager*, a type of catapult with the capacity to throw stones and rocks over considerable distances. Onagers were often used to hurl clay balls filled with a combustible substance that exploded when it struck its target. The Romans also adapted and improved the *polybolos*, a repeating catapult that, like a modern-day machine gun, used a chain drive to fire several dozen bolts from a wooden box without the need to reload after each shot. And, as in the case of European armies a millennium later, the Romans also innovated in the organization of technology to maximize its military effectiveness. In the legions, every Roman *century*, or company of 80 soldiers, was issued a ballista and expected to train a small group to become expert in its use. In addition, an engineering corps was organized to supervise military construction as well as to fire the larger and more complex ballistae and onagers in battle.

The Roman interest in Greek technology may have begun with weapons. However, to build and use—to say nothing of *improve*—Greek weapons effectively, the Romans had to develop an understanding of the mathematical and scientific principles behind the weapons. This, the Romans set out to do. Wealthy Roman families employed Greek tutors for their children and sent their sons to study in Athens and Rhodes. The Romans, to be sure, were not without technology. They were expert in a variety of areas such as bridge and road building. However, their conquest of Greece gave the Romans access to science, mathematics, and technology superior to their own, and they made good use of the opportunity. As in the case of military technology, the Romans often found ways to improve what they appropriated.

The Greeks, for example, had developed and made extensive use of the watermill, an important device that uses a water wheel to convert the energy from free-flowing or falling water into a source of power with which to grind grains and produce flour. The two main components of the watermill, the waterwheel and toothed gearing, are Greek inventions. After learning the basic principles, the Romans improved the technology of the watermill and applied the principle to other problems. The Romans built water-powered sawmills, stamp mills, and water-powered trip-hammers for use in mining operations.

Another basic piece of technology, the crane, was invented by the Greeks and improved by the Romans. The crane is a ubiquitous type of machine equipped with a hoist, ropes, or chains used to lift and move heavy objects. Cranes are used in loading, construction, and assembly. As we saw above, Archimedes used a crane and hook to lift Roman warships out of the water before dropping and smashing them. Greek cranes were powered by people or donkeys. The Romans improved upon the design and harnessed cranes to waterwheels, greatly increasing their power and making it possible to use very large cranes in heavy construction near streams, rivers, and waterfalls.

The Greeks, quite possibly Archimedes himself, also invented the wooden screw that the Romans used in a myriad of devices. The Greeks developed the gear, which the Romans used in wagons and carts. The Greeks invented the winch, the pulley, and the hoist, all of which became staples of Roman construction, mining, and commerce. The Greeks invented the screw press, which the Romans put to work in the production of wine and olive oil.

All in all, when they conquered Greece, the Romans substantially raised their own technological level. The Romans, moreover, disseminated the technologies they appropriated and adapted throughout their empire—thus throughout Europe—sometimes making use of Greek military technologies to subjugate new territories into which they would bring other technologies that were, themselves, often Greek in origin. Thus, for example, with their Greek-derived crossbows, onagers, ballistae, and so forth, the armies of the early Roman Empire crossed the Danube on a bridge built by Greek engineers to conquer Dacia (modern-day Romania). In addition, of course, to death, destruction, and slavery, the Romans brought architecture, engineering, mining, and agriculture as well as the water wheels, wine presses, screws, gears, and other devices they had learned from the Greeks. Within a century, of course, Dacian tribes like the Carpi were allied with the Goths and were using the Greco–Roman technology they had acquired from their conquerors to drive the legions back across the Danube.

IMITATION

Conquest is not the only route through which war disseminates technology. War and preparation for war also encourage societies to imitate one another's promising military technologies. Often enough, imitation of a military innovation requires assimilation of a whole new set of technologies with both civilian and military applications. In this way, copying swords may require learning to build plowshares. There are several ways in which military technologies developed by one society can spread to others. These include secondary use, simple observation, voluntary technology transfers, reverse engineering, and espionage.

Of course, several of these avenues of diffusion do not require warfare. Commercial competitors often imitate one another's products and even engage in industrial espionage to ferret out one another's secrets. In many cases, however, there is resistance on the part of established interests, both military and civilian, to the introduction of new ideas and new technologies that threaten the existing order and their power and prominence in it. Established nineteenth-century physicians disputed the germ theory of disease as early twentieth-century physicists resisted the idea of quantum theory. Peacetime navies commanded by battleship admirals denied the value of aircraft carriers that, among other things, would enhance the power of their rivals within the navy. American auto executives in the 1960s were confident that the huge, gas-guzzling vehicles upon which their careers and profits had been built would always rule the road and dismissed Japanese auto engineering innovations. The list of examples is endless.

War, however, puts enormous pressure on societies to identify and assimilate useful innovations. Though it offers no guarantee that innovation will prevail, in war, the penalty for failing to acquire and learn to use important new technologies or modes of organization can be quite severe. Hence, in wartime, the objections of established interests to innovation are more likely to be brushed aside as detrimental to a society's chances of survival. War-driven acceptance of innovation takes many forms. During World War II, for example, Joseph Stalin decided it was better to follow the example of other armies and reduced the power of the Red Army's political officers while increasing the authority of the army's professional soldiers to make tactical decisions.[12] Apparently Comrade Stalin disagreed with the slogan of America's post-war peace movement and decided it was *not* better to be "red than dead."

The most obvious and, perhaps, most common vehicle of military technological diffusion is what might be termed secondary use. This term simply refers to one state or society acquiring and using weapons built by another. The method of acquisition might be theft, purchase, or even battlefield scavenging. For instance, as I noted previously, long before they were fully conquered, some indigenous North American tribes acquired and became quite proficient in the use of firearms. Sometimes they purchased these weapons from traders; sometimes they were issued weapons in exchange for service in the US military; in some instances, they acquired them through raids and theft. Whatever the precise mode of acquisition, this form of secondary use represented a very limited transfer of technology. Indigenous tribesmen learned how to fire weapons but lacked the technological base from which to actually build firearms and produce ammunition for them. Generally speaking, the wider the technological gulf between the recipient and source of military technology transfers, the more likely that the transfer will be limited to secondary use.

This principle usually holds true in the case of a major source of secondary use today, namely, arms sales. The United States sells tens of billions of dollars of arms every year, mainly to nations in the Middle East and Asia. Most of America's Middle Eastern customers, Saudi Arabia in particular, have little in the way of manufacturing capability, much less a sophisticated arms industry. These recipients of American arms are dependent upon the United States for maintenance, spare parts, and ammunition, hence the transfer of technology is very minor. America's Asian customers, on the other hand, most notably Japan and Taiwan, have very large and sophisticated manufacturing bases and could probable copy the American weapons they purchase. These nations are, however, constrained from so doing by agreements with the United States, as well as a calculation that it would be too expensive and politically risky to build the most sophisticated weapons in their own factories. While the Japanese and Taiwanese undoubtedly examine and are capable of reverse-engineering the aircraft and anti-missile systems they purchase, the actual technology transfer is limited.

Whenever weapons are sold to a technologically sophisticated customer, however, there is a risk that the weapons transfer will not be limited to secondary use but will rather be reverse-engineered so that their secondary users learn the principles required to build them. Israel, for example, had sufficient technological capability to reverse-engineer the weapons it purchased from the United States and other suppliers and to use them as the foundations of its own arms industry. According to press reports, Israel routinely makes use of the underlying technologies of weapons it purchases from the United States.[13] Of course, to build a modern arms industry, the Israelis also had to

develop the ability to manufacture sophisticated computer and electronic components, and today Israel boasts an enormous number of
technologically advanced start-up firms that serve both the military
and civilian markets.[14] In this way, the transfer of military and civilian
technology went far beyond the narrow secondary use that might have
been intended by Israel's arms suppliers.

In some instances, nations have been able to purchase weapons,
components, and plans on the international arms market from third-
party suppliers. Such purchases often circumvent any restrictions that
might have been place to prevent secondary users to build their own
weapons. Indeed, in several cases, nations seeking to acquire modern
arms technology have purchased American or other Western firms in
possession of such know-how. The Chinese have sought to buy American technology firms. The Iranians, it has recently emerged, were able
to acquire a factory in Germany that had the ability to manufacture
components that might have been useful in Iran's nuclear weapons
program.[15] Of course, one might say that there is nothing new here.
Nineteenth-century British and German arms manufacturers sold their
wares and their nations' technologies to the United States and any
other nation that could pay for them.[16]

Reverse-engineering has been an important element in the dissemination of military technologies. Unlike simple secondary use, reverse-
engineering requires a level of technology similar to that of the society
that produced the weapon or weapons system in the first place. The new
user must be able to grasp the engineering principles represented by the
weapon and possess an industrial base capable of producing copies of
the weapon. Thus, the extent to which basic technology is actually
transferred may be militarily important but limited in scope. Often-
cited examples of reverse-engineered weapons include the Soviet Tu-4
bomber, which was directly copied from the American B-29 bomber.
The Soviets had a chance to closely examine the B-29 during World
War II when several American planes on missions over Japan developed problems and landed on Soviet territory. Similarly, the Soviet
K-13/R-3S air-to-air missile was a reverse-engineered version of the

American AIM-9 Sidewinder. The Soviets were able to examine the American missile after one fired by a Taiwanese fighter hit a Chinese MIG without exploding. Today, Iran claims to have reverse-engineered the American Predator drone and to have produced its own version of the American unmanned aerial vehicle (UAV) that has proven to be a useful weapon in America's arsenal.

Again, while reverse-engineering can be militarily useful, the actual extent to which technology can be transferred in this way is limited. Only those who already possess a level of technology sufficient to understand the principles embodied by the weapon and to build factories capable of making their own versions can benefit from reverse-engineering. A Predator drone somehow captured by a tribal group in the jungles of South America would not offer much in the way of benefits to them.

Another very common vehicle for the diffusion of military technologies is simple observation. One nation, observing a potentially useful weapon or weapons system fielded by others, may endeavor to build its own version of the weapon. Like reverse-engineering, imitation—though an important form of flattery—is not a particularly powerful instrument of technology diffusion. Weapons can only be copied by societies whose own level of technology is comparable to that of the society that produced the weapon. Thus, copying is more likely to diffuse weapons than engineering skill or scientific understanding. Take the case of naval power in late eighteenth- and early nineteenth-century Europe.

Political scientist Michael Horowitz writes that during the first half of the nineteenth century, Great Britain was the world's dominant naval power—a dominance based upon heavily armed, wooded-hulled sailing ships. However, the British observed the launch of a new French ironclad, steam-powered vessel, *La Gloire*, whose armor was capable of withstanding British gunfire. When the British also analyzed reports of the clash between the *Monitor* and *Merrimack* in America's Civil War, they quickly shifted their production of warships first to iron and then to steel.[17] The use of these materials and steam rather than wind power allowed the construction of warships much larger than any that had been built before and permitted their builders to mount huge guns with rotating turrets on the vessels' decks. Indeed, the new guns, with their own armored turrets, were too heavy to be mounted at a ship's sides and had to be installed midship, and ships redesigned to remove obstacles to the rotation of their turrets.[18] The construction and deployment of these ships required changes in naval organization and methods of training, the development of new technologies in the production of steel, as well as the development of turbine engines capable of powering the enormous battleships and battlecruisers introduced by the Royal Navy in the early years of the twentieth century.

The 1906 launch of the HMS *Dreadnaught*, followed by a series of other powerful warships, as well as the reorganization of the Royal Navy's tactics emphasizing battle fleets of auxiliary vessels organized around capital ships, was closely observed by the world's other maritime powers—including in particular Germany and Japan. Many maritime powers halted their naval construction programs while they considered how to best respond to the British innovations.[19] Several of these states possessed adequate levels of technology, as well as the organizational and financial capabilities, to imitate the British and proceeded to do so. Germany, for example, concluded that the new British warships represented a significant change in naval warfare that rendered existing vessels and fleets obsolete. Germany possessed a large and modern steel industry as well as the industrial infrastructure to build powerful warships on the British model. German military planners, moreover, had little difficulty understanding the organizational and tactical changes introduced by the British and adapted them for their own use.

In a similar vein, Japan was eager to imitate the Royal Navy's new warships and tactics. In its efforts to build a modern navy following Commodore Perry's 1853 visit, Japan had adopted the British Navy as a model for its own ships and tactics.[20] For a half century, Japan had worked to build an industrial base that would allow it to compete with the West. By the turn of the century, Japan possessed an adequate level of technology to copy the new British warships. What the Japanese were not able to do for themselves, the British were more than happy to do for them. Britain viewed Japan as a counterweight to its rival Russia and encouraged Japanese naval modernization, selling the Japanese ships, large-caliber naval guns, and technologies and helping Japan to organize its own naval academy modeled on the British naval academy at Dartmouth. The Japanese were, as a result, able to quickly copy the new British warships and assimilate the British naval tactics designed to make best use of the ships. Ironically, of course, within a few years the Japanese used their new navy to attempt to drive the British from Southeast Asia.

Dissemination by observation was also important in the case of the tank. Tanks were introduced by Great Britain toward the end of World War I. The British believed that tracked, armored vehicles had the potential to penetrate heavily defended German trenches and pave the way for successful infantry assaults. Though early British tanks were slow and cumbersome and prone to mechanical breakdowns, it was evident to all sides that the tank could become a formidable weapon. The Germans decided to copy the British tanks but did so in a desultory manner until the British offensive of 1918, in which large numbers of improved British tanks, attacking in waves, were able to achieve decisive breakthroughs and penetrated deep behind the German lines.[21] Watching their defense lines crushed by massed British armor convinced the Germans that the tank was, indeed, a powerful weapon. This realization came too late to affect the outcome of the war, since Germany soon capitulated, but it was to have a profound impact on German planning for the next war.

After the Versailles Treaty was signed, the army of the new German republic was severely limited in size and weaponry and could build no tanks. The Germans circumvented this restriction by entering into an agreement with the Soviet Union. The Soviet military, too, had been impressed with reports of the power of British armor and, indeed, during the Russian Civil War, had faced a small number of tanks fielded by the White Russian Army. After the Communist victory, Soviet officers had studied theories of armored warfare and very much wished to copy British tanks, but Soviet factories lacked the technological capability to build modern tanks. The Germans proposed a deal. The two nations would collaborate on tank design, with the Germans providing technical assistance for tanks that would be built in the USSR. Officers from both nations would train in a tank school established in the Soviet city of Kazan.

From this beginning, the German and Soviet armies both developed powerful tanks and doctrines of armored warfare emphasizing what the Germans would call *blitzkrieg*, or lightning war, and the Russians would call "deep battle." In both cases, the emphasis was on the use of massed tank formations to break through, envelop, and cut off enemy forces with infantry following to exploit the armored advances. Initially, the Germans and Soviets both copied British tank designs. Gradually, however, they introduced improvements, but, of course, when the Nazis came to power in Germany, this episode of German–Soviet cooperation came to an end. Within a few years, tank officers who had trained together at Kazan faced one another in battle. Interestingly, the Germans had provided the technical expertise in the 1920s but by the 1940s the Soviets had learned to build better tanks, including the T-34, generally thought to have been the best tank of the war. Indeed, the Germans found themselves copying the armor from the T-34 for their own tanks.

Again, successful imitation requires a level of technology similar to that possessed by the nation whose weapons are being imitated and is, as a result, not the most robust mechanism of technology transfer. British tanks were easily copied by the Germans and Russians. Germany and Japan, along with the United States and, to a lesser extent, France, Italy, and Russia, were able to copy British naval innovations. These nations already possessed the level of technology needed to build British-style battleships and battle cruisers and, once shown an example, imitated it with relative ease. Those who did not possess the technological ability already could not copy the ships.

This limitation is not true in the case of a fourth form of imitation—voluntary technology transfer. Technology transfer differs from, say, arms sales, insofar as the donor or seller provides not only finished weapons but also donates or sells the technology needed to manufacture and maintain the weapons. This sort of sale or donation involves a more substantial transfer of technology than the simple sale or donation of the weapons themselves. Understanding the technology may allow the recipient to move forward scientifically or technologically and move on to produce other civilian and military products that might previously have been beyond their reach. Such transfers take place for a number of reasons and, despite frequent efforts on the part of technology-rich nations to prevent their technological assets from being acquired by others, such flows are difficult to control. In some instances, nations are willing to share military technology with their allies in order to promote its use against their enemies. As noted above, in the early twentieth century, Great Britain shared naval technology, including plans for the construction of modern warships, with Japan as part of its effort to blunt Russian power. This transfer of technologies is a classical case of a tactic that seemed to be a good idea at the time, but was discovered out later to have been rather problematic.

In other cases, a transfer of technology involves civilian technologies that turn out to have military uses. Take, for example, the enormous transfer of American manufacturing technology to the Soviet Union that took place before and during World War II. During the 1920s and 1930s, the Soviet leadership was quite conscious of the fact that the USSR's level of industrial development was far behind that of Western Europe and the United States. Always fearing attack from the capitalist West, the USSR was especially anxious to develop its armaments industries. Accordingly, the USSR contracted with American industrial firms to build plants such as the Kama River truck factory, in which Soviet engineers learned how to build modern trucks—a skill set that transferred quite easily to the manufacture of military vehicles.

Today, the United States seeks to monitor and prevent the transfer of technologies with military potential. In practice, such transfers take place every week. American corporations often sell technological know-how to foreign purchasers. These corporations usually claim to have been unaware that the technology had military applications. In 2011, for example, the United Technologies Corporation, a major American defense contractor, paid a $75 million fine for selling engine-control software to China that the Chinese used to build that nation's first military attack helicopter.[22] The firm's Pratt and Whitney subsidiary had initially claimed to be unaware that the software had potential military uses, but then acknowledged that some of its executives had made false statements to the government when denying the allegation.

In some instances, foreign governments will demand a transfer of technology as a condition for purchasing American products. In a recent case, Brazil threatened to purchase military aircraft elsewhere if the United States continued to impose restrictions on technology transfers. Brazil wanted to sell twenty-four aircraft containing US-built components to Venezuela. The components had been sold to Brazil with the stipulation that they could not be transferred to a third nation. Brazil declared that if the United States refused to lift this restriction, it would award a fighter plane contract worth as much as $7 billion to a French or Swedish company rather than an American firm.[23]

A recent case of voluntary technology transfer poses grave dangers. Nuclear technology developed in Pakistan was sold to both North Korea and Iran. The technology was sold by prominent Pakistani engineer Abdul Qadeer Khan, possibly with the connivance of some Pakistani officials. North Korea has tested an atomic bomb it was able to develop with the help of Khan's information, and Iran is making every effort to build its own nuclear weapon. Iran asserts that it seeks nuclear technology for peaceful uses, while North Korea enjoys threatening the United States with a nuclear attack. In all likelihood, both states are lying.

The Khan case also illustrates another common factor in voluntary technology transfer—the internationalization of scientific training. Every year, American and European universities train thousands of scientists and engineers in the most advanced technologies. Some of these individuals remain in the countries where they received their training, but the majority return home with the skills they have acquired.

Abdul Khan, for example, was trained in Germany, the Netherlands, and Belgium. In the Netherlands, Khan had access to documents concerning gas centrifuge technology, an important element in the fabrication of nuclear bombs. Of course, America's own atomic bomb was originally devised by scientists trained in Germany. No doubt, engineers trained in the Roman army later built ballistae for the Goths.

Finally, there is the matter of espionage. Since ancient times, nations have relied upon spies to inform them of one another's plans and capabilities. One important form of espionage is collection of information on the use and manufacture of weapons. In some instances, espionage has provided information that allowed one or another nation to copy complex weapons systems that it might not easily have been able to develop on its own. In the 1940s, for example, Soviet spy rings penetrated American security and copied the plans and designs for American nuclear weapons. This intelligence coup allowed the Soviet Union to build an atomic bomb years earlier than its scientists and engineers might have been able to construct such a weapon on their own.

In recent years, China has been quite active in the realm of technological espionage. Chinese agents allegedly were able to acquire microwave submarine detection technology, space-based intercept systems, electromagnetic artillery systems, submarine torpedoes, aircraft carrier electronic systems, and various other military technologies. Recently, a Chinese citizen, Sixing Liu, was sentenced to seventy months in federal prison for attempting to transfer information about the "disk resonator gyroscope," a device that allows drones, missiles, and rockets to hit targets without satellite guidance, to the Chinese military. Liu was employed by US defense contractor L-3 Communications, where he had access to the gyroscope.[24] Similarly, Chi Mak, another L-3 employee, was convicted of passing information on the navy's quiet drive submarine propulsion technology to China, while another Chinese agent was convicted of acquiring American microwave submarine detection technology for China.

Of course, China is not the only nation that uses covert means to acquire American military technology. In recent years, Russian agents have been accused of attempting to export US military equipment and technology, and a number of Iranian agents have been apprehended seeking to obtain American technology and hardware for Iran's military and nuclear programs.[25]

Mid twentieth-century Soviet atom spies generally had to physically obtain or photograph documents and components. While this traditional form of espionage continues to be important, today's spying also includes cyberattacks on computer systems that store useful military and technological information. In recent years, computer attacks, mainly originating in China, have targeted a number of American defense firms, including Northrop Grumman, whose computer systems contain valuable information on American military systems. What, if any, technology was transferred through these attacks has not been made public.[26]

IMITATION IS MORE THAN JUST A FORM OF FLATTERY

War and preparation for war provide nations with a powerful incentive to identify and copy one another's useful military technologies. Whatever form such imitation takes, with the exception of simple secondary use, imitation of a foreign military innovation may allow—or indeed, require—learning and assimilating whole new sets of technologies with both military and civilian applications. As I observed earlier, copying swords may teach societies how to build plowshares.

Take the case of jet propulsion. Work on jet engines had been undertaken in Britain, France, and Germany during the 1920s. In the 1930s, however, German industrialist Ernst Heinkel saw the possibility of attaching a jet engine to an airplane. Along with an engine designed Hans von Ohain, Heinkel built the He 178, the world's first jet plane. With subsequent technical improvements, the Germans were able to build the world's first jet fighter, the Me 262, which entered combat in 1944. The *Messerschmitt* jet could attain a top speed of about 550 miles per hour, which was more than 150 miles per hour faster than conventional Allied fighter aircraft. The Me 262 was quite successful in downing Allied bombers, particularly after the introduction of a two-seat version with radar gave it an enhanced ability to fly and fight at night.

The Me 262 was introduced too late in the war to have any appreciable effect. Other air forces encountering the German jet fighter, though, recognized its clear superiority to piston engine aircraft, as well as to the British Gloster Meteor, a somewhat more primitive jet fighter developed by the British. Accordingly, Allied forces made every effort to capture an Me 262 for study, hoping to copy its design and technology. The US Army Air Force had created an intelligence effort dubbed "Operation Lusty," tasked with acquiring German aircraft and weapons technologies. No Me 262, though, was captured until the end of the war, when both the Americans and Soviets were able to seize a number of the jets in fairly good condition. The United States shipped nine of the Me 262s, along with other German equipment, to an airfield in Newark, New Jersey for study. There the German planes were reverse-engineered and immediately became the basis for America's jet fighter and jet bomber programs.

Within a few years, of course, jet engines were being used to power commercial airliners. With improvements in their power, reliability, and fuel efficiency, they soon replaced piston engines on most large civilian aircraft. The jet engine has dramatically shortened flight times and reduced the costs associated with travel and commerce. Copying the sword produced a very important plowshare. Of course, jet technology had been under development before the war and had not been exclusively intended for military purposes. This point, however, raises the larger issue of how technology is transferred between civilian and military uses, a question to which we shall now turn.

CIVIL-MILITARY TECHNOLOGY TRANSFERS

There is a long-standing argument about whether the military should be seen mainly as a producer or as a consumer of technology. That is, does the military develop new technologies that turn out to have civilian applications or does it make use of—"militarize"—technologies that were initially developed for civilian purposes? It is certainly possible to think of examples of both phenomena. The microwave oven was an accidental spin-off of military radar. The Internet is an outgrowth of the ARPANET created by the Advanced Research Projects Agency (ARPA), an entity later renamed the Defense Advanced Research Projects Agency (DARPA), created in 1958 by America's Defense Department to develop advanced technologies. ARPA was a response to the Soviet launch of Sputnik, the world's first orbital satellite, and devised the ARPANET to link the nation's various research computers through a packet switching network that would allow these computers to communicate almost instantaneously with one another. The basic technology for the ARPANET is still the technology underlying the Internet.

At the same time, there are many examples of civilian technology that became militarized. Sonar, the device used by every navy to search for enemy submarines, was initially developed after the sinking of the *Titanic* as a device that might be used to detect icebergs in bad weather. The military value of airplanes was not immediately perceived and was still being debated in the 1930s. And, the tank, it might be said, is essentially a farm tractor that has been modified to carry a bit of armor and a gun.

Though there are many examples of spin-offs in both directions, in general, the military develops rather than initiates new technologies. That is, some technology developed by engineers or scientists who are mainly curious and had no particular application in mind will turn out to have military possibilities. If these come to the attention of military authorities they will invest resources in perfecting the technology and exploiting its military potential. This investment may, in turn, lead to technological improvements that serve the civilian economy in a benign spiral.

Take radar, for example. Nineteenth-century radar experimenters such as Heinrich Hertz found it interesting that radio waves could be reflected from solid objects. Hertz and other scientists who studied the phenomenon had no particular interest in its practical applications. In the 1930s, however, as the likelihood of war increased, military authorities in several nations became interested in the idea of a system that might be able to detect enemy aircraft before they reached their targets. In 1934, the British Air Ministry funded a study that led to the construction of a working prototype system designed to detect aircraft, which became the basis for the radar network that served Great Britain very well during the 1940 Battle of Britain. Today, of course, in addition to its military uses, radar is essential to the civilian aircraft and shipping industries, to say nothing of its role in food preparation through the microwave oven.

In a similar vein, the physicists who studied the secrets of the atom in the late nineteenth century were driven by scientific curiosity, not military possibilities. It was a long time before the potential military applications of atomic energy were understood and brought to the attention of the military. In 1939, a group of eminent German–Jewish physicists who had been forced to flee Germany and emigrate to the United States became concerned that Nazi Germany might develop an atomic bomb. As noted in chapter 1, two of these men, Leo Szilard and Albert Einstein, in consultation with Edward Teller and Eugene Wigner, sent a letter to President Franklin D. Roosevelt, in which they described the possibility that a new type of weapon of unprecedented power could be built, based upon the principle of nuclear fission. Such a weapon, they said, could destroy a city with one blast. Moreover, the letter went on to say, it was possible that Nazi Germany had already begun work on a nuclear bomb.[27] Once nuclear energy had been harnessed, the possibility for civilian spinoffs became evident. Nuclear reactors provide a significant fraction of the word's energy, though concerns about safety and the storage of nuclear waste materials have limited their use.

Roosevelt received this letter several days after the German invasion of Poland and was sufficiently concerned to authorize the creation of an advisory committee, which in turn funded the beginnings of what became the Manhattan Project, a government-funded crash program that built the atomic bomb. The military did not invent the atomic bomb. Rather, it provided the funding and organization that took a civilian scientific theory and used it to create a weapon.

A similar story could be told about microelectronics. The transistor and the semiconductor emerged from the work of scientists and engineers working in private or university laboratories beginning in the late nineteenth century. In the 1970s and 1980s, however, mindful of the military importance of these developments, the US Defense Department provided an enormous amount of funding for microelectronic research, which served as the foundation for new weapons and communications systems as well as tens of thousands of civilian devices.

Today, the military is investing heavily in robotics and artificial intelligence—technologies that were not initially devised for military purposes but whose military uses were apparent, as in the example of the LS3 discussed at the beginning of this chapter. The military believes that robotic warriors may play a role in future wars.[28] At the same time, military-funded research in robotics and artificial intelligence may produce enormous changes in medicine, industry, and society more generally. Perhaps, when military funding boosts some technologies it disadvantages other technologies that are then left behind. Proponents of green energies often make this point. Nevertheless, in most realms, war and technological progress seem to go hand in hand.

CHAPTER 3

WHY WAR MITIGATES GOVERNMENTAL BRUTALITY

All governments rely upon force to compel obedience and keep dissent in check. Some regimes, indeed, seem prepared to treat their own people in a very brutal manner if it suits their purposes. In the twentieth century, Stalin's Soviet Union, Mao's China, and Pol Pot's Cambodia, among others, murdered tens of millions of real or imagined enemies among their *own* citizens, often through policies of deliberate starvation. Chairman Mao was fond of observing that the quality of a revolutionary could be measured by the number of people he had killed.[1] The sheer scale of the Soviet, Chinese, and Cambodian governments' atrocities against their own citizens may have been unprecedented, but many other regimes have made up in simple ferocity what they lacked in reach and ambition.

Throughout early modern Europe, for example, some of those who broke the law or otherwise incurred the wrath of the authorities were commonly subjected to whipping, branding, amputation of hands and ears, and blinding. Other offenders were subjected to ever more hideous tortures, drawn and quartered, burned alive, and, of course, hanged at the whim of one or another sadistic ruler.[2] Every modern-day government is certainly capable of mistreating its citizens. Most Western regimes, however, and many others as well, tend to abjure outright brutality in favor of what at least purports to be more humane systems of governance. Ironically, one of the reasons for this shift is centuries of warfare. In order to maximize the power they can exert abroad, governments have been compelled to restrict its use at home.

It is, of course, commonly believed that in times of war, rulers are inclined to govern even more harshly than in peacetime, perhaps justifying mistreatment of their subjects by the demands of national security. This idea is captured by the Roman proverb, *inter arma silent leges*: In time of war the laws are silent. It is certainly true that even liberal regimes are capable of restricting civil rights and violating civil liberties during wartime. The United States government, for example, restricted the right of habeas corpus during the Civil War, placed limitations on free speech during the First World War, interned Japanese-Americans during the Second World War, and currently curtails various civil liberties as it prosecutes the "war on terror."

But, despite such examples, over time war actually has been associated with a gradual lessening rather than an increase in the most overt forms of governmental brutishness. Particularly during the past quarter millennium, military necessity has frequently impelled rulers to turn to their subjects for support. Millions of ordinary individuals have been expected to serve in their nations' armed forces, to work long hours in defense plants, to pay burdensome taxes, and to volunteer for a variety of home-front activities. While a regime might seek to compel its subjects to undertake such activities, coercion alone is usually not very productive.

Take the example of military conscription. An effective system of conscription requires a fairly substantial level of popular support for the regime that is ordering its citizens to serve. Efforts to conscript members of an unwilling or hostile populace are frequently met with evasion, resistance, and violence.[3] A well-known example is that of early nineteenth-century Egypt, where Mehmet Ali attempted to conscript peasants into his new national army without first inculcating in them any sense of national loyalty or obligation. The result was a high level of popular resistance. To escape conscription, families abandoned their homes and villages while entire regions rebelled against the government. Some prospective conscripts resorted to such tactics as gouging out their own eyes or amputating fingers so as to be unfit for military service.[4] During the unpopular Vietnam war, few Americans of draft age resorted to such extreme tactics, but tens of thousands avoided service by using the courts to fight induction, decamping for Canada, or seeking to document medical disabilities that did not require actual self-mutilation.

In order to build popular support against foreign foes, regimes at war often find it necessary to rely more on persuasion and less on brute force in dealing with their own subjects. Indeed, such regimes frequently offer their people concessions and incentives, sometimes including both material benefits and political rights, to induce them to work, sacrifice, and fight. Even despotic rulers like Stalin, when embattled, have made an effort to convince their truculent subjects that they are, in fact, *citizens* with a stake in the regime's survival. To put it another way, in order to facilitate their use of hard power abroad, governments will often turn to soft—or at least *softer*—power at home.

Of course, concessions granted during wartime might be retracted when the danger passes. Governments, however, often find it difficult to rescind benefits once they are granted. Take, for example, the case of women's suffrage in England. During the First World War, women (initially only those with relatives in the armed services) were given the right to vote for the duration of the war. By the time the war ended, though, the idea of revoking women's voting rights was hardly discussed.[5] What begins as a temporary wartime concession can quickly become a permanent entitlement, vigorously defended by its recipients and by the state institutions established to organize and distribute the regime's largesse. Revocation of wartime benefits, moreover, is not without some risk. How many citizens will be willing to sacrifice for the next war if they are cheated of the rewards promised for the last one?

WAR MAKES CITIZENS

During the medieval and early modern eras, wars were fought by small feudal levies and professional or mercenary armies, and the funds to pay for military conflicts usually were borrowed from local or international financiers. Military logistics consisted mainly of looting and scavenging as the army made its way through the countryside.[6]

During the eighteenth and nineteenth centuries, however, especially in Europe, changes in the character of military force and international conflict substantially increased the costs and difficulties associated with the maintenance of national power, independence, and territorial integrity and gave rulers a strong incentive to attempt to enlist their subjects' active cooperation in the defense of the state.

To begin with, war and preparation for war became constant rather than intermittent facts of life during this century. Every European state found it necessary to construct a large standing army, which it maintained in a constant state of readiness to answer threats from other powers. In addition, every state began the creation of a reserve force that could be mobilized in time of crisis to augment its regular forces. Normally, all adult males were required to perform regular military service followed by service in the reserves, which typically included a period of military training each year. War and preparation for war had been intermittent—albeit frequent—features of European political life. Now preparation for conflict had become a permanent and full-time aspect of every state's existence.[7]

Citizen Soldiers

Second, the size of military forces increased dramatically at this time. In the mid-seventeenth century, the forces that could be mustered by, say, Prussia hardly numbered more than 40,000 men. Even at the height of the War of the Spanish Succession in 1712, the size of the British army barely reached 75,000 men. Only France, the wealthiest and most populous state in Europe, could field more than 100,000 soldiers before the eighteenth century. Beginning with the French revolutionary and Napoleonic eras, though, the size of national military forces began to increase substantially. The Jacobin *levee en masse* of 1793 produced 300,000 volunteers and conscripts for the republic's armies. By 1813, Napoleon was able to draft some 1.3 million of his countrymen. He drafted another one million for the campaigns of 1813 and 1814. Napoleon's *Grande Armee* assembled for the Russian campaign numbered 700,000 men. By the end of the nineteenth century, even these numbers were dwarfed by the standing armies of the major European powers. In 1874, the French standing army numbered some 1.75 million soldiers; the German army had approximately 3.5 million. By 1897, French forces including reserves numbered 3.5 million, and Germany fielded 3.4 million men. In World War I, the French were able to place more than three million soldiers in the trenches of the western front.

These huge forces, moreover, were mainly national armies. Prior to the eighteenth century, armies were composed of mercenary or forcibly impressed troops whose nationality was of little or no consequence. Armies were multilingual or multinational, held together by iron discipline and material incentives. But as the need to maintain permanent reserve forces impelled rulers to rely more heavily upon their own subjects to fill the military ranks, during the eighteenth and nineteenth centuries the earlier multinational armies began to give way to more or less exclusively national forces. The construction of national armies, of course, was associated with the development of the idea that military service was a duty and an obligation of all male citizens.

Of course, even while most of Europe still relied on mercenaries and professional soldiers, the British colonies in North America were already fielding armies of ordinary citizens. England had urgent missions for its own professional troops elsewhere and consistently urged its North American colonies to provide for their own defense against the French in Canada, the Native Americans on the frontier, and the Spanish in the South and West. Later, colonial militiamen made up the bulk of Washington's army. Their short tours of duty reduced their military effectiveness, but the militia's enthusiasm for the cause sometimes made up for what it lacked in training and discipline. The colonies' part-time soldiers had other virtues as well. When they returned home they performed the vital service of holding their communities to the patriot cause, often by intimidation or violence, so that the Continental Army had continuing access to its recruitment base and to most of the food produced in the colonies.[8]

By the twentieth century, the major European powers as well as the United States were able to field enormous armies composed of a mix of conscripts and volunteers. America's army in World War I, for example, consisted of three million draftees and 700,000 volunteers. During the Second World War, ten million conscripts were inducted into the armed services along with five million volunteers. Another five million Americans were given deferments for work in war industries. Similarly, the British government introduced universal service in 1939, quickly conscripting 1.5 million men. In 1942, Britain began conscripting women, who were assigned to nonmilitary duties. Eventually, 3.2 million men were conscripted and another 1.4 million volunteered. The Soviet Union conscripted roughly thirty million men for military service in the Second World War and assigned millions of women to serve in defense plants.

Money

The expense of conflict increased substantially during the eighteenth and nineteenth centuries. Obviously, the permanence and increased size of military forces meant increased expense. The permanent maintenance of enormous standing armies and reserve forces required vast expenditures even during peacetime for food, pay, supplies, transport, and weapons. At the same time, technological advances in military tactics and weaponry, including artillery, communications, transport, and munitions, increased the cost of equipping an effective fighting force. Moreover, the industrial revolution made it possible for each nation—and thus necessary for all nations—to produce vast quantities of rifles, machine guns, field guns, and munitions. Early-modern states had relied upon a patchwork of taxes and borrowing, but these were wholly inadequate to finance the accelerating costs of war and preparation for war.

Beginning in the eighteenth century, European governments had little choice but to broaden their revenue base to the public at large. In addition to imposing income and poll taxes, states began to sell securities in denominations small enough that ordinary citizens, not just bankers and financiers, might purchase them. These new mechanisms produced a steady and substantial flow of revenue. But in broadening the base for revenue collection, the state also enlarged the population whose loyalty and support it had to cultivate. With expanded taxation came demands for expanded representation and citizen participation, as well as increased stature for representative institutions.

These developments were similarly important in the United States. The United States began life as a nation with the sort of broadly based revenue system that European states reached only after centuries of trial and error. Local and state governments relied heavily upon ordinary citizens for their financial needs from the earliest days of the republic, making use of property taxes, poll taxes, and widely distributed certificates of indebtedness that circulated as currency in $1 or $2 notes. Reliance upon such certificates of indebtedness was one of the factors that forced colonial governments to pay attention to the views of ordinary citizens. If a government lost public confidence, its notes would no longer be accepted, and its ability to meet its obligations would be threatened.

After the revolution, the new federal government was prohibited from levying direct taxes and was financed via land sales and tariff and customs duties supplemented by moderate borrowing in national and international credit markets. During the Civil War, however, its need for revenue increased so dramatically that the government could not secure sufficient funds from domestic banks and financiers. European investors, for their part, had no confidence that the Union would prevail on the battlefield and were reluctant to purchase US securities.[9] This situation forced the federal government to turn to new forms of revenue extraction, including income taxes, bond sales to small investors, and the issue of a variety of legal tender notes in small denominations. All these revenue devices depended upon a measure of popular acceptance and left the government financially dependent upon popular confidence to meet the Union's military expenses, which ultimately totaled the then-astronomical sum of more than $4 billion.

One major source of federal revenue was the sale of government bonds to small investors. In 1862, Treasury Secretary Salmon P. Chase invited Ohio Republican banker Jay Cooke to attempt to place $500 million in government bonds that could not be sold to domestic banks or foreign investors. Cooke developed a plan to market these securities to ordinary citizens who had never before purchased government bonds. He thought he could appeal to the patriotism of ordinary Americans, and he believed that widespread ownership of government bonds would give ordinary Americans a greater concern for their nation's welfare.[10] Cooke established a network of 2,500 sales agents throughout the North and used the press to promote the idea that purchasing government securities was both a patriotic duty and a wise investment. In every community, Republican Party organizations worked hand-in-hand with Cooke's sales agents, providing what historian Eric McKitrick calls the "continual affirmation of purpose" needed to sustain popular support and the regime's finances through four long years of war.[11]

During the First World War, all the major powers dramatically increased taxes on individual incomes and made use of bond sale campaigns to persuade citizens to contribute to the war effort. Germany's government, for example, conducted nine bond drives during the course of the war, through which it raised nearly two-thirds of the military expenditures required by the war effort. Great Britain raised more than a billion pounds in a public campaign that urged the British people to "Lend your money to your country." In the United States, the government urged Americans through "borrow and buy" campaigns to participate in what were called "Liberty Loans" and "Victory Loans." The Liberty and Victory Loan campaigns were conducted by the War Loan Organization, which was organized into sales, speaking, and publicity bureaus. Bonds were sold in denominations as low as $50, and purchase on an installment plan was allowed so that even impecunious citizens could participate. Tens of thousands of volunteers sold the bonds throughout the nation. For those too poor to afford these bonds, the government also sold thrift stamps, war savings certificates, and small bonds in schools, post offices, and factories. Stamps cost as little as twenty-five cents each. A sheet of sixteen thrift stamps could be exchanged for and interest-bearing $5 bond. Stamps and savings certificates were also sold by an army of civilian volunteers.[12]

During the Second World War, the United States also significantly broadened its tax base. The 1942 Revenue Act increased the number of households subject to the income tax from thirteen million to twenty-eight million. At the same time, the government launched bond campaigns that eventually produced $50 billion in revenues to help finance the war effort. American workers were encouraged to enroll in the payroll savings plan. Under this scheme, workers agreed to have 10 percent of their income automatically deducted from their paychecks and invested in savings bonds. By the end of the war, some twenty-eight million workers were participating in the plan.

Wartime Production

By the end of the eighteenth century, the large-scale industrial production required for an effective military effort not only increased the cost of armed conflict but also made the factory worker as much a soldier in the war effort as the infantryman in the front line. During the First World War, the United States alone produced 3.5 million rifles, 226,000 machine guns, 3,000 bombers and more than 630 million pounds of gunpowder. During the course of World War II, America's defense plants produced 1,200 major warships and 124,000 other vessels, 100,000 tanks and armored vehicles, 310,000 aircraft, 40,000 artillery pieces, 12 million rifles and carbines, and 41 billion rounds of ammunition. The Soviet Union, despite having to evacuate its major defense industries to the Ural mountains after the Germans overran Western Russia, managed to build more than 90,000 tanks, 137,000 military aircraft, and more than 400,000 artillery pieces.[13]

These prodigious efforts required enormous armies of production workers, including millions of women, willing to work long hours undertaking physically strenuous and often dangerous tasks.

In Britain and the United States, during both world wars, millions of women joined the industrial workforce to replace men who had been called to the military. In Britain during World War I, women became the mainstays of the munitions industry, and in the United States the number of women in the workforce increased by more than five million during World War II. These women were celebrated by the heroic symbol of "Rosie the Riveter," first presented in the eponymous 1942 song written by Redd Evans and John Loeb. Rosie was said to be a tireless worker in a defense plant, who was doing her part to help the American war effort. Rosie had her counterparts in other belligerent nations. Canadian wartime posters, for example, featured a female assembly line worker named "Ronnie, the Bren Gun Girl." In the Soviet Union during World War II, tens of millions of women replaced men in the nation's factories and on the farms. After the German invasion, some 2,500 Soviet defense plants had hastily evacuated thousands of miles into the Soviet interior. Here, millions of women, along with men too old or too young for the military, worked to build the tanks and aircraft and other weapons upon which the USSR depended. Generally, defense workers were expected to work a sixty-six-hour week with one rest day per month. There were no holidays, and compulsory overtime was the norm. In the initial months after the evacuation of industry to the Ural Mountains, the conditions of life were primitive, to say the least. Workers slept in caves or tents, and factories had no walls or roofs. Nevertheless, without the weapons being produced, the USSR would collapse.

Voluntarism

States at war during the past two centuries have relied upon their people not only to fight, pay taxes, and work, they have also depended upon millions of citizens to devote their time on a voluntary basis to engage in the hundreds of tasks necessary to support a nation at war. For example, the American Red Cross was an outgrowth of the voluntary relief efforts mounted to aid wounded soldiers during the Civil War.

During World War I, the Red Cross received a government charter and built a network of 3,500 chapters with some twenty million volunteer members.[14] During the First World War, the Red Cross, along with the YMCA, organized voluntary efforts to provide spiritual, recreational, and medical support for soldiers at home and abroad. Similar efforts were made by such voluntary organizations as the Knights of Columbus, the Salvation Army, and a host of others. And, as noted above, the administration's all-important bond drives depended upon armies of volunteers who organized bond rallies and sold bonds to their neighbors.

During the Second World War, volunteer efforts in every community were organized to support bond sales, to recycle materials that might be useful for the war effort, and to mount a civil defense effort in case enemy bombers appeared over the nation's skies. One unusual group of volunteers called itself the Women Airforce Service Pilots (WASPs). The WASPs consisted of some one thousand women pilots who volunteered to fly new warplanes from factories throughout the nation to East coast ports for shipment to Europe. The 1,200 WASPs allowed a similar number of male pilots to be assigned to combat duties. During the war, the WASPs flew more than 12,000 aircraft to their ports of embarkation. They also towed targets for flight students engaged in gunnery practice, crews engaged in anti-aircraft practice, and functioned as test pilots for new aircraft.

Volunteers also played a major role on the British home front in both world wars. Hundreds of thousands of men too old or infirm for military service volunteered for the Home Guard, where they some manned some 1,500 anti-aircraft guns, served as sentries, and watched for German aircraft and parachutists. Tens of thousands of women volunteered to serve in a variety of military auxiliary forces. For example, members of the Women's Auxiliary Air Force (WAAF) served as radar operators and plotters and operators of barrage balloons, and played a key role in directing British fighters to intercept German bombers during the Battle of Britain. Another group of women volunteers replaced the farm workers called to serve in the military. During both the First and Second World Wars, the Women's Land Army (WLA), engaged in farm work. In the Second World War, some 90,000 WLA workers ensured that Britain would not starve despite the German blockade of its shipping.

FROM COERCION TO PERSUASION

As governments came to depend upon popular willingness to engage in such voluntary activities, along with a willingness on the part of millions of individuals to serve in the military, pay taxes, buy bonds, and work long hours in factories, governments also found it necessary to rule less through force and more through persuasion. In other words, war gradually impelled regimes to show their own people what Gramsci called the velvet glove, rather than the mailed fist, of state power.

Propaganda

An early manifestation of this shift in modes of governance was the rise of propaganda as a major governmental tool. The term *propaganda* simply refers to a campaign of information and ideas, whether true or false, designed to persuade some audience to support a particular cause or political leader. Similar information and idea campaigns used to promote products and services are usually called advertising. The term *propaganda* apparently derives from the Catholic Church's *Congregatio de Propaganda Fide*, or Congregation for Propagating the Faith, established in 1622 to encourage the spread of Catholic teachings in non-Catholic realms.

The term *propaganda* has a negative connotation because of its association with Nazi Germany and Stalin's USSR. Accordingly, the US government refers to its own propaganda efforts as "public information." Propaganda, however, should be seen in a more positive light. Governments able to rule entirely through force and fear have no need to employ propaganda to persuade their citizens of anything, though they may aim propaganda at external audiences they do not control. Domestic use of propaganda suggests that a government is, for one or another reason, interested in courting popular support and approval. Every government, of course, makes use of both force and propaganda but, in what we might call the most martially experienced states, the balance seems to favor carrots over sticks. The US government, for one, generally incarcerates or—as we have learned—sometimes kills only those who have proven extremely resistant to its public information efforts.

In ancient times, long before the term was introduced, secular rulers made use of propaganda, mainly to bolster the morale of their own troops before battle and to attempt to unnerve the enemy forces facing them. For example, in the campaign against Athens during the fifth century BCE, Spartan troops were told, "We must not then fall short of our fathers' standards, nor fail to live up to our own reputation. For, the whole of Hellas is eagerly watching this action of ours . . . Think, too, of the glory, or, if events turn out differently, the shame which you will bring to your ancestors and to yourselves, and with all this in mind follow your leaders . . ."[15]

Writing in the fourth century BCE, Kautilya recommended the use of propaganda to confuse and demoralize opponents. "In the enemy's territory they shall advertise, in particular, the appearance of gods and his receiving arm and treasury from divine sources. Whenever there is an opportunity (e. g., when interpreting questions to gods [*devaprasna*] through oracles, omens, the crowing of crows, body-language, dreams, bird calls, and animal noises), they shall proclaim the meaning to be victory for the conqueror and defeat for the enemy. Any appearance of a meteor in the constellation stars of the enemy's birth shall be proclaimed by a beat of drums as an omen of the imminent defeat of the enemy."[16]

In the seventeenth century, with the expanded use of printing presses and the development of copper plate that permitted posters to be quickly printed, propaganda could be aimed at a larger audience. This became evident during the Thirty Years' War, when the pen and the sword were said to have forged a "formidable alliance."[17] Much of the propaganda produced in the seventeenth and eighteenth centuries had an external rather than internal target. That is, government propaganda was aimed more at undermining the morale of the troops, supporters, and subjects of an opposing regime than rallying support among the government's own subjects. For example, when Gustavus Adolphus of Sweden entered the war on the side of the Protestant forces, he launched a propaganda campaign aimed at the subjects of the various German principalities that his troops invaded. His "War Manifesto," along with a host of other leaflets and pamphlets, was widely circulated. These propaganda tracts were designed to justify Gustavus's involvement in the war as an effort to liberate his coreligionists from Papist tyranny. During the same war, Protestant forces sometimes waged propaganda campaigns against one another. Thus, the Lutheran stronghold of Saxony issued pamphlets and posters attacking the Calvinist forces in the Palitinate.[18]

Rulers saw propaganda as a potential source of disorder and discontent and preferred to employ censorship at home and propaganda abroad. An echo of this idea can be found in the policies of the Soviet Union before World War II. The USSR relied on censorship and brute force at home while using many forms of propaganda to trumpet its achievements abroad. For decades, the Soviet Union sponsored the Communist International and a host of cultural and political institutions designed to promote Communist ideology and the idea of the USSR as a utopian society deserving of respect and support throughout the world. This effort was enormously successful for a number of decades. Everywhere in the world, dedicated Communists worked vigorously to promote the interests of the Soviet Union, in some cases committing acts of espionage and treason against their own nations for what they saw as a higher purpose.

In Western Europe during the late eighteenth century, the advent of the citizen soldier led regimes to direct more of their propaganda efforts toward domestic rather than foreign audiences. This new direction in propaganda was first manifest in America, whose colonial governments relied exclusively on volunteer militia forces before, during, and after the Revolutionary War. Militiamen could not be compelled to fight and had to be persuaded. As a result, with the beginnings of the revolt against Britain, colonial pamphleteers, newspaper editors, and others were long-accustomed to the idea of appealing to public opinion to advance their cause.

Virtually every action of the Royal Government was presented in a negative light, and its significance exaggerated by colonial publicists, to inflame popular sentiment and bring recruits flocking to the revolutionary cause. Paul Revere's inflammatory cartoons of the Boston Massacre, a minor event in which British troops fired on rioters, were circulated throughout the colonies to exemplify British brutality. Samuel Adams earned the title "master of the puppets" for his anti-British propaganda in the *Boston Gazette*. In the aftermath of the 1773 Boston Tea Party, Adams worked through the Boston Committee of Correspondence to flood the colonies with distorted news stories portraying the British as cruel occupiers of the helpless city of Boston. During the war itself, virtually every colonist read Tom Paine's propaganda treatises, "Common Sense," "American Crisis," and "Rights of Man." "These are the times that try men's souls," Paine wrote. "The summer soldier and the sunshine patriot will, in this crisis shrink from the service of his country . . . Tyranny, like hell, is not easily conquered; yet we have this consolation with us, that the harder the conflict the more glorious the triumph."[19]

These American efforts prefigured the propaganda efforts of France's post-revolutionary regimes. Besieged on all sides by the armies of the anti-French coalitions, and with the old royal army in disarray, the National Assembly called upon the French nation to come to the defense of the fatherland. The National Assembly created a Committee on Public Instruction, later replaced by the Committee on Public Safety, to rally the nation on behalf of the revolution and the French nation. This committee issued posters and pamphlets and chose the iconic figure of "Marianne" as the symbol of French liberty, to be displayed on statues and posters throughout the nation. Propaganda agents were instructed to distribute patriotic pamphlets and journals, particularly the *Soiree de camp*, aimed at military units, and the *Bulletin*, an official government mass-circulation daily newspaper. The *Bulletin* was posted throughout the nation to present the regime's view of domestic and international events. The result of these efforts was a "nation in arms." As one observer put it, "A force appeared that beggared all imagination. Suddenly war again became the business of the people—a people of 30 million, all of whom considered themselves to be citizens."[20]

Propaganda efforts continued under Napoleon Bonaparte. Napoleon made use of publications, art, theater, and music to rally the nation to his rule and to fight in his imperial wars. The artist David became the regime's chief visual propagandist, providing paintings and statues of Napoleon. Great architectural works were commissioned to celebrate the regime's achievements. The *Moniteur* became the official government newspaper, distributed free to the army. Festivals and public ceremonies reminded the French of the nation's grandeur and Napoleon's achievements. "Miss no opportunity to give the ceremonies a solemn, inspirational character," Napoleon told organizers.[21] In 1810, Napoleon established the "Direction General de l'Imprimerie et de la Librarie" to oversee French cultural and literary activity. Books, plays, and lectures were scrutinized to make certain that their content was favorable to the regime. Works of history were commissioned that placed the government and—especially—the emperor in a favorable light.

This enormous propaganda effort, like the earlier and more modest effort of the National Assembly, demonstrated not so much the French regime's power as its dependence upon favorable popular opinion. Napoleon governed with a light hand at home, never subjecting the French citizenry to the terror of the revolutionary days. He was fond of asserting that newspapers could be more effective than bayonets and claimed that without an ability to control and shape information, "I wouldn't last more than three months."[22] The chief goal of Napoleonic propaganda was to ensure the popular support that would produce a continuing flow of recruits and conscripts into France's armies. Napoleon presented himself as the soldier–emperor, had history books rewritten to emphasize French martial glory, and organized a host of festivals and public ceremonies emphasizing military themes. To make certain of the popular support—and recruits—that would provide the hard power for his military efforts abroad, Napoleon made use of soft power at home.

In time, Napoleon's chief antagonist, Great Britain, followed this example. The British government sponsored new publications such as the *Anti-Jacobin* to promote the patriotism needed to raise the money and armies that would be required to resist the French nation-at-arms. Cartoons, popular songs, pamphlets, and even nursery rhymes were commissioned to convince all classes of British society to contribute to the war against France. A new "British War Song," was published that called upon all Englishmen to quit their rustic labors and change their scythes to sabers. This British propaganda effort was accompanied by a campaign to suppress pro-French newspapers, publicists, and politicians. For most Englishmen, however, this was an era when their government and king called upon them for support more than it sought to compel their obedience. Generally, the government used the press at home and turned its bayonets abroad. Indeed, because of the press, the regime hoped to have more bayonets to turn toward the Channel.

This same pattern was manifest during the First World War. All the major combatants, of course, sought to silence antiwar media and political groups. The United States, for example, instituted wartime censorship of the mail and enacted the Espionage Act and the Sedition Act aimed at silencing opponents of the war effort. But in Britain and America, as well as France and Germany, governments focused mainly on maintaining support at home in order to increase the force they would be able to project abroad. In this war, not only would soldiers be needed, but factory workers and farmers, too, in order to provide the military equipment and food needed to sustain a modern war effort. Citizens would have to be asked to redouble their efforts with both scythes and sabers.

In Britain, initial enthusiasm for the war led to a rush of volunteers for the armed forces. Popular enthusiasm, however, waned as the war dragged on, producing hundreds of thousands of casualties as well as hardships and shortages at home. To cope with the morale problem, the British government created the National War Aims Committee (NWAC) to develop a domestic propaganda campaign. The NWAC commissioned news stories, posters, rallies, and films to promote patriotism and present the Germans as despicable and brutal figures.

Films, in particular, were aimed at working class audiences whose members were expected to provide most of the workers and troops needed in the war—and whose Labour Party leaders had been least ardent in their commitment to the necessity of military action. Films such as *Britain Prepared*, *The Battle of the Somme*, and *Hearts of the World* were commissioned by the NWAC to tout the heroism of British soldiers and to present the Germans as murderous occupiers of French and Belgian villages. Posters and news stories glamorized wartime factory work and extolled the heroism of the tens of thousands of women who volunteered to work in munitions plants.

In the United States, the Wilson administration made a major effort to mobilize popular support for the war and for the civilian factory production that would be needed to sustain the war effort. The chief instrument for eliciting popular support was the Committee on Public Information (CPI), chaired by journalist and publicist George Creel. The CPI launched a massive public information and news management program aimed at promoting popular enthusiasm for the war effort. This program included the dissemination of news favorable to the Allied cause; the publication of patriotic pamphlets, films, photos, cartoons, bulletins, and periodicals; and the organization of war expositions and speakers' tours. Special labor programs were aimed at maintaining the loyalty and productivity of the work force. Much of the CPI's staff was drawn from the major advertising agencies. According to Creel, the work of the committee "was distinctly in the nature of an advertising campaign . . . our object was to sell the war."[23]

The CPI's program was a temporary wartime effort. Within several months of the armistice, much of the government's opinion management apparatus was disbanded. The work of the CPI, however, demonstrated the value of persuasion as a tool of governance and led to a permanent expansion of government opinion management efforts during the New Deal. The enlargement of the scope of governmental activity that began during the Roosevelt era was accompanied by an explosion of official public relations efforts to convince the public of the value of these new programs. Each new governmental department, agency, bureau, office, or committee created a public relations arm to persuade the citizenry to cooperate with its programs and support its objectives. Perhaps the government could not force Americans to accept every new program, but they might be persuaded.

This idea was articulated by Chester Bowles, then-director of the new Office of Price Administration (OPA). Under Bowles's leadership, the OPA had developed an extensive public relations program whose budget drew congressional scrutiny. Bowles's defense of the program is recalled in his memoirs:

> At one point Congress threatened to cut our information budget. I testi-
> fied that if they deprived us of the means of explaining our programs to
> the people, our requirements for investigators and inspectors to enforce
> our regulations would be greatly increased. With a $5 million annual
> budget for information, I said I could keep the American people reason-
> ably informed about our regulations and their own obligations and rights
> as citizens. But if Congress cuts this $5 million, I would have no alter-
> native but to make a public request for $15 million to hire law enforce-
> ment inspectors to prosecute the many people who, often through their
> own ignorance and lack of information, had acted illegally. If Congress
> preferred this, it was their prerogative. I myself preferred persuasion to
> police-state tactics.[24]

During the Second World War, of course, each of the major combatants devoted considerable attention to the manipulation of public opinion and the maintenance of popular support for the war effort. The government of Nazi Germany, one of the most savage regimes in modern history, focused its brutality upon Jews, Russians, and others it deemed to be its enemies. Ordinary Germans were quite well treated by the Nazi state, and one manifestation of that relatively benign treatment was the fact that the government relied much more upon persuasion than force to impel Germans to support the war effort. The *Gestapo* and other police forces employed only a handful of agents to monitor the activities of ordinary Germans. These selfsame Germans, however, were subjected to a barrage of propaganda to ensure their support for the regime. The Reich Ministry of Public Enlightenment and Propaganda, under the leadership of Joseph Goebbels, was charged with what Goebbels termed the "mental mobilization" of the German people for war. The ministry made use of film, newsreels, and especially the radio to persuade the German people to support the government, to accept the hardships of war and to fight to the last. Goebbels believed that radio was a particularly important propaganda instrument. Radio manufacturers were provided with government subsidies to build inexpensive receivers so that every German home would have a radio with which to receive the regime's propaganda broadcasts.

In Great Britain, the Ministry of Information (MOI) was charged with administering wartime censorship of the press and aiming a steady stream of propaganda at the public. The MOI made some use of radio and posters and print propaganda, but its officials believed that, given the public's general propensity to disbelieve what it read or heard on the radio, film was a far more potent instrument than any of the others. With MOI backing, the British film industry produced hundreds of feature films dealing with the war. Many of these films, viewed every week by tens of millions of citizens in Britain's 4,000 cinemas, depicted the heroic efforts of ordinary working-class English men and women to survive the hardships facing them as a result of the German attack and, of course, to defend their nation. Thus, British films not only depicted the heroic efforts of British troops, fighting against overwhelming odds, but also focused on the daily struggles of the British people. And films, along with posters, urged citizens at home to do their utmost for the war effort. One poster declared in bold letters, "Women of Britain, Come into the Factories and Back Them Up."[25]

Propaganda in the United States

In the United States, with the tacit and sometimes overt encouragement of the Roosevelt administration, which was anxious to break the hold of isolationism on American public opinion, the motion picture industry had begun to produce anti-Nazi films as early as 1940. The most famous of these was *Confessions of a Nazi Spy*, starring Edward G. Robinson. In the film, Nazi Germany is depicted as intent on world domination and presenting a clear and present danger to the United States. Robinson, in the role of an FBI agent, asserts that through espionage and subversion Germany has already embarked on a war against the United States. Toward the conclusion of the film the audience is warned that continued isolationism will leave the United States and its way of life vulnerable to German attack from within and without.

By 1940, Hollywood studios were producing many feature films and film shorts promoting American rearmament and attacking Germany. Warner Brothers offered to make any film short on the need for military preparedness free of charge. At the Roosevelt administration's request, MGM produced a film on foreign and defense policy entitled *Eyes of the Navy*, which dramatically presented the importance of a strong national defense and an activist foreign policy. Other studios followed with films bearing such titles as *I Wanted Wings*, *Dive Bomber*, *Flight Command*, *Navy Blues*, *Buck Private*, and *Tanks a Million*. Even the comedy team of Abbott and Costello promoted preparedness with their humorous depiction of national military service, *Caught in the Draft*. Other important films presenting anti-German themes or warning of the need for preparedness included *A Yank in the RAF*, in which a young American flier shows his countrymen how to fight the Nazis, and Warner Brothers's *Sergeant York*, the story of America's greatest World War I hero, Alvin York, who put aside his pacifism to serve his country. York himself attended the film's New York premiere along with Eleanor Roosevelt and General John Pershing. York declared that if Americans stopped fighting for freedom, "then we owe the memory of George Washington an apology."[26]

President Roosevelt personally thanked the movie industry for its "splendid cooperation with all who are directing the expansion of our defense forces." The White House showed its gratitude to Hollywood by ordering the Justice Department to settle, on terms favorable to the studios, an antitrust suit it had brought against the major film producers a few years earlier. Roosevelt also intervened to secure a reduced sentence for Joseph Schenk, head of Twentieth-Century Fox, who had been convicted of income tax evasion.

During the war itself, the Hollywood studios focused on such themes as the danger posed by Nazi Germany and its Japanese ally, the threat of foreign spies and saboteurs, the need for national unity, the importance of American leadership in the world, patriotism and sacrifice, and, above all, the indomitable American spirit. Once aroused, said Hollywood, Americans would show their mettle and bring Hitler and his friends to their knees.

A film that presents many of the main themes of World War II propaganda is, of course, Warner Brothers's 1942 feature *Casablanca*, which starred Humphrey Bogart and Ingrid Bergman. In this film, Bogart portrays Rick Blaine, an embittered American who owns Rick's Café in Casablanca, then under the rule of the Vichy regime. Gathered at the café are refugees from Nazism from many lands. Though Rick claims to be an apolitical cynic, it turns out that he, like America itself, had fought against the Germans before and only needed to be reminded of his duty. The reminder comes in the form of Ilsa Lund (Ingrid Bergman), Blaine's long-lost love, who arrives at Rick's with her husband, Czech freedom fighter Victor Laszlo (Paul Henreid). Laszlo reawakens Rick's latent heroism and resolve. Rick decides to reenter the fight against Nazism, even though it means giving up Ilsa. He tells her that the stakes outweigh their own love and lives. Rick tells Ilsa he has a "job to do," a phrase often heard by Americans in the military.[27]

Rick even inspires the sleazy, collaborationist French commandant, Captain Renault (Claude Raines), to join him in the battle against the Germans. Thus, the film intimates, Americans need to be reminded of their duty and must put personal concerns aside for the duration of the war. Inspired by American leadership, moreover, the other nations of the world—even the sometimes craven French—will do their duties as well. With America reawakened, the outcome is no longer in doubt. "I know our side will win," Laszlo tells Rick as they part.[28]

During the war, the Roosevelt administration established a number of agencies designed to mobilize popular sentiment, bolster civilian morale, and encourage military service. The largest of these was the Office of War Information (OWI), whose mission was the enhancement of public understanding of the war, coordination of government information activities, and oversight and liaison with the press, radio, and motion pictures.[29] In other words, the OWI was in charge of coordinating wartime propaganda. The OWI's Bureau of Publications produced pamphlets and essays on topics relevant to the war effort. For example, the OWI produced a 123-page pamphlet entitled "Battle Stations For All," designed to explain to ordinary Americans how taxation, rationing, and bonds contributed to winning the war.[30] Similarly, the OWI's Domestic Radio Bureau worked with the radio networks to encourage popular entertainers to incorporate war-related themes into their acts. At the OWI's behest, Jack Benny told his audience, "When we buy those bonds, remember we're not doing the government a favor. We're the government! This is my war, and your war! So let's get rolling."[31]

Among the most important offices within OWI was the Bureau of Motion Pictures (BMP), which was charged with seeking to ensure that the movie industry would help to promote the nation's war effort. According to published BMP guidelines, the first question filmmakers were to ask themselves before beginning a project was, "Will this picture help win the war?"[32]

For the most part, though, the Hollywood studios operated more-or-less independently of the government, though they often submitted scripts for review and consulted with various civilian and military agencies on their propriety. One 1942 feature film, however, was actually commissioned by the OWI. This was the documentary film *The World at War*, produced and edited by Samuel Spewack and distributed to theaters through MGM, Twentieth-Century Fox, Paramount, Warner Brothers, and RKO. The film makes use mainly of newsreel material to trace the origins and history of the war and to explain to Americans the need to fight the Axis. The film revisits the years before the war when the German–American Bund and isolationists such as senators Nye and Wheeler sought, according to the film, to confuse Americans and leave them unprepared to defend their nation. *The World at War* goes on to show German and Japanese atrocities, some of the footage taken directly from Nazi films. After viewing the film, *The New York Times* film critic Bosley Crowther wrote, in 1942, "Spread across the face of America, *The World at War* should stimulate a grim resolve."[33]

In the United States, propaganda was also an important instrument in the government's effort to finance the war effort. The 1942 Revenue Act, adopted in the wake of the Pearl Harbor attack, was a turning point in the history of American income taxation. The act raised rates, cut exemptions, and lowered the threshold of income subject to taxation so that some forty million Americans would now be required to pay income taxes.[34] This expansion of America's tax base meant that tens of millions of lower and middle-income Americans with no prior experience in this realm would now be required to file income tax returns, an idea that most found confusing and daunting. And, given the numbers involved, the Internal Revenue Service would be hard-pressed to enforce the law. The IRS lacked the administrative capacity or database to allow it to assess the accuracy and veracity of the tax filings of tens of millions of Americans.

Anticipating that collection could be a major problem, Treasury officials launched a two-pronged campaign to encourage taxpayer compliance. First, the Treasury Department presented tax payment as a patriotic duty and launched an extensive propaganda campaign to convince Americans that paying taxes was a form of sacrifice required to win the war. In this campaign, Jewish film studios and radio networks, as well as Jewish composers and media personalities, played an active role. For example, at Treasury Secretary Henry Morgenthau's behest, the composer Irving Berlin wrote a song performed by Danny

Kaye and played incessantly on the radio, entitled "I Paid My Income Tax Today," aimed at lower-income Americans who previously had not been asked to pay federal income taxes:

> I said to my Uncle Sam,
> "Old Man Taxes here I am,"
> And he was glad to see me,
> Lower brackets that's my speed,
> Mr. Small Fry yes indeed,
> But gee—I'm proud as can be.
> I paid my income tax today.
> I'm only one of millions more.
> Whose income never was taxed before.
> A tax I'm very glad to pay,
> I'm squared up with the USA.
> You see those bombers in the sky?
> Rockefeller helped to build them, so did I.
> I paid my income tax today.[35]

Similar forms of propaganda were used to promote bond sales, which actually raised more money than income taxation during the war years. Of the war's $350 billion cost, income taxes accounted for $164 billion and bond sales for about $185 billion. More than eighty-five million Americans were persuaded to buy war bonds in sales promoted by the Treasury Department's War Advertising Council. Many of America's major artists, singers, and actors were mobilized to promote bond sales. But, the name most closely associated with World War II bond sales became Berlin's. At Morgenthau's request, he also wrote the song *Any Bonds Today?* based on his popular tune *Any Yams Today?* which had been sung by Ginger Rogers in the 1938 musical *Carefree*. The Berlin song, for four years, served as the anthem of America's war bond drives and was performed by the era's most famous bands and singers, including the Andrews Sisters, the Tommy Dorsey Orchestra, Dick Robertson and Kay Kyser.[36]

The tall man with the high hat and the whiskers on his chin,
Will soon be knocking at your door and you ought to be in,
The tall man with the high hat will be coming down your way,
Get your savings out when you hear him shout, "Any bonds today?"
Any bonds today?
Bonds of freedom,
That's what I'm selling,
Any bonds today?
Scrape up the most you can,
Here comes the freedom man,
Asking you to buy a share of freedom today,
Any stamps today?
We'll be blessed,
If we all invest,
In the USA.
Here comes the freedom man,
Can't make tomorrow's plan,
Not unless you buy a share of freedom today.
First came the Czechs and then came the Poles,
And then the Norwegians with three million souls,
Then came the Dutch, the Belgians, and France,
Then all of the Balkans with hardly a chance.
It's all in the book if only you look,
It's there if you read the text,
They fell ev'ry one at the point of a gun—America mustn't be next.
Any bonds today?
All you give,
Will be spent to live,
In the Yankee way.
Scrape up the most you can,
Here comes the freedom man,
Asking you to buy a share of freedom today.[37]

World War II bond drives were not just efforts to raise money. They were also undertaken precisely in order to build a sense of national spirit and purpose. Before launching the bond drives of World War II, Morgenthau consulted carefully with political scientist Peter Odegard, an expert in public opinion, who believed that a bond sales campaign could bring Americans closer together, producing a more united America. Odegard wrote, "Behavior begets belief quite as often as belief begets behavior. Public opinion is as much a product of what the public does as what it thinks. The experience of participation in a joint effort breeds community of purpose, conveys a sense of national direction, creates what is commonly referred to as morale. National unity is not so much the precursor as the product of united action."[38]

Retrospectively, World War II is sometimes seen as "the good war," a conflict that united Americans in the face of an existential threat. In point of fact, Americans were deeply divided before the Japanese attack and not definitively united after Pearl Harbor. Partisan and ethnic differences could well have become the basis for wartime division, especially as the human and pecuniary costs of the war escalated.[39] One key to American unity during the war was the fact that Americans were the recipients of a steady diet of material emphasizing the need to support the war effort. From the radio, the cartoons and the movies, the nation learned that Americans must buy bonds, pay taxes, serve in the military and fight until "the job" was done.

Propaganda in the USSR

The prewar Soviet regime was among the most repressive and murderous governments on the face of the earth—a fact it sought to hide with a sustained propaganda campaign aimed heavily at foreign audiences. During the war, however, Stalin found that brute force would not impel the Soviet people to fight and work to resist the German invasion and reduced his dependence upon coercion in favor of a greater reliance on persuasion. Soviet propaganda instruments turned from an external to an internal emphasis to persuade the people of the various Soviet nationality groups—the Russians in particular—to work and fight for the motherland.

The Stalinist regime hardly became the kingdom of heaven and, until Stalin's death in 1953, continued its murderous efforts to intimidate potential critics and opponents. During the war years, however, the regime learned to make fuller use of persuasion—a program to which it returned in the postwar era. Beginning in 1942, Soviet propaganda shifted from socialist to nationalist themes in an effort to mobilize Russian patriotism. Russia and the Motherland replaced the USSR and Communism as the values to be defended.[40] A new national anthem was written and played in place of the "Communist Internationale." Russian Orthodox churches were reopened. The war was presented in the press, motion pictures, and lectures to the troops by their commissars and *politruks* (political workers) as a fight to prevent the Russian motherland from being defiled by German beasts.[41] According to most observers, these propaganda themes were extremely effective in building morale among the troops and maintaining the spirit of the hard-pressed civilian population.[42]

Within the army, the politruks not only enforced discipline but also lectured the troops on their duties to the motherland and the bestiality of the Germans. During the first eight months of the war, more than 130,000 political workers were mobilized and assigned to combat units.[43] These efforts were generally thought to have played an important role in stiffening the will of Soviet soldiers to fight against terrible odds in the early months of the war.[44]

In terms of more general forms of persuasion, the Soviet film and media apparatus was organized to exhort the frightened and exhausted citizenry to fight the Germans. Sergei Eisenstein's film *Alexander Nevsky*, the story of a Muscovite prince who defeated the Teutonic Knights in the thirteenth century, had been produced in 1938 but withdrawn in 1939 after the Nazi–Soviet pact. In 1942, it became required viewing.[45] Mikhail Romm's *Girl No. 217* showed Russian audiences the brutal treatment of a Russian girl held as a slave by a German family.[46] Mark Donskoy's *How the Steel Was Tempered* was a story of Ukrainian resistance to the Germans in 1918.[47] Donskoy's *The Rainbow* was about a woman partisan, Olena, who is brutally tortured by the Germans but refuses to betray her comrades.[48] These and hundreds of films like them were shown throughout the war to fan feelings of Russian nationalism and hatred for the Germans.

Equally important were the press accounts in *Pravda* and the official army newspaper, *Red Star*. These accounts emphasized the heroism of Soviet troops and the bestiality of the Germans and were often accompanied by commentary from Ilya Ehrenburg, a writer who became one of the most famous newspaper correspondents in all the Soviet Union during the war years. Ehrenburg's accounts from the front lines, published in *Red Star*, called upon every Soviet citizen to kill the Germans. "If you have killed one German," he wrote, "kill another. There is nothing jollier than German corpses."[49] Ehrenburg's articles were read by every literate soldier in the Red Army as well as by millions of civilians and helped to crystallize popular feelings and hatreds—particularly in 1941 and 1942 when all seemed to be lost. Ehrenburg's articles helped inspire the hundreds of thousands of popular militiamen and women, or *opolchenie*, who turned out to dig trenches, build fortifications, and fight to defend Soviet cities.

At the end of the war, Stalin, increasingly paranoid and violent, had little further interest in seeking popular cooperation and turned to a policy of fierce reprisal against those nationality groups he deemed to have been disloyal during the war. Stalin sent hundreds of thousands of Ukrainians, Latvians, Estonians, Volga Germans, and others to camps in remote regions of the USSR. Jewish officials and military officers, who had made a major contribution to the war effort, were purged, arrested, and murdered. Millions of ordinary citizens were arrested for petty crimes, and the population of Soviet labor camps increased sharply. After Stalin's death, however, the new Soviet leadership recalled the lesson of the war years, reduced its level of internal repression—even emptying and closing the main Soviet penal camps—and stepped up its internal propaganda efforts, seeking to persuade more than force citizens to obey.

THE CARROT AND THE STICK

Every regime seeks to elicit popular cooperation through a mix of coercion and persuasion—carrots and sticks. In wartime, regimes often learn the effectiveness of carrots, and begin to sharpen their instruments of persuasion. Opinion management becomes the norm, and when it is done effectively, ordinary citizens are hardly aware of the manipulation. Many Americans are aware that since the New Deal, thousands of press releases written by government agencies are seamlessly incorporated into news stories every week. Indeed, more than half the news stories appearing in America's daily newspapers are actually based on press releases—many from government agencies. Some local television "news" stories are actually "video press releases."

The video release is a taped report, usually about ninety seconds long, the typical length of a television news story, designed to look and sound like any other broadcast news segment. In exchange for airing material that serves the interests of some advocate, the television station airing the video release is relieved of the considerable expense and bother of identifying and filming its own news story. The audience is usually unaware that the "news" it is watching is actually someone's canned publicity footage.

One recent example of a video news release that caused some controversy was a pair of ninety-second segments funded by the US Department of Health and Human Services (HHS) in 2004. After Congress enacted legislation adding a prescription drug benefit to the Medicare program, HHS sent a video release designed to look like a news report to local TV stations around the nation. Forty television stations aired the report without indicating that it came from the government. The segment was introduced by local news anchors reading from a government-suggested script. The anchor read, "Reporter Karen Ryan helps sort through the details," of the new Medicare law. Then, against the backdrop of film showing President Bush signing the law and the reactions of apparently grateful senior citizens, an unseen narrator, speaking like a reporter, presented the new law in a positive light.

"The new law, say officials, will simply offer people with Medicare more ways to make their health coverage more affordable." The segment concluded with the sign-off, "In Washington, I'm Karen Ryan reporting." Viewers were not told that the entire "news" story was distributed by the government. Nor were viewers informed that Karen Ryan was not a reporter at all. She was an employee of the ad agency hired by the government to create the video release.[50] In response to criticism, an HHS spokesperson pointed out that the same sort of video news release had often been used by other administrations and were commonly used by other government agencies, private firms, and interest groups. "The use of video news releases is a common, routine practice in government and the private sector," the spokesperson said. "Anyone who has questions about this practice needs to do some research on modern public information tools.[51]

We could be offended or upset by this use of propaganda and manipulation—or recall the testimony of Chester Bowles cited above. If not for its tools of persuasion, the government would hire more police and prosecutors and use "police state tactics," as Bowles said, to enforce its regulations. If that is the choice, and it often may be, we might well prefer the happy voice of Karen Ryan to the angry yells of the police agent.

Warfare and Welfare

War has not only taught governments the uses of propaganda; it has also shown them how to fashion another type of "carrot" designed to elicit popular support and obviate the need for coercion. This second carrot consists of national social welfare systems. War, preparation for war, and military rivalry were important factors, though not the only factors, leading to the development of the welfare state. As historian Bruce Porter has observed, "The historical linkages between war and the welfare state are too close and too extensive to dismiss as mere coincidences of chronology. The experience of total war on the 'home fronts' of Europe greatly facilitated the emergence of welfare states all across the continent . . ."[52]

Of course, America's first national welfare program, the post–Civil War pension system, was created in the aftermath of the struggle in order to provide assistance to Union Army veterans and their survivors. In Great Britain, the First World War saw the creation of the Welfare and Health Section of the Munitions Ministry, established to look after the health of the many women undertaking defense work in government and private factories. The motive of this effort was by no means altruistic. Illness and injuries among women workers would deprive the British war effort of badly needed workers. The needs of women workers also played a role in the expansion of child welfare services and the extension of free public education to all children under the age of fourteen. The impetus for the creation of a Ministry of Housing began during the war, as Britain's first public housing program was promoted under label, "homes fit for heroes."[53]

World War I also played an important role in bringing about the development of new welfare programs in France. To encourage worker productivity in the defense industry, the French Ministry of Munitions introduced a number of new safety and health regulations, including such benefits as maternity leave, job guarantees, medical care, and housing. These new benefits became a model for French industry The government also intervened to defer rent payments, require minimum wages, and otherwise gain the support of working-class citizens for the war effort.

Similar patterns manifested themselves during World War II. Germany, of course, already had a well-established welfare state built in the aftermath of the Franco–Prussian War and German unification. During the Second World War, it rewarded its citizens for their service with plunder taken from the nations conquered by German troops. Trainloads of captured goods arrived in Germany until reverses at the front ended the flow of this wartime booty.

At the beginning of the Second World War, the British government established the Interdepartmental Committee, chaired by Sir William Beveridge, to consider reforms in the realm of social insurance and worker's compensation. The Beveridge report, entitled "Social Insurance and Allied Services," was published in 1942. The report declared that, "Each individual citizen is more likely to concentrate upon his war effort if he feels that his Government will be ready in time with plans for a better world."[54] The Beveridge report gave rise to the enactment of some legislation during the war, including the Butler Education Act of 1944 establishing a Ministry of Education and a system of government-funded secondary education for all students. Immediately after the war, Britain created its National Health Service and built a comprehensive social insurance program as outlined in the report.

In a similar vein, the Japanese welfare system was also built in response to World War II. The Japanese program included national health insurance, old-age pensions, and housing assistance for the families of workers and soldiers. Why did Japan introduce a comprehensive welfare system during the war? According to East Asia scholar Gregory Kasza, the reasons included the importance of maintaining a healthy workforce and military recruitment base and the importance of inducing all members of Japanese society to work, fight, and sacrifice to the utmost to ensure the nation's survival.[55] In other words, the construction of a welfare system was tied to the government's desire to maintain popular support for the war effort.

In the United States, the 1944 GI Bill promised returning soldiers a variety of benefits, including low-cost mortgages, low-interest loans to start businesses, a year of unemployment compensation, and education subsidies that sent more than two million veterans to America's colleges and universities.

In all these nations, what governments learned in wartime was remembered after the war. Welfare benefits were not rescinded, welfare states continued to grow, and governments relied more on persuasion and less on coercion.

War and Voting Rights

And finally there was the right to vote. Nineteenth-century proponents of suffrage expansion believed that the franchise would give subjects a sense of ownership of the state and inspire them to fight for their country. A Swedish slogan of that period captured the idea. It was: "one man, one vote, one gun." The slogan's more contemporary echo seems to have dropped the last part of the trio. Modern warfare transformed politically voiceless subjects into citizens. World War I was associated with a great wave of suffrage expansion in Europe and North America as governments sought to mobilize support for the war effort.[56] In both Canada and Britain, under the Wartime Elections Act women with relatives serving in the armed services were given the right to vote for the duration of the war. The government apparently believed that a woman with a vote would have reason to urge her husband, son, or brother to make whatever sacrifice was needed for victory.[57]

Of course, war and voting rights had been closely connected in the United States long before the First World War. During the American Revolution, the property and freehold requirements that restricted the right to vote came under severe attack. Men of military age demanded the right to vote as a condition for accepting the risks and hardships of military service. The issue of suffrage reform was therefore linked to the more general question of independence. Advocates of independence supported extension of the right to vote because they recognized that soldiers with voting rights would have a personal stake in the success of the revolution. Politicians with pro-British sympathies opposed the elimination of the various property restrictions that limited voting rights.[58] For its part, the Continental Congress sought to encourage the martial spirit and loyalty of state militiamen by recommending that all non-commissioned militia officers be elected by their men.

After the war, veterans and their political supporters demanded expansion of the suffrage as a reward for their wartime sacrifices. "The soldier is as much entitled to vote as the Captain of the company or the Colonel of the regiment," thundered the Fredericktown, Maryland, *Hornet*.[59] Some opponents of suffrage reform argued that military service was its own reward and that the true burden of the war actually had been borne by the civilians who had been required to "pay heavy taxes to support you in the field, endure all that anxiety which the patriot feels for his suffering country . . . [and had not the] . . . privilege of shining in the heroic page."[60] Members of one Pennsylvania militia company answered this argument forcefully by appearing at the polls fully armed. They were allowed to cast ballots.[61]

In the late 1790s, anticipation of possible American involvement in a war against the French revolutionary regime led to another wave of suffrage expansion. In Maryland, for example, Michael Taney introduced a bill in 1797 establishing universal white manhood suffrage. Taney pointed out that Maryland militiamen might soon be called up for service. He urged the legislature to avert the difficulties encountered during the revolution, when the state had been compelled to expand the suffrage because its militiamen had been reluctant to fight unless they were given the right to vote.[62] A number of states substituted tax-paying requirements for the freehold restriction, thus achieving nearly universal white, male suffrage. This process continued during the War of 1812.

War and the Making of Citizens

In wartime, a number of governments have learned that their capacity to use force abroad could be enhanced if they reduced their use of force at home. Using propaganda, welfare, and voting rights, among other tactics, at least some regimes were able to transform their sometimes-sullen subjects into citizens willing to sacrifice, fight, and die for the nation, the motherland, the fatherland, or some other imagined community. When they need popular support, states seek to transform their subjects into citizens. In Great Britain, women became citizens during World War I when the government needed their work and sacrifices in defense plants. In the United States, the Irish became citizens during the Civil War when their blood was needed to save the Union.[63] In some respects, African Americans in the United States began to be treated as citizens during the Korean War, when the Truman administration added them to the military roster and sent them to fight.

Once the transformation from subject to citizen is complete, it is usually irreversible. Citizens sometimes have rights and powers with which to guard their status and, as noted above, governments must consider where they would derive their support in the next war if they reneged upon agreements made in the previous one. Of course, governance through persuasion is still governance, and citizens who are not persuaded may still find themselves subject to the iron fist hidden within the velvet glove. Nevertheless, the almost-casual daily brutality practiced by rulers in an earlier era has, in many parts of the world, largely been banished from political life. And, for most "citizens," this is a blessing.

CHAPTER 4

WAR AND ECONOMIC PROGRESS

HAS THE UNITED STATES LOST ITS IMMUNITY TO IMPERIAL OVERREACH?

Wars are often costly and futile, but in modern times war, as a phenomenon, has served as a great spur to economic development. In the modern world, military success requires a strong economic base to support the armies, weapons, training, and logistics needed to prevail in serious or protracted combat. When more developed nations face less developed foes on the battlefield, the former generally prevail.[1] This fact has impelled quite a few regimes facing external threats to concern themselves with their nation's prosperity and level of economic development.

It might, of course, seem reasonable to assume that all ruling groups would seek to enhance their nation's prosperity and pursue policies that promote economic development. Unfortunately, however, this is not the case. Rulers often view economic change, however beneficial to the nation as a whole, as a threat to their own power and prerogatives. Take an example from the recent history of Nepal. A rural village was able to obtain sufficient funds to purchase a Swiss-made watermill capable of powering such machinery as a press to make oil, as well as a sawmill. These capabilities would have allowed the village and, indeed, the entire locality to take an important economic step forward. Unfortunately, however, the government saw the enrichment of this village as a threat to its own power and ordered the mill shut down, saying the community had no authority to undertake such a project. This action was consistent with the government's earlier opposition to roads and schools, which were seen as possibly subversive influences.[2] Students of economic development will confirm that this is not an isolated case.

Of course, particularly benign regimes or those like the commercial oligarchies that ruled the early-modern Netherlands or post-revolutionary United States, might be naturally inclined to focus on national prosperity. Many rulers, however, seem more interested in their own welfare and power than the economic welfare of the nation. Imperial China's mandarins, as we saw in chapter 1, viewed exploration and the potential for transoceanic trade as politically disruptive and put a halt to China's early lead in these areas. Many ruling groups have seen economic development mainly as a source of instability and a threat to their own power. When, however, regimes face strong external challenges, they may see matters in a different light. Threats from other states can force even the most conservative regimes to bolster their own economic strength, whatever internal challenges this may pose, lest they be defeated by stronger foes. As Paul Kennedy observed, "The largest and most sustained boost to the financial revolution in Europe was given by war."[3]

ENGLAND

Precisely this calculus prompted Britain's rulers to launch a "financial revolution" in the late seventeenth century that paved the way for England's eighteenth-century industrial revolution. During the seventeenth century, Britain was regularly embroiled in wars. These included conflicts with Spain and France, the wars of the Three Kingdoms, the Commonwealth Wars with Holland and Spain, the Anglo–Dutch wars of Charles II, the two rebellions faced by James II, and unremitting warfare during the reigns of William III and Anne.[4] This century of warfare convinced Parliament and the British Crown that major financial changes were needed. As Mark Kishlansky noted, "War finance was no longer an extraordinary expense that members of Parliament were occasionally summoned to provide: it was central to the workings of the royal budget." This fact "drove the modernization of taxation, credit, and finance."[5]

Britain's ensuing financial revolution entailed the construction of a stable structure of public revenue and credit to replace the patchwork of taxes and borrowing that had characterized public finance in the early modern era. This financial revolution was a direct response to Britain's military needs and challenges in the seventeenth century. One building block of this new fiscal structure was the establishment of a central bank, the Bank of England, to facilitate raising long-term loans at a lower rate of interest than the short-term debt to which the government had frequently resorted. The bank was founded in 1694 as a temporary wartime expedient following the crushing defeat of the English fleet by the French in the 1690 Battle of Beachy Head in the Nine Years' War between the French and an English–Dutch alliance. Their victory gave the French temporary control over the English Channel and seemed to pose the threat of a French invasion of England. The feared invasion never came to pass, and the British fleet in the Channel was reinforced. Nevertheless, the Beachy Head defeat convinced the British government that it must build a far more powerful fleet if it was to secure its position of power in Europe.

The cost of building a fleet capable of wresting control of the sea from France and protecting English commerce from privateers, while meeting other government needs as well, was estimated to be the enormous sum of £1.2 million. The government had already borrowed heavily to fight the French and to battle an Irish revolt instigated by the recently deposed James II. As a result, William III's government found itself unable to borrow more money except at usurious interest rates. The solution, first proposed by Scottish banker William Paterson, was to identify a group of wealthy individuals who would subscribe to the loan. In exchange, these individuals would be incorporated as the "Governor and Company of the Bank of England," entitled to an 8 percent annual dividend on their investment, and given substantial control over the government's credit as well as the sole right to issue bank notes (later called *pounds*) in England. Within two years of its founding in 1694, the bank had loaned the Treasury 1.2 million and issued £887,000 of notes to private customers.[6]

During this same period, changes in the law promoted the development of joint stock companies and the emergence of a market in government and private securities. Just between 1688 and 1695, the number of joint stock companies in England increased from 22 to 150.[7] Stock in these companies quickly came to be publicly traded and soon were the foundation for a liquid securities market in which company stocks, long-term bonds, and other investments could be traded.[8] The existence of a secondary market encouraged investors to purchase bonds and stock and effectively lowered interest rates for both the government and the private sector.

To bolster its creditworthiness, the government also rationalized its system of taxation and placed it primarily under the control of the Treasury. The state's ability to borrow, of course, depended upon its creditors agreeing that it had the means and intention to pay its obligations. Reform of the British tax system in the years preceding the Glorious Revolution of 1688 and proceeding more quickly during the Nine Years' War (1688–1697), helped to create this necessary level of investor confidence.[9] Prior to 1688, tax collection was supervised by a hodgepodge of local government officials, private tax farmers, parliamentary appointees, and a small number of royal officials. The result was that some taxes were seldom collected and no single body could coordinate government income with government expenditures to provide an overall picture of the government's financial status.[10] After 1688, however, the government began to replace old taxes and confused modes of collection with a unified system of customs, excise, and land taxes collected by trained and closely supervised royal officials. The result was a steady and dependable flow of revenue that financed the government's expenditures and convinced creditors that the purchase of long-term government securities was a safe investment.

Thus, in response to wartime needs, by the end of the seventeenth and beginnings of the eighteenth centuries, the British government had built a firm tax base and institutions that provided an adequate supply of money and credit to wage war. This England did with considerable success over the next several decades, building a fleet that gave Britain naval superiority over almost any possible combination of its European rivals. During the Seven Years' War, for example, the Royal Navy easily swept the French from the seas.[11]

England's financial revolution spurred its subsequent industrial revolution in two ways. First, the establishment of the Bank of England, the expansion of the banking industry, the development of firm state control over the money supply, the enhanced credibility of government debt, and the expansion of the securities market were all essential preconditions for commercial and industrial development.[12]

Second, the wave of military—especially naval—construction made possible by the financial revolution served as what William McNeill called "a great bellows" for the expansion of commerce and industry. To begin with, contracts for supplying the British navy with supplies expanded commercial activity throughout the British Isles and even as far away as New England and Canada, where timber for masts was purchased. Provisioners of meat, beer, and biscuits for the Royal Navy fed a population of as many as 60,000 sailors. This stimulated the growth of commercial agriculture in several parts of Great Britain and Ireland, as well as promoting the expansion of commerce and market relations throughout the realm.[13] Subsequently, a decade of war against revolutionary and Napoleonic France produced enormous demand for a variety of commodities, particularly those made of iron such as artillery. The production of cannons led to the development of a new industry based around coke-fired blast furnaces.[14] Improvements in iron production, in turn, helped bring about improvements in steam engines, innovations in railways, and, subsequently, the construction of iron ships.

FRANCE

French industrial development was, in turn, spurred by the obvious military advantages that industrial innovation gave her British rivals. For example, in the 1780s the British introduced superior techniques for smelting iron. Using a process known as "puddling," British iron-masters were able to melt iron inside a coke-fired furnace in such a way as to remove impurities that made it possible to shape it to any desired form or thickness at a relatively low cost. The iron was then passed through heavy rollers that eliminated the need for the expensive and wasteful hammering that had previously been needed to shape it.[15] This process was useful in the manufacture of a variety of products, one of which was cannons. Using the puddling process allowed the economical manufacture of large numbers of very efficient artillery pieces, including some small enough to be easily transported on the battlefield.

Observing this British development, the French sought to improve their own artillery by building a smelting plant employing the latest British technology. The plant was to be linked by canal and rivers to a naval gun foundry. The idea was obviously to allow the French navy to use British technology to build large numbers of its own inexpensive guns for its ships and harbor defenses.[16] The technology would, of course, also have civilian uses.

Imitation was not a one-sided affair. French military innovations such as heavily armored warships were also copied by the British, and this naval design, in turn, became the basis for the steel-hulled commercial vessels that replaced the wooden hulls that had been the mainstays of ship design for centuries.

In its efforts to compete with Britain, France was hampered by an antiquated financial system unable to support increasing levels of military spending, to say nothing of industrial and commercial development. For example, during most of the eighteenth century, French warship design was as good as, if not better than, that of the British. France, however, had difficulty financing the construction of enough ships and guns to match the British effort. The chief problem was France's lack of an institutional equivalent of the Bank of England, after the 1720 collapse of the *Banque Royale*, to provide long-term financing for naval and other expenditures. As a result, when the French built or repaired a warship, purchased provisions for crews, moved a fleet from one station to another, and so forth, the government was forced to secure short-term credit at high rates of interest. Thus, the British were able to build and operate warships far more economically than the French, an ability that more than compensated for the higher quality of French ships.[17]

One expedient to which the French government resorted was inflation of the currency, which, over time, led creditors to demand ever-higher interest rates on government loans.[18] In the 1770s, even the French government's ability to obtain short-term credit was compromised when an acute shortage of tax revenue relative to growing military expenditures forced the government to suspend payment on most of its loans. This effective default meant that the government was, for a time, unable to secure new credit at even the most usurious interest rates.[19] And, of course, the government's financial distress led it to call for the Estates General to help it raise money, setting into motion the events leading to the French Revolution.

French government finances understandably remained in disarray throughout the revolutionary period. Napoleon Bonaparte, however, sought to build a financial system with the ability to finance his military goals. To this end, in 1803 Bonaparte authorized the creation of a Bank of France, which, it was hoped, would enable the French government to match England's ability to obtain long-term credit on favorable terms. This bank, however, was very cautious in extending credit, perhaps recalling the experience of its predecessor in 1720. Thus, under both the Napoleonic regime and the soon-restored Bourbon monarchy, the government relied mainly on private banks to fund its debt. This practice had costs and benefits. The cost was a higher rate of interest, but the benefit was the growth of private banking. From the 1830s onward, particularly under the urging of Napoleon III, major private banking houses including Comptoir, Credit Mobilier, and Credit Foncier offered long-term financing not only for the government, but also for industrial corporations and railroad construction. These banks and their peers financed France's industrial revolution.

As in the British case, France's industrial revolution was, at least in part, driven by military spending. For example, during the 1840s, France took a position of world leadership in the design and manufacture of steam-powered vessels—an innovation with major military and commercial applications. France's opportunity to take such a leadership position came about because of the conservatism of the Royal Navy, which had a vested interest in wooden-hulled, sail-powered vessels and worked actively to discourage the development of other technologies. Seizing the opportunity, the French designed ships protected by armor plate and carrying guns that fired explosive shells. These vessels were extremely heavy and required powerful steam engines to propel them.[20] These military innovations encouraged an expansion of French iron foundries and engineering works. And, of course, determined to prevent the French from attaining a position of naval superiority, the British were forced to drop their own opposition to the development of new types of ships and to match French advances. In this way, military competition contributed to industrial development in both nations.

GERMANY

Many subsequent industrializers were also driven by military goals or necessities. Take the case of Germany. During the 1850s and 1860s, Prussia fought a series of wars against Denmark, Austria, and France. To finance these military efforts, the Prussian government turned to private bankers like Gerson Bleichroeder. In the 1850s, Bleichroeder had formed a consortium of German banks that financed the expansion of the German rail network. This brought him to the attention of Otto von Bismarck, who paved the way for Bleichroeder to organize a consortium of banks that financed Prussian mobilization during the

1859 Franco–Austrian war. Bleichroeder subsequently arranged the loans that financed the Austro–Prussian war and Franco–Prussian war that paved the way for German unification under Prussian auspices.

After German unification, the government made a major effort to spur the sort of industrial development that would increase German military power. One important step was the creation of a central bank, the *Reichsbank*, which would finance the government's needs as well as provide credit for foreign trade and German industrialization. For the new German government, rapid industrial development was essential to supporting Germany's military and political ambitions. The Reichsbank provided credit, set interest rates, and issued a new unified currency to replace the currencies of the formerly independent German states. New rules and regulations were designed to encourage the development of a host of other credit institutions at the regional and local levels to ensure an ample supply of credit for commercial and industrial borrowers.[21]

Germany's financial revolution played a major role in making Germany a major industrial and military power, with banks providing the long-term financing that facilitated German industrialization and the growth of German military capabilities. The latter two developments reinforced one another. With the help of the banks and spurred by military expenditures, German coal and steel production soon outstripped that of any other European nation. Germany also became the world's leader in such fields as electronics, optics, and chemicals. A great deal of this development was driven by the German government's desire to build a fleet able to do battle with the British. And, indeed, by the close of the nineteenth century, Germany boasted the world's second largest fleet and posed a serious threat to British naval supremacy in the North Atlantic.[22] German nationalists declared, with some justification, that Germany brought, "an army, a navy, money, and power to the world."[23]

THE UNITED STATES

America's nineteenth-century financial and industrial development was driven by military necessity more than military ambition. Necessity, of course, took the form of America's bloody Civil War. Prior to the Civil War, America's national government had few responsibilities and was able to finance its limited expenditures through tariffs and customs duties, occasionally supplemented by small-scale borrowing in national and international credit markets. During the Civil War, however, the government's need for revenues increased so dramatically that the government could not secure sufficient funds from the traditional sources—domestic banks and financiers. European investors, for their part, had no confidence that the Union would prevail on the battlefield and were reluctant to purchase US securities.[24]

The federal government therefore turned to new forms of revenue extraction, including excise taxes on manufactured goods, a tax on incomes, bond sales to small investors, and the issue of a variety of legal tender notes, some interest-bearing and some not, in small denominations. All these revenue devices depended upon a measure of popular acceptance and, as we saw above, left the government financially dependent upon popular confidence to meet the Union's military expenses, which ultimately totaled more than $4 billion. By the end of the war, excise and income taxes had produced more than $1.2 billion in revenues. A moderately progressive income tax was enacted in 1862. A levy of 3 percent was imposed on all incomes below $10,000, with the rate rising to 5 percent on incomes above that level. In 1864 and 1865, the income tax act was amended, eventually providing for rates of 5 percent on incomes below $5,000 and 10 percent for those earning more than that amount.[25]

As mentioned in chapter 3, a third major revenue instrument introduced during the Civil War was the sale of government bonds to small investors. In 1862, Treasury Secretary Salmon P. Chase invited Ohio Republican banker Jay Cooke to attempt to place $500 million in government bonds that could not be sold to domestic banks or foreign investors. Cooke developed a plan to market these securities to ordinary citizens who had never before purchased government bonds.[26] He thought he could appeal to the patriotism of ordinary Americans, and he believed that widespread ownership of government bonds would give large numbers of ordinary citizens a greater concern for their nation's welfare.[27]

Cooke pushed the idea that purchasing government securities was both a wise investment and a patriotic duty. His network of 2,500 sales agents throughout the North sold these bonds to an eager public. Knowing the difficulty of retaining popular support and the regime's finances over four long years of war, Republican Party organizations worked with Cooke's sales agents in every community to provide what historian Eric McKitrick calls a "continual affirmation of purpose."[28] By 1863, all the bonds had been sold and most were in the hands of private citizens rather than financial institutions.

A final revenue instrument introduced during the war was the issue of $450 million in legal tender notes. Some of these so-called "greenbacks" bore interest, and others could be redeemed for twenty-year government bonds. The bulk of the greenbacks, however, were unredeemable "fiat money." Issued in the form of payment on existing government debt, the greenbacks constituted an interest-free loan from the general public to the government. After the war, the constitutionality of federally issued paper money was challenged and, eventually, upheld by the Supreme Court.[29]

The revenue instruments devised during the Civil War became important parts of the national government's revenue collection efforts during the ensuing decades. The income tax was declared unconstitutional by the Supreme Court in 1895 and then reinstated by the Sixteenth Amendment in 1913. During the late nineteenth and early twentieth centuries, business and financial interests, along with the Republican Party that spoke for them, opposed the income tax and advocated financing the federal government through the sale of large-denomination bonds. Bondholders, unlike taxpayers, derived private profit from financing the operations of the federal government, and a government sustained by bonds tended to be attentive to the institutions and people who bought bonds.

Their participation in the primary and secondary markets for Civil War–era debt provided financiers based in the United States with a great deal of marketing experience and a much stronger financial base than they had previously possessed.[30] Such financiers as Jay Cooke, Daniel Drew, James Fisk, Jay Gould, Edward Harriman, J. P. Morgan, and Joseph Seligman not only traded in government bonds but also used the capital acquired in this way to deal in commodities and undertake lucrative military contracts. Fisk, for example, made millions selling textiles and other commodities to the government. In Europe, where war seemed unremitting, such financiers had an ongoing role in sustaining the state revenue needs and selling supplies to the military. In the United States, by contrast, during the period after the Civil War the army was largely disbanded and direct governmental spending declined sharply.

Nevertheless, the federal government was compelled to deal with the matter of the enormous debt it had acquired to prosecute the war. Between 1860 and 1866, the national debt had increased from a mere $65 million to nearly $3 billion, a sum amounting to nearly 30 percent of the gross national product of the Union states. This mountain of debt curtailed private investment by absorbing capital that might otherwise have been used to finance private endeavors. At the same time, much of this debt had been acquired when the fate of the Union was still in doubt and, hence, was obtained at rates of interest well above current market levels.[31]

The Treasury Department realized that it needed to move expeditiously to repay or refund its outstanding obligations. This was accomplished through the issuance of new US government securities bearing considerably lower rates of interest than those marketed during the war. Some of the proceeds from the sale of the new bonds were used to retire the old debt. A strong effort was also made to sell these new securities in Europe in order to bring new capital into the country that would be available for industrial and commercial development. Many of the same financiers who had made millions during the war, like Joseph Seligman, were now involved in refinancing the government's accumulated wartime debt.

The profits that Seligman, Fisk, and the others had made during the war and postwar periods financing the government's debts were, in turn, used to finance America's postwar industrial development. The single most important element of industrial development was railroad construction, which provided the nation with a unified continental market and promoted general economic and industrial expansion. The government worked to promote railroad construction by giving land grants to firms in exchange for their agreement to build rail lines. Such land grants were an important subsidy but did not provide the capital actually needed to lay track and purchase equipment. This is where the role of private financiers was critical. Financiers like Seligman or Drew would arrange to loan a railroad corporation the funds needed for construction and to begin operation in exchange for bonds secured by the value of the land grant that the railroad received from the federal government. In this way, private financiers were responsible for the government's success in promoting railroad construction—the key to America's subsequent industrial development.

Thus, as was the case in Europe, military needs set into motion a financial revolution that, in turn, paved the way for industrial development in the United States. For all its horrors, war served as the great engine of development.

LATER INDUSTRIALIZERS

It is worth noting that many, if not all, of the nations that subsequently worked to develop their economies were driven, to a greater or lesser extent, by a desire to compete militarily with the developed world. Thus, after seeing the heavily armed steam warships of the 1853 American squadron commanded by Commodore Matthew Perry, the Japanese government recognized that it would be unable to defend itself against a Western power unless it developed its own economy and military capabilities. Japan began by establishing modern financial institutions including the Bank of Japan, networks of commercial banks, property rights, stock exchanges, and corporate law.[32] These institutions were designed to integrate Japan into the international financial system and to give the government and private entrepreneurs access to the foreign capital and equipment Japan would need to develop its economy. Initially, Japan raised capital in the London financial markets, purchased machinery in England and Germany, and worked to build a fleet along British lines, purchasing warships in England and securing the services of British naval experts.

Tsarist Russia worked to modernize its economy after the military debacle of the Crimean War demonstrated that the developed nations had far outstripped Russia militarily. Subsequently, the Soviet Union, convinced that it would eventually be attacked by the capitalist world, sought to develop an industrial base that would support a powerful Red Army that would defend the state. And, of course, for the Chinese Communist regime, military modernization has been at the forefront of the "Four Modernizations" called for by Zhou Enlai and Deng Xiaoping. As was true in the eighteenth century, war and the threat of war have continued to provide an enormous incentive for economic development.

DEVELOPMENT AND MILITARY PROWESS

Charles Tilly famously declared that war makes states and states make war. One might add to Tilly's observation that economically developed states make war more successfully than their more backward counterparts. In a recent empirical study, political scientist Michael Beckley has shown that level of economic development is the single most important variable explaining military outcomes over the past century or so. In hundreds of battles, says Beckley, the more economically developed side consistently outfought the poorer side on a soldier-for-soldier basis.[33]

States with a higher level of economic development are usually likely to have better weapons, but in the modern era sophisticated weapons can often be acquired by primitive fighters. More than weapons, though, economic development is likely to be associated with better communications, intelligence, and medical care. Armies deployed by developed states are usually better able to repair equipment in the field. Officers and soldiers from economically developed states are likely to possess higher levels of education and training and to be more adept at operating complex weapons systems that often link troops to sensors, satellites, and command centers.[34] Generally speaking, as Eliot Cohen has noted, a less developed state can acquire the weapons that form the "teeth" of a modern army, but it is far more difficult to acquire these other capabilities, including training, that form the "tail" of a modern military force and give it its superior striking power.

Of course, some militarily ambitious states and even non-state actors have endeavored to develop shortcuts to military power that do not require long-term economic development. The two most evident of these shortcuts are the acquisition of weapons of mass destruction and the use of various forms of so-called "asymmetric warfare" designed to threaten more powerful opponents with unacceptable losses if they engage in battle. The former strategy seems currently associated with North Korea and Iran and the latter strategy with a number of non-state actors targeted by America's "war on terror."

As to weapons of mass destruction, most notably nuclear weapons, there is little doubt that even the most primitive state possessing such weapons could pose a threat to the lives of millions of individuals in the developed world. Such a state, however, would be highly unlikely to use its weapons. While a North Korea or, perhaps, an Iran or other so-called "rogue state" might do harm to a more developed state, it would risk total annihilation by the forces of that state or its allies. By acquiring nuclear weapons, an otherwise weak state actually does little to advance its place in the world. If a rogue regime actually used its weapons it would risk total destruction in retaliation; and, if a more heavily armed developed power became convinced that a rogue was actually contemplating the use of nuclear weapons against its territory, the pressure for a preemptive strike of its own would be considerable. Thus, in some respects, weak states with nuclear weapons increase the military risks to themselves.

As to asymmetric warfare, this is hardly a tactic through which poor states can make themselves great powers. Terror attacks against the United States and other developed nations can be bloody and frightening to the civilian populace. However, they represent no real threat to a developed nation's security. And, as exemplified by the US response to the September 11, 2001 terrorist attacks in New York and Washington, such acts are likely to provoke severe retaliation. In response to the 9/11 attacks, the United States destroyed the governments of Afghanistan and Iraq, killed tens of thousands of individuals in those and other Middle Eastern countries, and continues to maintain a troop presence and to undertake targeted assassination campaigns via "drones," or unmanned aerial vehicles, throughout the Middle East. Asymmetric warfare is a term that describes desperation tactics used by the weak against the strong. The strong usually prevail.

ECONOMIC STRENGTH AS A RESULT OF MILITARY POWER

Generally speaking, the world's dominant military powers seek to use that power to enhance their economic power, thus establishing a virtuous cycle in which military and economic might reinforce and enhance one another. One example, of course, is Great Britain during the eighteenth and nineteenth centuries. The British financial and industrial revolutions allowed Great Britain to become the world's greatest power, particularly in the maritime realm. At its peak, Britain's Royal Navy was generally larger and more combat effective than the next two or three largest European fleets. Naval strength served British economic interests as Britain used its fleet to expand the British empire at an average annual pace of 100,000 square miles between 1815 and 1865.[35]

Perhaps not all portions of this empire were economically beneficial to Britain but, in general, its overseas possessions gave Britain privileged access to commodities and raw materials and a more-or-less captive market for British manufactured goods. The Royal Navy and occasional "boots on the ground" also protected British property and investments in regions such as Egypt, whose own rulers often showed insufficient respect for the property rights of foreigners. For example, in 1882, British warships bombarded Alexandria in a response to a threat by the new Egyptian government to expropriate British bondholders with investments in Egypt.[36] For more than a century, international and intraempire trade and investment, protected by the Royal Navy, made Britain the world's wealthiest as well as its most powerful nation.

In a similar vein, America's economic power in the middle decades of the twentieth century allowed it to vault to a position of military preeminence at the end of World War II. In 1945, America's naval fleet consisted of 1,200 major warships and its air fleet boasted more than 2,000 heavy bombers. Its aircraft carriers and marine amphibious divisions gave the United States the capacity to project power throughout the world and, of course, it briefly possessed a monopoly on nuclear weapons.

As the British and others had in the past, America used its power to rebuild much of the world's economic system in a way that generally served American economic interests. The post–World War II economic settlement, more or less imposed upon the Western world by the United States (as Russia was imposing a self-serving economic settlement on its domain), included a number of elements. The first was privileged American access to strategic materials—particularly oil. This was accomplished in part by an American anticolonialist policy that pressured Great Britain to surrender its colonial possessions that, like the oil-rich kingdoms of the Middle East, quickly became American protectorates. Second, through such institutions as the International Monetary Fund, the World Bank, and the General Agreement on Tariffs and Trade (GATT), the United States strongly promoted a program of free trade from which it expected to benefit as the world's greatest manufacturing power. Third, through these and other institutions, the United

States became the major source of international credit and the American dollar became the world's reserve currency. Credit allowed foreign governments and industries to purchase American goods, and the role of the dollar as a reserve currency gave the United States great leverage and flexibility in international bond and money markets.

British world preeminence lasted little more than a century, coming to an end as a result of the rise of other military and economic powers like America and Germany and the ruinous costs of two major wars in the twentieth century.[37] And, of course, a number of authors have argued that American "global economic and military leadership is also in the process of coming to an end as America faces new economic and military rivals such as China." In his well-known book, *The Rise and Fall of the Great Powers*, historian Paul Kennedy asserts that the American decline is in large measure a result of the tendency of great powers to rely too heavily on military might and spend excessively on warfare. "If too large a proportion of the state's resources is diverted from wealth creation and allocated instead to military purposes, then that is likely to lead to a weakening of national power over the longer term," Kennedy declared.[38]

To Kennedy and other theorists of American decline, there seems to be a kind of inevitability to the process. Great powers amass wealth, build powerful military forces with which to defend and promote their military power, spend too much on their military efforts, and go into a period of decline. If the United States succumbs to this sort of imperial overreach, which is by no means certain, it will be in large measure because of a set of decisions initiated during the Cold War in the name of national security. As I have observed elsewhere, what could be called the dark side of American exceptionalism is the nation's often excessive willingness to go to war.[39]

If, however, the United States is able to avoid this sort of imperial decline, thanks will in no small measure be due to the prescience of James Madison, who was determined to place the constitutional war power in the collective hands of Congress. Madison thought, correctly, that executives, be they kings or presidents, had a tendency, *contra*

General Lee, to become too fond of war. Congressional war powers, Madison thought, would leash what he and Jefferson liked to call the "dogs of war." Presidents and kings tended to see only the benefits of war while Congress, representing those who actually fought and died in wars, tended to be more cognizant of the costs.[40] Congressional war powers, coupled with a lively popular politics, provided an element of self-correction to compensate for the nation's often excessive bellicosity. Historically, after every war or skirmish, the United States sharply curtailed its military spending and went back to its mundane economic and civil pursuits. Political scientist Ira Katznelson refers to this pattern as expressive of America's "flexible capacity" to meet its military needs.[41] Though, as we shall see in chapter 5, some wartime agencies were occasionally able to avoid postwar retrenchment by blending into the civilian bureaucracy. Congressional war powers coupled with popular politics helped to forestall America's militarist and imperialist inclinations. America could be a great power without committing itself to full-blown imperialism and succumbing to imperial overreach.

In particular, the American government's reliance upon ordinary citizens to fight as well as finance war efforts has often sparked significant mass political mobilization both in support of and in opposition to presidential war policies. To begin with, the recruitment of troops—especially through conscription—and concomitant efforts to rally citizen support for military undertakings often energizes popular political organization and activity both in support of and in opposition to the war effort. For example, as political scientist Theda Skocpol has shown, the Civil War and both world wars prompted the formation of hundreds of patriotic, civic, and service organizations such as the Grange, the Women's Christian Temperance Union, and the Red Cross.[42] Some organizations were sponsored by the government itself. For instance, the American Farm Bureau Federation was organized with federal assistance during World War I to spur food production. Similarly, the Knights of Columbus received government support in exchange for its advocacy of military service for working-class Catholics. Many of these groups became politically active, promoting causes ranging from labor reform to temperance.

At the same time, individuals and groups asked to bear the costs of war often feel emboldened to make new political demands and seek new political rights. As we saw earlier, in both America and Europe, war has been closely associated with expansion of suffrage. Revolutionary War militiamen called to place their lives at the service of the nation thought themselves just as entitled to vote as their betters who risked only property. Indeed, the revolutionary militia was known as a breeding ground for radical democrats. In 1776, the Philadelphia Committee of Privates, an organization of Pennsylvania militiamen, advised voters to "Let no man represent you disposed to form any rank above that of Freeman."[43]

The sentiments of armed militiamen could not be ignored in the suffrage debates that followed the success of the revolutionary cause. Throughout the colonies, citizen soldiers pressed for and helped to win expanded voting rights. Organizations of state militiamen demanded an end to property restrictions for suffrage on the ground that those asked to fight should not be barred from voting. In Maryland, groups of armed militiamen went to the polls in 1776 demanding to vote whether or not they could meet the state's existing property requirements for voters. In some instances, those denied the right to vote threatened to refuse to continue to fight. The result in Maryland and other states was a general expansion of suffrage during the revolutionary period designed to accommodate the demands of those Americans being asked to fight. Subsequently, the War of 1812 led to suffrage reforms in a number of states on the argument that "men who were good enough to fight were good enough to vote."[44] Women's suffrage in the United States, as in England and Canada, was partially brought about by the First World War, on the basis of the notion that women were more likely to support the war effort if they possessed the right to vote.[45] Most recently, the Twenty-Sixth Amendment, lowering the voting age to 18, was designed in part to bolster support among young men who were then being conscripted for service in the Vietnam War.

While energizing the government's supporters, mobilization for war can also galvanize foes of the government's military efforts. Virtually every American war has engendered opposition from one or another quarter, and often opposition to war has been the basis for passionate rhetoric and intense bouts of organizational activity. Abolitionists, for example, castigated the 1846 Mexican War as a campaign to expand slavery and organized a fierce, if ultimately ineffective, movement to oppose President Polk's policies. Though its opponents failed to block the war, their organizational efforts helped bring about the creation of the Free Soil party, which subsequently became a major component of the Republican coalition.[46]

In protracted conflicts, the hardships, casualties, and dislocations suffered by citizen soldiers and their families can inflame antiwar sentiment and escalate the formation of political opposition to continued fighting. Resistance to military conscription often becomes a major focus of these efforts. The Civil War draft was bitterly resisted in many parts of the North and ignited major riots in New York and other cities in 1863.[47] The New York riot lasted four days before it was finally quelled by police and military authorities. So serious was the threat of continuing civil disorder that more than ten thousand soldiers were detached from the Army of the Potomac to garrison New York in the riot's wake.[48] Opposition to the draft and growing popular weariness of the war very nearly led to Lincoln's defeat in the 1864 presidential election. Draft resistance was a major problem during the First World War, when socialist organizers urged draft-age men to refuse induction, and thousands of men were arrested for failing to register with their draft boards.[49] During the Vietnam War, liberal foes of American intervention in Indo-China encouraged draft resistance and made conscription a major political issue.[50] Even World War II, a conflict that had overwhelming popular support, saw limited but vocal draft resistance.[51]

Finally, even after the cessation of hostilities, former critics of the war, including even some veterans, search out political vehicles through which to express their alienation while other Americans who served in the military organize to trumpet their patriotism and to seek recognition for their sacrifices. Thus, many individuals initially politicized by their opposition to the Vietnam War became active in the left-liberal "New Politics" movement of the 1970s.[52] New Politics supporters dominated the Democratic Party convention in 1972 and secured the party's presidential nomination for liberal South Dakota Senator George McGovern. In subsequent years, New Politics activists played important roles in the consumer, environmental, feminist, and other "postmaterial" political movements.[53] In a similar vein, many American war veterans joined organizations like the Grand Army of the Republic (GAR) after the Civil War or the American Legion after the two world wars. These organizations became significant actors in American politics, pressing not only for such matters as the extensive system of veterans' pensions and benefits made available after the Civil War and World War I, and under the post–World War II GI Bill, but for broader political goals as well. The GAR was a powerful force in Republican Party politics in the late nineteenth century, while the American Legion became an important conservative pressure group during the twentieth century.

These wartime and postwar mobilizations of new political forces, in turn, created new opportunities for political entrepreneurship on the part of sympathetic or even merely ambitious members of Congress. Occasionally during the war, but most often in the peacetime aftermath of military conflicts, groups in the Congress have endeavored to reach out to the movements energized by the war. Members of Congress have espoused these groups' causes, advocated their views, and appealed to their solidary concerns and material interests—in the case of veterans, for example, joining and associating themselves with veterans' groups and activities and providing pensions, bonuses, and other benefits. In these ways, groups in the Congress have been able to link themselves to energetic new political forces which, for their part, now have a stake in supporting congressional power *vis-à-vis* the executive branch. These alliances with new political forces often allowed postwar congresses to accomplish what the nation's foreign foes could not—take on and defeat the president.

In the wake of the Mexican War, a number of northern congressional

Democrats, including such New York "Barnburners" as David Wilmot, Preston King, and John A. Dix, turned against the national administration.[54] These members of Congress aligned themselves with the antislavery forces that had mobilized throughout the North in opposition to the attack on Mexico and subsequent American territorial expansion. This strengthened antislavery coalition became the basis for the Free Soil party and, later, for the creation of the Republican Party. Antislavery forces in Congress harassed and weakened the Fillmore, Pierce, and Buchanan administrations. Though Pierce was able to secure the enactment of the 1854 Kansas–Nebraska act, repealing the Missouri Compromise, in an attempt to appease both sides in the slavery controversy, the end result was to irrevocably divide the Democratic Party.

During the concluding years of the Buchanan administration, the new Republican Party controlled the House of Representatives. Republicans asserted that the power of the presidency should be curbed and established a special committee under the leadership of Representative John Covode of Pennsylvania to investigate the general topic of improper presidential efforts to influence congressional deliberations. The Covode committee charged President Buchanan with using bribes and other unsavory tactics to secure the enactment of legislation he favored and recommended ways of reducing presidential influence in the legislative process.[55]

In a similar vein, in the aftermath of the Civil War, members of Congress opposed to President Andrew Johnson's Reconstruction policies relied heavily upon the political support of the most important Union Army veteran's organization, the Grand Army of the Republic. At its peak, the GAR enrolled nearly a half-million members along with hundreds of thousands of their family members in its auxiliary organizations. The GAR supported the adoption of the Fourteenth Amendment, which the president opposed, and generally favored the radical Republicans' harsh policies toward the defeated South rather than the conciliatory program espoused by Johnson. Radical Republicans relied upon GAR grassroots support against Johnson's efforts to influence the outcome of the 1866 congressional elections. Subsequently, in 1867, Johnson attempted to oust Secretary of War Edwin M. Stanton, in defiance of the new Tenure of Office Act, which required congressional approval for the dismissal of cabinet officers. Many Republican radicals were convinced that Johnson's action was a prelude to some form of coup d'état and asked the GAR to march a detachment of Union veterans to Washington to protect the Congress. House Speaker Schuyler Colfax reported that explosives had been stolen in New York and were being brought to Washington to blow up the capitol. The GAR prepared, unnecessarily as it turned out, to march on Washington at a moment's notice.[56] To emphasize the importance of the alliance between the president's congressional foes and the GAR, during the impeachment proceedings against President Johnson, the GAR's national commander, Congressman John Logan of Illinois, served as one of the House impeachment managers.

A similar pattern of congressional alliances with emergent political forces manifested itself after the two world wars. After World War I, President Wilson's congressional opponents made common cause with German and Irish Americans and postwar isolationists to block American participation in the League of Nations and, thereby, to destroy the Wilson presidency.[57] The Germans and Irish had, from the beginning, opposed support for Great Britain in the European conflict but had been silenced by the administration's wartime suppression of dissent. But even many Americans who had supported the war were shocked by the carnage and disillusioned by the results. Now they opposed having "An American army policing the world and quelling riots in all peoples' back yards."[58] Interestingly, the treaty's most vehement foe, Senate Majority Leader Henry Cabot Lodge of Massachusetts, was himself a Rooseveltian internationalist who had supported America's entry into the war. Lodge, however, harbored a deep personal hatred for Wilson and was prepared to align himself with isolationists if to do so would thwart the president. Other Republicans had been angered by Wilson's wartime arrogation of power and were now eager to cut the president down to size and, especially, to derail any ambitions Wilson might have to seek a third term.[59]

After the Second World War, President Truman's congressional foes courted the support of patriotic veterans' groups like the American Legion and the Catholic War Veterans in their investigations of alleged Communist penetration of the executive branch. The American Legion, in particular, organized nation-wide, antisubversive seminars, publicized and enforced blacklists, supported anti-Communist members of Congress like Richard M. Nixon, and lent their political clout to the efforts of HUAC and the McCarthy committee.[60]

During the late 1960s, groups in Congress aligned themselves with liberal forces that mobilized against the Vietnam War to undermine Lyndon Johnson's presidency in the late 1960s. This "New Politics" alliance remained active in American politics during the following decade and played an important role in the ouster of Richard Nixon. During Johnson's second administration, liberals—who had initially supported the war—turned against it largely because military needs began to divert substantial resources from Great Society social programs to which liberal Democrats were strongly committed. Liberals were joined by some civil rights leaders, like Dr. Martin Luther King Jr., who viewed the war as a diversion of national energy and attention from the nation's effort to end segregation.[61] Supported by segments of the national news media, liberal forces began to criticize not only the administration's war policies, but patterns and practices that had become commonplace in the years since World War II: lax Pentagon procurement practices, Pentagon public relations activities, domestic spying by intelligence agencies, and the hiring of former military officers by defense contractors.[62]

Growing opposition to the war among liberals encouraged some members of Congress, notably Senator J. William Fulbright, chair of the Senate Foreign Relations Committee, along with such senators as George McGovern, Wayne Morse, and Ernest Gruening to break with the president.[63] Fueling the growth of opposition to the war was the fact that increasing numbers of citizen soldiers, including conscripts, were being sent to fight in the jungles of Southeast Asia, where they suffered substantial casualties.[64] Initially, the system of deferments and exemptions surrounding military conscription ensured that most of the draftees would be drawn from working-class and minority households—a segment of society not well represented in the political process or in possession of ready access to the media and, hence, vulnerable to wartime exactions. In 1967, however, foes of the war charged that the draft was racist in character because its burden fell so heavily on minority communities.

Stung by these charges, President Johnson set in motion a set of changes in the draft law that limited student and other upper middle class deferments. As critics had hoped, the result was increased opposition to the war from more influential social strata who now saw *their* children placed at risk. Between 1968 and 1970, tens of thousands of young men claimed conscientious objector status or presented dubious medical excuses, while tens of thousands more refused to register or destroyed or returned their draft cards.[65] Others clogged the federal courts with challenges to draft orders. Antiwar sentiment among congressional liberals intensified in 1967 and 1968, and Senator Eugene McCarthy launched a bid to deny Johnson the 1968 Democratic nomination. Though he almost certainly would have been renominated despite liberal opposition, Johnson was politically wounded and chose to withdraw from the race. Antiwar Democrats became an important element in the New Politics coalition which, in 1974, forced President Richard Nixon from office in the wake of the Watergate scandal.

After Nixon's resignation, congressional Democrats enacted a number of pieces of legislation designed to curb presidential power. These included the Budget and Impoundment Control Act to enhance congressional power in the budget process, the Ethics in Government Act to facilitate future prosecution of wrongdoing in the executive branch, and the Freedom of Information Act to open the files of executive agencies to congressional and media scrutiny. Congress also strengthened its own investigative arm, the General Accounting Office. Other legislation, such as the War Powers Resolution, specifically struck at presidential war and foreign-policy powers.

Thus, in the wake of the Vietnam War as in a number of other instances, important groups within Congress were able to take advantage of war-induced political mobilization to do battle with the White House. The importance of war as an incubator of new political forces that could appeal to the Congress helped to place limits on America's martial propensities. On the one hand, military exigencies have frequently allowed chief executives to demand—and have compelled congresses to give—vast new powers to the president. On the other hand, however, the new political forces often brought into being by war have allowed groups in the Congress an opportunity to forge political alliances that then enabled them to lay siege to the White House and retrieve some or all of the power that had been surrendered to the president. Again, as we shall see, some wartime agencies and powers survived by tunneling into the civilian bureaucracy. Nevertheless, this democratic self-corrective can be seen as a vaccine against imperialist overreach developed by "Dr. Madison."

An echo of this pattern helped bring an end to the wars in Iraq and Afghanistan, pressing Presidents Bush and Obama to end the fighting and bring American troops home sooner than they wanted. But, during the fights over these and other American military actions during the past quarter century, it became evident that congressional ability to leash the dogs of war has declined considerably.

THE END OF THE MADISONIAN SOLUTION

Unfortunately, several developments during the last quarter century have weakened and frayed, though not yet cut, the constitutional leashes and muzzles fashioned by Mr. Madison. These include the expansion of unilateral presidential war powers, making it more difficult for America's system of checks and balances to operate effectively, and the advent of forms of military engagement that reduce the mobilizational effects of war.

As to the first of these, a statute enacted in 1947 began the construction of the unilateral presidency and the erosion of Congress's role in military affairs. The was the 1947 National Security Act, which reorganized the military services by separating the air force from the army and abolishing the historic division between the War Department and Navy Department. All three military branches were now placed within a single National Military Establishment, later renamed the Department of Defense (DoD), under the leadership of a civilian cabinet officer—the secretary of defense. The 1947 act also created the Central Intelligence Agency (CIA) to coordinate the government's activities in the realms of information gathering, espionage, and covert operations. Finally, the act established the National Security Council (NSC), chaired by the president and including the major cabinet secretaries, the chairman of the Joint Chiefs of Staff, the three service secretaries, and a number of other high-ranking officials. The NSC was to assist the president in coordinating national security planning and decision making. Taken together, the 1947 National Security Act created the basis for what later critics would call the "imperial presidency."

Presidential Control of the Military

To begin with, the 1947 act was an important step in the professionalization of the military services and their subjection to presidential control. America's military effort had historically depended upon state militias, which often answered as much to governors, senators, and members of Congress as to the president. During the Civil War, for example, many politicians secured gubernatorial commissions in state militia units and through them, as well as through the state governors, Congress frequently sought to interfere with Lincoln's military plans. Presidential control of the military was enhanced at the beginning of the Spanish–American war when Congress passed the 1898 Volunteer Act. Under its terms, the general officers and their staffs of all state militia units, now renamed the National Guard, were to be appointed by the president rather than the state governors. The 1903 Dick Act further increased presidential control of the nation's military forces by authorizing the president to dissolve state guard units into the regular army in times of emergency, while the 1916 National Defense Act gave the president authority to appoint all commissioned and noncommissioned guard officers in time of war. The 1916 act also began the creation of the national military reserves, which eventually supplanted the state units as the force employed to fill out the military's ranks in time of emergency.[66]

While these pieces of legislation gradually gave the president and the military brass in Washington fuller control over what originally had been primarily state forces, the long-standing division of the military into two cabinet departments—War (army) and Navy—had undermined presidential control. Historically, each of the services, as well as branches within the services, most notably the Marine Corps and, more recently, the Army Air Corps, had their own ties to supporters in the Congress and used these to circumvent their nominal superiors. For example, during the First World War, the Marine Corps mobilized its allies in Congress to induce the president to accept their participation in the American expeditionary force over the objections of the secretary of war, the secretary of the navy, and General Pershing, the force's commander.[67] In a similar vein, between the wars, some lawmakers became enchanted with the idea of military aviation and supported General Billy Mitchell's quixotic crusade against the War and Navy departments. Over the objections of the president and the secretary of war, Congress enacted the 1926 Air Corps Act, which made the air corps a virtually autonomous entity within the army.[68] Even more important, the War Department and the Navy Department presented Congress with separate budgets and competing visions of the nation's military needs and priorities. The annual struggle for funding between the two service branches, complete with competing testimony by the nation's foremost military authorities, opened the way for increased congressional intervention into military decision making.

The 1947 National Security Act created a single secretary of defense responsible for all defense planning and the overall military budget. As amended in 1949, the act diminished the status of the individual service secretaries, who were no longer to be members of the president's cabinet or the National Security Council. Instead, the individual service secretaries were to focus on manpower and procurement issues and to report to the secretary of defense and his assistant secretaries. To further centralize military planning, the 1949 amendments created the position of Chairman of the Joint Chiefs of Staff (JCS) to denote the officer who was to serve as the principle military advisor to the defense secretary and the president. By creating a more unified military chain of command and a single defense budget, the National Security Act diminished Congress's ability to intervene in military planning and decision making and increased the president's control over the armed services and national security policy.

In 1948, under the auspices of the first secretary of defense, James Forrestal, the chiefs of the three military services met at Key West and negotiated a set of agreements on missions and weapons that were expected to mute inter-service squabbles and the congressional intervention that inevitably ensued. For several years, some resistance to the newly centralized military regime manifested itself within the services. The eventual result, though, was a clear chain of command with the president at the top and Congress out of the loop.

Intelligence and Planning

In addition to centralizing military decision making, the 1947 National Security Act increased the White House's capacities for foreign policy and security planning, intelligence gathering and evaluation, and covert intelligence operations. The first of these results stemmed from the creation of the National Security Council. The council itself was never more than a loose-knit presidential advisory body and seldom had any independent influence. Beginning during the Kennedy presidency, however, the NSC staff became an important presidential instrument. Truman and Eisenhower relied upon the State Department's policy planning staff and the JCS staff for policy analysis and advice.

These groups, however, did not work directly for the president and had other institutional loyalties. Kennedy expanded the NSC staff and designated McGeorge Bundy, an Ivy Leaguer and former intelligence officer, to serve as his special assistant for national security affairs and head of the NSC staff. During subsequent presidencies, the NSC staff—eventually consisting of nearly two hundred professional employees organized in regional and functional offices, along with the national security assistant—became important forces in the shaping of foreign and security policy, often eclipsing the State Department and its leadership. For example, when he served as Richard Nixon's national security assistant, Henry Kissinger effectively excluded the secretary of state, William Rogers, from most foreign policy decision making. Similarly, during the Carter administration, the president allowed his national security assistant, Zbigniew Brzezinski, to marginalize Secretary of State Cyrus Vance. Both Rogers and Vance eventually resigned.[69]

The construction of a national security bureaucracy within the executive office of the president made possible the enormous postwar expansion of presidential unilateralism in the realm of security and foreign policy. Beginning with Truman, presidents would conduct foreign and security policy through executive agreements and executive orders and seldom negotiate formal treaties requiring Senate ratification. Presidents before Truman—even Franklin D. Roosevelt—had generally submitted important accords between the United States and foreign powers to the Senate for ratification, and had sometimes seen their goals stymied by senatorial opposition. Not only did the Constitution require senatorial confirmation of treaties, but before Truman, presidents had lacked the administrative resources to systematically conduct an independent foreign policy. It was not by accident that most of the agreements—particularly the secret agreements—negotiated by FDR concerned military matters where the president could rely upon the administrative capacities of the War and Navy departments.[70]

The State Department's policy planning staff—and especially the NSC staff—created the institutional foundations and capabilities upon which Truman and his successors could rely to conduct and administer the nation's foreign and security policies directly from the oval office. For example, American participation in the International Trade Organization (ITO), one of the cornerstones of US postwar trade policy, was based on a sole executive agreement, the GATT Provisional Protocol, signed by President Truman after Congress delayed action and ultimately failed to approve the ITO charter.[71] Truman signed some 1,300 executive agreements and Eisenhower another 1,800, in some cases requesting congressional approval and in other instances ignoring the Congress. Executive agreements take two forms: congressional–executive agreements and sole executive agreements. In the former case, the president submits the agreement to both houses of Congress as he would any other piece of legislation, with a majority vote in both houses required for passage. This is generally a lower hurdle than the two-thirds vote required for Senate ratification of a treaty. A sole executive agreement is not sent to the Congress at all. The president generally has discretion over which avenue to pursue. All treaties and executive agreements have the power of law, though a sole executive agreement cannot contravene an existing statute.[72] During the Truman and Eisenhower presidencies, barely two hundred treaties were submitted to the Senate as stipulated by Article II of the Constitution.[73] The same pattern has continued to the present time. Indeed, two of the most important recent international agreements entered into by the United States, the North American Free Trade Agreement and the World Trade Organization agreement, were confirmed by congressional executive agreement, not by treaty.[74]

Indeed, it is worth noting that in recent years, through a combination of executive orders and institutional changes, presidents have been able to sharply reduce congressional authority in the realm of trade policy. The 1934 Reciprocal Trade Agreements Act gave the president expanded authority to negotiate trade agreements with other countries and reduced Congress's ability to interfere with or reject such presidential agreements. In 1974, similar authority was granted to the president to negotiate the reduction of non-tariff barriers under so-called "fast track" procedures, which limit congressional power to overturn presidential decisions.[75] The 1974 Trade Act also expanded the role of the US Trade Representative (USTR), an office originally authorized by Congress in 1962 and established by President Kennedy via executive order in 1963. The USTR has enhanced the institutional ability of the White House to set the nation's overall trade policy agenda, often relegating Congress to the task of vetoing specific measures within a larger plan—a reversal of the constitutionally mandated relationship between the two branches.

In a similar vein, the policy planning staff and NSC opened the way for policy making by executive order in the areas of security and foreign policy. Executive orders issued to implement presidents' security policy goals have been variously called National Security Presidential Directives (NSPD) and National Security Decision Directives (NSDD), but are most commonly known as National Security Directives or NSDs. These, like other executive orders, are commands from the president to an executive agency.[76] Most NSDs are classified, and presidents have consistently refused even to inform Congress of their existence, much less their content. Generally, NSDs are drafted by the NSC staff at the president's behest. Some NSDs have involved mundane matters, but others have established America's most significant foreign policies and security postures. As mentioned above, NSD 68, developed by the State Department's policy planning staff prior to the creation of an NSC staff, set forward the basic principles of containment upon which American Cold War policy came to be based. A series of Kennedy NSDs established the basic principles of American policy toward a number of world trouble spots.[77] Ronald Reagan's NSD 12 launched the president's massive military buildup and force modernization program, while his NSD 172 began the development of an antimissile programs. Thus, the creation of new administrative capabilities gave presidents the tools through which to dominate foreign and security policy and to dispense with Congress.

Presidential power was further augmented in the 1947 act by the creation of the CIA, which became a centrally important presidential foreign policy tool. The CIA gave the president the capacity to intervene in the affairs of other nations without informing Congress or the public. At the president's behest, the CIA undertook numerous covert operations and clandestine interventions in foreign countries during the Cold War and afterward. The agency's covert operations branch was established by a top secret presidential order, NSD 10-2, issued in June 1948. These operations were to include propaganda, economic warfare, sabotage, subversion, and assistance to underground movements.

The US government was to be able to "plausibly disclaim responsibility" for all covert operations.[78] Carrying out successive secret presidential orders, usually framed as NSDs, the CIA overthrew the Iranian government in 1953 and installed the shah, who ruled Iran for the next quarter century. During the 1950s, the CIA also overthrew governments in Guatemala, Egypt, and Laos that were deemed to be unfriendly to the United States.[79] The CIA helped organize and, for a number of years, subsidize anti-Communist politicians and political parties in Western Europe. In some instances, of course, CIA operations resulted in embarrassing failures such as the abortive "Bay of Pigs" invasion of Cuba in 1961. Nevertheless, covert CIA operations have been used by presidents to advance American interests in virtually every corner of the globe—literally from Afghanistan to Zaire. From its inception, the CIA was a presidential instrument with the Congress exercising little or no supervision over its activities. Indeed, until the 1970s the agency lacked procedures for even responding to congressional concerns about its activities. Such procedures were not deemed necessary. To the extent that Congress was even informed about CIA operations, such information usually came after the fact.[80] In the wake of the Vietnam War and Watergate investigations, both houses of Congress, to be sure, established intelligence oversight committees with subpoena powers and budgetary authority over intelligence agencies. Nevertheless, Congress continues to acquiesce in the notion that intelligence is an executive function, and congressional intervention in the operations of the CIA and other intelligence agencies has been superficial at best.[81]

For the most part, the nation's new intelligence capabilities were directed outside its own borders. Truman hoped to avoid infringements on the civil liberties of Americans and opposed Director J. Edgar Hoover's efforts to expand the domestic intelligence activities of the FBI.[82] By executive order, however, Truman created a Loyalty Review Board, which brought together a number of World War II programs designed to screen prospective government employees and to investigate charges of treasonable or disloyal conduct. Individual agencies were authorized to develop their own loyalty programs.[83] Truman also issued a number of executive orders, establishing a classification system for government secrets that ultimately led to the classification of millions of pages of documents and allowed the president and the various federal agencies to stamp as "secret" almost any information they chose not to reveal to the public and the Congress.[84] This policy continued under subsequent presidents and continues today as the National Security Agency conducts "secret" monitoring of Americans' phone and email conversations, and other agencies engage in secret renditions and interrogations of terrorist suspects. We shall return to this topic in chapter 5.

FROM CITIZEN SOLDIER TO MILITARY PROFESSIONAL

As the expansion of presidential war powers reduced the role of Congress, another set of developments reduced the immediate impact of war on the citizenry and, hence, the potential for war to produce popular mobilization. Foremost among these developments was the professionalization of the American military. For two centuries, America had relied upon citizen soldiers to fill the ranks of its armed forces and spurned the idea of a professional army as being inconsistent with democratic values. In the wake of the Vietnam War, however, presidents and military planners realized that dependence upon citizen soldiers could impose serious constraints upon the use of military forces. The risks facing citizen soldiers provided opponents of the use of military force on any given occasion with a potent issue to use against the government. The casualties and hardships borne by citizen soldiers, moreover, reverberated through the society and might, as the Vietnam case illustrated, fuel antiwar movements and resistance to military conscription. University of Chicago economist Milton Friedman, who served as a member of the Gates Commission created by President Nixon to examine the elimination of military conscription, argued that three-fourths of the opposition to the Vietnam War was generated by the draft.[85] Citizen soldiers might be appropriate for a national war in which America was attacked and domestic opposition driven to the margins. Anti–Vietnam War protests, however, convinced President Richard Nixon and his successors that an army composed of professional soldiers would give them greater flexibility to use military power when they deemed it necessary.[86]

Accordingly, Nixon ended the draft in 1973 and began conversion of the military into an all-volunteer force of professional soldiers. The presumption was that sending military professionals into battle would spawn less popular and political resistance than deploying reluctant conscripts, and this supposition seems to have been bore out. Indeed, in 2002, some opponents of President George W. Bush's buildup of American forces for an attack against Iraq argued for a renewal of conscription precisely because they believed that president would be constrained from going to war if the military consisted of draftees.[87] Members of this new professional force, moreover, especially those recruited for its elite combat units, receive extensive training and indoctrination designed to separate them from civilian society, to imbue them with a warrior ethic emphasizing loyalty to the group and organization as primary values, and to reduce their level of integration into the larger society.[88] This training is designed to immunize the military against possible contagion from antiwar and defeatist sentiment that may spring up in civilian America and appears to have produced a military, especially an officer corps, that views itself as a distinct caste.[89]

To a significant extent, the current military lives as a state within a state, subject to its own rules, norms, and governance.[90] Many are recruited from families with a strong military tradition and from areas of the country, primarily the South and West, where conservative politics and support for the military are widespread.[91] This is a military better prepared for the idea that war is a normal state of affairs and whose members are less likely to complain to the media and members of Congress about the hardships and dangers they may endure in their nation's service. The creation of this all-volunteer force has sharply reduced the constraints upon the use of military power and rendered it more difficult to mobilize opposition to the continuing use of military force once a campaign is launched. Thus, for example, while the national news media and opposition politicians sought to make an issue of the American casualties suffered during the occupation of Iraq in 2003, the public's response was muted. Military families were generally prepared—albeit not pleased—to accept the risks to which their loved ones were exposed. They were trained to be "stoical" in the words of defense analyst Eliot Cohen.[92] Most Americans, secure in the knowledge that their children would not be called upon to serve in the armed forces, were more concerned with other political issues.[93]

Taking professionalism a step further and removing war even further from the popular political domain is the presidential use of private military contractors. Thousands of heavily armed private contractors were employed by American public and corporate entities in Iraq in 2003 and 2004 to provide security and other services for US operations. These contractors were involved in intense fighting alongside regular US troops in the spring of 2004 and incurred significant casualties.[94] Indeed, the existence of these private soldiers was brought to the attention of the American public in March, 2004, when four employees of "Blackwater, USA," a North Carolina security firm, were ambushed and killed in the Iraqi town of Fallujah and their bodies mutilated and dragged through the streets. The four men, former army special operations personnel, were serving as security officers for American firms working in Iraq.[95] Later that year, eight Blackwater commandos, assisted by the firm's helicopters, repelled an attack by Shiite militiamen against the US headquarters in the town of Najaf. At the peak of the fighting, the various US security firms working in Iraq formed an operational alliance to share intelligence and resources.[96]

The ability of private firms to deploy heavily armed, professional soldiers has given presidents access to military capabilities outside the scope of public or congressional scrutiny. Indeed, several recent presidents have employed private military contractors to engage in activities that Congress has expressly declared US military forces could not undertake. For example, when authorizing assistance to Columbia to prosecute the "War on Drugs" in the 1990s, Congress placed strict limits upon the use of American military forces to support the Columbian military. US forces were prohibited from engaging in counterinsurgency efforts and from providing assistance to Columbian military units with poor human rights records. The Clinton administration, however, believed that drug gangs and antigovernment insurgents were often difficult to distinguish and found it difficult to identify Columbian military units with unblemished human rights records. Accordingly, the administration employed private military contractors, at a cost of roughly $1 billion, to circumvent what it saw as burdensome congressional restrictions. The use of private contractors allowed the administration to claim it was following the letter of the law and, at the same time, to provide "deniability" and political cover if military plans went awry.[97] Thus, MPRI was given a contract to develop the Columbian government's overall military plan and another contractor, Northrup Services, was engaged to provide technical specialists for such tasks as staffing radar sites.

Two additional firms, Virginia Electronics and DynCorp, provided what amounted to fully equipped combat troops. Virginia Electronics employed former US Navy Seals to operate gunboats along the supply lines used by Columbian rebel groups, while DynCorp provided training and support for the Columbian Air Force. According to many reports, DynCorp pilots actually flew combat missions against Columbian rebel groups.[98] Private military contractors also were employed by the Clinton administration in Bosnia, Angola, Equatorial Guinea, and Liberia to circumvent congressional restrictions on the use of

American military forces.[99] In these and many other instances, military contractors have provided presidents with the means to pursue their own policy goals without having to defer to congressional views and priorities.

While a more professional and centralized military might diminish the political constraints on presidential war making, it could not fully eliminate them. Many Americans might be willing to accept the idea of sending professional soldiers into harm's way, especially if their own children were not subject to conscription. But, even professional soldiers are Americans with hometowns, parents, relatives, and friends, and the Vietnam conflict had demonstrated that American casualties could become a political liability and, ultimately, a constraint on the use of military force. This problem was one of the factors that led successive administrations to search for means of waging warfare that would minimize American casualties. After the carnage of the Civil War, American military doctrine had already begun to emphasize technology and maximum firepower in order to keep casualties low and maintain public support.[100]

In the years after the Vietnam War, the military services invested tens of billions of dollars in the development of cruise missiles, drone aircraft, precision-guided munitions, and a multitude of other advanced weapons systems capable of disabling or destroying America's opponents while reducing the risks to which American troops were exposed.[101] Thus, in the 1990 Persian Gulf War—and even more so in the 2001–2002 Afghan campaign, precision-guided weapons inflicted enormous damage on enemy forces and gave US troops all but bloodless victories. In the 2003 Iraq War, pilotless aircraft, precision-guided munitions, battlefield computers, and new command-and-control technology helped bring about a rapid victory over substantial Iraqi forces with what once might have been seen as impossibly low casualties.[102] Military analysts have pointed to these developments—sometimes called a revolution in military affairs—as indicative of a technological revolution in the conduct of war.

Like past transformations in military tactics, however, this one has been caused as much by political as technological or exclusively military factors.[103] At any rate, to the extent that US casualties can be limited to smart bombs and pilotless aircraft, popular opposition to the use of military force is less likely to become a political problem. After one Predator drone aircraft was downed, an air force officer involved in the program said, "It was on page six of the *Washington Post*. If that had been a [manned] F-16, it would have been page one."[104] In 2012 and 2013, with most American combat troops removed from the Middle East, the Pentagon and the CIA continue to send hundreds of drones every month against suspected terrorists. While some in the media question this practice, few Americans show any interest. Unmanned drones fired at shadowy enemies seem more like a video game than a war.

IMPERIAL OVERREACH?

America's Constitution and its lively popular politics offered some protection from the sort of imperial overreach and decline described by Paul Kennedy. Whatever imperialist inclinations America manifested tended to be self-correcting. War was quickly followed by popular mobilization, Congressional opposition, and a return to civilian concerns. Today, this pattern seems to have come unglued. War has less impact on civilian politics than it once did thanks to the professionalization of the military. If the use of robots continues to grow, the citizenry will have even less reason to become agitated about military conflicts. At the same time, presidential unilateralism and congressional marginalization have made a shambles of Constitutional checks and balances. The Constitution gave Congress the power to declare war. What a quaint and forgotten idea! Having become a more imperial republic, the United States no longer seems immune from imperial decline.

CHAPTER 5

BEATING SWORDS INTO MALIGN PLOWSHARES

SURVEILLANCE, SECRECY, AND POPULAR GOVERNMENT

War gives states reason to mitigate their brutality and even—at least—go through the motions of soliciting citizens' views on matters of leadership and policy. I would, however, be remiss if I did not address the issue of war and state power—an issue that has begun to loom large for Americans.

War, as the late Charles Tilly often reminded us, expands state power.[1] And, for better or worse, power justified by and created for use in war is, more often than not, converted into peacetime uses. Political economist Robert Higgs has shown that in the United States, after each of the world wars, many federal agencies built to support the war effort found new civilian tasks, survived postwar bureaucratic demobilization, and expanded the government's capacity to direct the nation's civilian economy and society.[2] Thus, for example, after the end of the First World War, the War Finance Corporation, which had been created to help essential war industries secure adequate financing, lived on until 1925. That year, the agency was officially liquidated but was reborn in 1934 under the name Reconstruction Finance Corporation. Similarly, the Railroad Administration, which operated the nation's railroads during the war, was officially closed in 1920. Many of its powers, however, were then transferred to the Interstate Commerce Commission.

The same pattern was manifest after the Second World War. While many wartime agencies were dismantled, others were quietly renamed or saw their functions and powers transferred to other agencies. Thus, when the Employment Service and the Reemployment and Retraining Administration were closed, their offices and functions were taken over by the Labor Department. When the Foreign Economic Administration was closed, its jurisdiction was assigned to the State Department. The Smaller War Plants Corporation was nominally closed, but was actually absorbed by the Commerce Department. The list goes on. An administrative state built by war redeploys some of its now-excess administrative capacity to regulate the civilian economy.

Some might welcome, or at least be untroubled, by such a postwar expansion of the government's mundane administrative capabilities. However, in a rather perverse conversion of swords into plowshares, coercive capabilities built for war may also be turned to peacetime uses. Indeed, following many periods of significant American military combat, legislation and institutional mechanisms created to further the war effort were not liquidated but were, instead, redirected at the government's domestic foes. Thus, even after the First World War ended, a number of radicals were prosecuted under the Espionage Act, which had been drafted to prevent opposition to the wartime draft. Similarly, the Bureau of Investigation, predecessor to the Federal Bureau of Investigation, was assigned the wartime responsibility of assisting the Committee on Public Information in building a favorable climate of opinion for the war effort by infiltrating and disrupting antiwar and pacifist groups such as the Socialist Party and the Industrial Workers of the World ("Wobblies"). With the end of the war, the Bureau of Investigation was not shut down but was, instead, assigned to investigate Communist influences in the United States. Bureau of Investigation agents led the 1919 and 1920 Palmer Raids aimed at rounding up suspected radicals. Under the authority of the still-in-force World War I Sedition Act, the bureau infiltrated suspect organizations with undercover informants and employed warrantless wiretaps to secure information.

In a similar vein, the 1940 Smith Act, enacted on the day the French capitulated to Nazi Germany, was aimed at compelling noncitizens to register with the authorities and established penalties for those advocating or seeking the overthrow of the US government. During the war, a number of Nazi sympathizers were prosecuted under the act. For example, in 1942 the government prosecuted George W. Christians, founder of an organization calling itself the "Crusader White Shirts," for attempting to spread pro-German literature to American soldiers. In 1944, thirty-three individuals accused of expressing pro-Nazi views were prosecuted under the act. When the war ended, the Smith Act was certainly not repealed. Instead, during the 1940s and 1950s the act was used to prosecute dozens of individuals accused of belonging to the Communist party. In 1949, ten defendants were sentenced to five years in prison and in 1956, 131 alleged communists were indicted and ninety-eight convicted and sentenced to lengthy terms in federal prison.

This discussion brings us to the main matter at hand—America's burgeoning regime of domestic secrecy and surveillance. Beginning with the First World War, the United States has undertaken the construction of massive programs of secrecy and surveillance justified by wartime and national security concerns. These programs, however, have survived every war, conflict, and national security emergency and now seem focused on the general American public posing, as we shall see, serious threats to popular freedom. It seems that beating swords into plowshares can produce very dangerous implements.

Government surveillance of communications, travel, and personal conduct has become a fact of American life. Revelations of extensive electronic surveillance by the National Security Agency (NSA) in the summer of 2013 caused considerable consternation in Congress and in the news media. Such surveillance, however, is not an entirely new phenomenon in the United States. As early as 1920, the Cipher Bureau, remembered today as the "Black Chamber," an office jointly funded by the army and the State Department, and arising from a World War I program, secretly inspected telegrams in the Western Union system. After the war, the Black Chamber, headed by Herbert O. Yardley, was disguised as a commercial code company headquartered in a nondescript New York City office building.[3] Yardley and his superior, General Marlborough Churchill, head of the army's Intelligence Division, had secured an agreement from Newcomb Carlton, the president of the Western Union Telegraph Corporation, allowing the Black Chamber to monitor the nation's telegraph traffic.[4]

Secrecy of electronic communications had been guaranteed by the 1912 Radio Communication Act. The act was superseded by wartime legislation and circumvented in the war's aftermath. Between 1920 and 1929, when the Black Chamber was closed by Secretary of State Henry Stimson, Yardley and his staff sifted through millions of telegrams looking for evidence of foreign espionage activities. Yardley later claimed to have ferreted out numerous plots and conspiracies, but there is little evidence from his writings that random snooping through the telegrams of ordinary Americans did much to enhance the nation's security.

Today, Yardley's Black Chamber seems a quaint relic of a long-forgotten past, as Americans find themselves subject to more or less constant government surveillance via electronic interception of telephone calls, examination of email communications and social media postings—to say nothing of ubiquitous security cameras now tied to crowd-scanning software, traffic monitoring, airport searches, and so forth. And, while Yardley and his staffers sifted through transcripts of telegrams by hand, peering at their contents, today the work is done by computers and analytic methods that allow the government to process and analyze enormous quantities of data looking for possible indications of illicit activity among seemingly disparate bits of information.[5]

Some in Congress and in the media are concerned with citizens' privacy, as well as their own, while police and intelligence agencies aver that their surveillance activities are of critical importance in the nation's ongoing struggle against crime and, of course, terrorism. Testifying before Congress in 2013, NSA officials, unwittingly echoing the assertions of their forebear, Yardley, declared that the agency's eavesdropping program had averted dozens of possible terrorist attacks. Needless to say, since the matters were highly classified, no actual proof of these assertions was proffered, and many members of Congress, including Senate Intelligence Committee Chairman Patrick Leahy (D-VT) expressed doubts about the agency's claims. Later the NSA conceded that its domestic surveillance programs had possibly thwarted only one terrorist plot, rather than the dozens initially claimed.[6]

Many Americans seem satisfied to believe that they are the beneficiaries rather than the potential victims of government surveillance. Those who have nothing to hide, goes the saying, have nothing to fear.[7] This view is, of course, rather naive. As law professor Daniel Solove shows, surveillance can entrap even the most innocent individuals in a web of suspicions and allegations from which they may find it extremely difficult to extricate themselves.[8]

Be that as it may, to couch the issue of government surveillance purely in terms of the conflict between security and privacy interests is to miss the larger question of political power in which this debate is embedded. Hobbes famously observed that the end or purpose of knowledge is power.[9] That is, both individuals and rulers seek knowledge about one another in order to exercise or resist the exercise of power. This Hobbesian observation becomes especially significant if we consider the role of knowledge in the context of popular government.

Popular government requires that citizens possess a good deal of knowledge about the actions of the state. Knowledge is necessary to permit citizens to evaluate rulers' claims and to hold rulers accountable for their conduct. In essence, citizens must undertake their own surveillance of the government and its officials as a precondition for exerting influence over them. This idea is captured in the ancient Athenian practice of the audit (*euthyna*) in which all civil and military officials, including even priests and priestesses, were periodically required to undergo detailed public examinations of their actions.[10] The results might then be debated in the popular assembly (*ecclesia*) which was, of course, open to all male citizens who had performed the requisite period of military service. In this way, surveillance through the audit directly empowered the citizenry.

At the same time, citizens' ability to exercise power also requires that they have considerable protection from the state's scrutiny. In point of fact, privacy may be a prerequisite for effective popular political action. To begin with, those intent on expressing anything but support for the groups in power need privacy to plan, organize, and mobilize, lest their plans be anticipated and disrupted. Terrorists are hardly the only ones who need privacy. Even in the mundane realm of partisan politics, the efforts of the party-out-of-power can certainly be compromised if the government becomes privy to its plans. Recall that the Nixon administration thought its surveillance activities, including the work of the infamous "plumbers' squad," could help it to undermine Democratic campaign plans in 1972.

Known political dissidents, moreover, always face some risk of official reprisal. Accordingly, at least some citizens may refrain from acting upon their political beliefs for fear that they will draw attention to themselves and become targets for tax audits and other government efforts to find evidence of criminality, cupidity, or other misconduct conduct that can be used against them. This is a realistic concern given a recent past in which agents of the FBI, seeking to compile damaging information on civil rights leader Dr. Martin Luther King Jr., secretly videotaped King's extramarital trysts and forwarded the tapes to his wife. More recently, in an echo of Richard Nixon's demand that the Internal Revenue Service investigate individuals on his "enemies list," so-called Tea Party groups and other conservative organizations found themselves the recipients of special scrutiny from the IRS. Privacy for political activities is, like the secret ballot, an important element of political freedom.

Indeed, this notion of the relationship between privacy and freedom of political expression is at the heart of the Constitution's Fourth Amendment, prohibiting unreasonable searches. While many currently see the Fourth Amendment as related to evidence in mundane criminal cases, the framers were well aware of the fact that government intrusions into private homes were often aimed at identifying papers, manuscripts, and books that might point to nascent efforts to foment political discontent.[11] Individuals whose private papers evinced dissenting political opinions might then be prosecuted for the crime of seditious libel (i.e., criticism of Crown officials) to forestall any public expressions of their views. As Justice Brennan wrote for a unanimous court in the 1961 case of *Marcus v. Search Warrant*, "The Bill of Rights was fashioned against the background of knowledge that unrestricted power of search and seizure could also be an instrument for stifling liberty of expression."[12] In her dissent in a recent case, Justice Ginsburg called attention to this original purpose and meaning of the Fourth Amendment as an instrument for protecting liberty of political expression.[13]

Thus, popular government requires a combination of government transparency and citizen privacy. To exercise influence over it, citizens must know what the government is doing. At the same time, citizens seeking to exercise influence over the government need protection from retaliation and intimidation. Unfortunately, however, objective conditions in the United States today are far from these ideals. Today, indeed, the state keeps more and more of its activities secret while the citizenry has less and less privacy.

SURVEILLANCE

After Yardley's Black Chamber was closed in 1929, the government briefly refrained from random or blanket surveillance activities. During the 1930s, though, the new Federal Bureau of Investigation (FBI) began to make extensive use of wiretaps, various listening devices, and postal surveillance against targeted groups such as suspected subversives and criminals, as well as President Franklin D. Roosevelt's chief political foes. As early as 1934, President Roosevelt asked FBI Director J. Edgar Hoover to monitor the activities of Louisiana Governor Huey Long, who had become one of FDR's most formidable political opponents and a potential challenger for the 1936 Democratic presidential nomination.[14] The 1934 Federal Communications Act expressly prohibited the interception of electronic communications, and the Supreme

Court subsequently held that evidence obtained from such intercepts could not be used in court. The FBI, nevertheless, decided that it was not bound by the legislation. This view was supported by President Roosevelt, who believed that the government's ability to intercept telephone calls was too important to be limited by legal niceties. In a 1940 memo, for example, the president authorized the FBI to use wiretaps when it believed that subversive activities might be discussed in the intercepted communication. Then as now, national security claims seemed to outweigh all other interests and became a pretext for surveillance programs that went far beyond any real security concerns.

During the 1940 presidential campaign, for example, the FBI reportedly conducted more than two hundred investigations of President Roosevelt's political foes, as well as those among his friends about whom the president harbored suspicions. For example, the FBI conducted physical and electronic surveillance of United Mine Workers President John L. Lewis, a nominal but wavering Roosevelt ally. Matters did not turn out to the president's liking when Lewis discovered that his telephones were being tapped and angrily confronted Roosevelt. FDR claimed to know nothing about the matter though the surveillance had, in fact, been undertaken on his orders.

Over the next three decades, the FBI's growing arsenal of electronic surveillance devices, nominally devoted to protecting the nation from spies and criminals, also provided political intelligence that served Roosevelt and his successors in the White House. Director Hoover also assembled information that could serve his own purposes. Through electronic and physical surveillance, Hoover created dossiers on hundreds, if not thousands, of important political figures. He used this information, especially if it included evidence of financial improprieties or sexual peccadillos, to intimidate or blackmail his foes or to reward allies by revealing embarrassing or unsavory facts about their own political opponents. Any bit of damaging information in a politician's FBI dossier could make that individual vulnerable to pressure from the bureau. As one former FBI executive explained, "The moment Hoover would get something on a senator, he'd send one of the errand boys up and advise the senator that we're in the course of an investigation and we by chance happened to come up with this [damaging information]. From that time on the senator's right in his pocket."[15]

One such politician whose FBI dossier was reportedly quite voluminous was Senator—later President—John F. Kennedy. Electronic eavesdropping had provided Hoover with such extensive knowledge of Kennedy's personal foibles that the president could not risk opposing, much less firing, the Director even though he apparently wished to do so. On one occasion, Hoover told Kennedy that electronic surveillance had revealed that the president was having an affair with a woman named Judith Campbell Exner, who also happened to be involved with Chicago gangster Sam Giancana.[16] Hoover's possession of this and other facts that might seriously have undermined Kennedy's presidency gave the director considerable leverage over the president.

Through the use of surveillance, threats to the FBI and its director could, as Hoover liked to say, be "neutralized." For example, in 1941, Congressman Martin Dies of Texas, then chairman of the House UnAmerican Activities Committee (HUAC), claimed that the FBI had been lax in its efforts to protect the nation from spies and subversives and informed the attorney general that he hoped to be named to replace Hoover as head of the agency. Upon learning of Dies's criticisms and efforts to supplant him, Hoover had his agents target the congressman for electronic surveillance. The FBI learned that Dies had taken a $2,000 bribe to help a refugee enter the United States. Hoover confronted Dies with the evidence but promised not to disclose the information or to seek an indictment so long as Dies did as he was told. Dies never again criticized the FBI or its director.

Or, take the case of Tennessee Senator Estes Kefauver. The senator headed the Senate Special Committee to Investigate Crime in Interstate Commerce and, in 1951, in a direct challenge to Hoover's preeminence in this realm, announced plans for televised hearings on organized crime in America. The hearings, seen in the early days of television, created a sensation and vaulted the previously obscure senator into a position of national prominence as gangster after gangster was called to testify before the television cameras. Many refused to answer questions, citing Fifth Amendment rights. This scene was repeated so frequently that "taking the Fifth" became a favorite slang expression. During the course of the hearings, the names of several of J. Edgar Hoover's friends and cronies including, Joseph P. Kennedy, oil millionaire Clint Murchison, and columnist Walter Winchell were linked to organized crime.

Hoover had been opposed to the hearings from the start because they seemed to imply that the FBI had been lax in its own duties. Now with some of his political allies implicated, Hoover examined the FBI's dossier on Kefauver and found evidence from electronic surveillance suggesting that the senator had accepted financial payoffs. Confronted with this material, Kefauver abruptly, and without explanation, ended the hearings. Not completely satisfied to merely neutralize the senator, Hoover then gave the damaging financial information, along with surveillance data containing evidence of Kefauver's marital infidelities, to Republican vice presidential candidate Richard Nixon for use against the Stevenson–Kefauver ticket in the 1952 presidential campaign.[17]

From the 1940s to Hoover's death in 1972, the FBI controlled thousands of wire taps and listening devices, covertly opened hundreds of thousands of pieces of mail each year, and examined thousands of cables sent from the United States to foreign countries. Every member of Congress was subject to surveillance, as was the Supreme Court and other important institutions and political figures. At its height, this system of surveillance gave the FBI and its Director considerable political power. Hoover, for example, provided Governor Thomas E. Dewey with material that helped him defeat his then-rival for the Republican presidential nomination, Governor Harold Stassen.[18] Hoover reportedly helped to secure the Supreme Court appointment of Chief Justice Warren Burger by the simple expedient of making certain that adverse information would be found and highlighted in the background checks of other potential nominees.

Hoover also played a major role in advancing the career of then-

Congressman Richard Nixon. In 1948, young Congressman Nixon was a member of HUAC. In that capacity, he became a leading figure in the sensational espionage case involving former Communist party activist Whittaker Chambers and State Department official Alger Hiss. Chambers accused Hiss of spying for the Soviet Union—a charge that Hiss resolutely denied. Nixon saw the case as a vehicle that might bolster his own political career. Director Hoover, for his part, saw Nixon as a potentially useful tool and ally and saw to it that Nixon was provided with information from the FBI's files on the case. Without publicly revealing his sources, Nixon used Hoover's help to take a lead role in the HUAC hearings. The attendant publicity made Nixon a political star and led to his being named Eisenhower's running mate in the 1952 presidential campaign. It almost goes without saying that Hoover began to build a thick dossier on Nixon to ensure that his new protégée could, if necessary, be encouraged to remember his political obligations. This dossier reportedly became important a quarter of a century later when President Nixon summoned Director Hoover to the oval office intending to order him to retire. A brief conversation ensued, and Director Hoover remained in office.

Hoover also provided Senator Joseph McCarthy with confidential FBI reports to bolster the senator's charges that government institutions had been infiltrated by Communist agents. At the same time, Hoover suppressed other information in the FBI's files dealing with the senator's substance abuse, moral deficiencies, and financial misdeeds. Of course, after 1954 when Hoover and President Dwight D. Eisenhower decided that the senator was becoming a political liability, some of this damaging information, collected via the FBI's electronic surveillance of the senator, was leaked to the news media and helped to destroy McCarthy.

The FBI's impact on the American political process went beyond the bureau's capacity to help or hinder the careers of prominent politicians. FBI surveillance also became a tool designed to destroy the left-wing and dissident political movements that J. Edgar Hoover and his allies viewed as inimical to their own vision of the American way of life. Beginning during the Eisenhower administration and continuing through the Kennedy and Johnson administrations, with the tacit assent of the White House and the approval of a number of congressional leaders, Hoover launched a series of illegal covert operations labeled Counter Intelligence Programs or COINTELPRO aimed at disrupting these groups. Most of these operations targeted civil rights organizations, anti–Vietnam War groups, women's rights groups, socialist organizations, and "New Left" groups such as the Students for a Democratic Society. A small number of COINTELPRO operations also targeted the Ku Klux Klan.

To begin with, COINTELPRO relied upon extensive surveillance of targeted groups. The FBI examined their mail, tapped their telephones, hid microphones in members' homes and offices, and sent informers to infiltrate the various organizations. The information collected through these surveillance efforts then became the basis for FBI campaigns of disruption and intimidation. Spouses were informed of one another's infidelities. Arrest records and sexual histories were leaked to the press or used to "neutralize" targeted individuals. Foreshadowing the potential uses of social media, unwitting individuals, found via electronic surveillance to have business, family, or personal ties to the bureau's targets, were sent derogatory information on the alleged subversives.

After a time, the FBI went beyond these tactics and brought criminal charges based upon planted evidence, instigated IRS audits, harassed unfortunate targets at their places of work and their children's schools, and sowed suspicion and distrust within targeted groups by planting false evidence indicating that one or more members were FBI informants. Rivalries among various groups were exploited—in several instances, leading to what amounted to gang warfare between the Black Panther Party and other black organizations. Local law enforcement officials were encouraged to conduct violent raids, which on several occasions led to the deaths of targeted individuals.

Particularly after the 1963 "March on Washington," civil rights leader Martin Luther King Jr. was targeted by the FBI, in the words of

Hoover's deputy, William C. Sullivan, as, "the most dangerous Negro of the future . . . from the standpoint of Communism, the Negro, and national security."[19] Based on this assessment, the FBI employed hidden microphones, phone taps, and other methods to place King and all his associates under extensive surveillance. Through these means, the FBI was moved to label two of King's white advisers, Stanley Levison and Jack O'Dell, as Communists. Though the electronic evidence was questionable, they forced King to disassociate himself from both men. The FBI also collected a good deal of electronic information on King's numerous extramarital flings, which Hoover shared with various politicians and, as mentioned above, with King's wife.

COINTELPRO was brought to a halt in 1971 when a group calling itself the Citizens' Commission to Investigate the FBI burglarized the small FBI field office in Media, Pennsylvania, and stole more than a thousand files. Some contained references to COINTELPRO and an NBC newsman, Carl Stern, won a federal suit to compel the FBI to release documents relating to the program. Hoover was forced to bring COINTELPRO, though not his routine surveillance activities, to an end.

The CIA: Operation CHAOS

Particularly during the 1960s, domestic surveillance activities were also undertaken by the Central Intelligence Agency (CIA). The CIA was established by the 1947 National Security Act that had also created the Department of Defense. The agency's main missions were foreign intelligence and counterintelligence activities, and the CIA was generally prohibited from engaging in intelligence collection activities within the United States. Soon after its creation, however, the CIA began to engage in domestic activities such as planting false stories in the American news media and recruiting agents from various American ethnic communities. To provide cover for its domestic activities, the CIA established a Domestic Operations Division, which operated various front companies that purported to be private business concerns.

In 1965, President Lyndon Johnson ordered the CIA to begin

investigating student opposition to the Vietnam War. Johnson was, of course, receiving intelligence from the FBI but was concerned that the aging J. Edgar Hoover was more concerned with proving that student leaders were receiving their instructions from the Communist party than objectively assessing the facts. Accordingly, and much to Hoover's chagrin, Johnson told the CIA to conduct investigations separate from and independent of the FBI's operations. The CIA assigned agents to infiltrate student groups and, sometimes working in cooperation with local police departments, engaged in a variety of physical and electronic surveillance efforts. The entire activity was labeled "Operation CHAOS."

In 1970, President Richard Nixon expanded CHAOS to include not only student antiwar groups but also a variety of other groups about whom the president entertained suspicions. These included women's groups, African-American organizations, and Jewish groups. Such groups were subjected to electronic surveillance, mail opening, infiltration, and physical surveillance including collection and inspection of their trash.

By 1972, the CHAOS program had produced card files on some 300,000 Americans and 1,000 groups that had somehow run afoul of CIA surveillance. Names and information were generally shared with other agencies and with foreign governments. Stories containing disinformation about such targeted groups as Students for a Democratic Society and Women Strike for Peace were planted in the press to discredit the organizations and, allegedly, covert CHAOS infiltrators acted as provocateurs, encouraging such groups to engage in illegal acts that would provide the basis for intervention by local law enforcement. News of the 1972 Watergate break-in, which involved two former CIA agents, E. Howard Hunt and James McCord, led agency executives to fear that any subsequent investigation would reveal the existence of the illegal CHAOS operation. CIA quickly closed CHAOS and transferred all its agents to other duties. CHAOS remained a secret until 1972, when details of the operation were reported by The New York Times.[20]

The NSA

During the years that J. Edgar Hoover was expanding the FBI's surveil-lance activities and the CIA was being asked to target domestic groups, another federal agency was developing its own capacity to monitor Americans through their communications. This was the National Security Agency (NSA) created by President Harry Truman in 1952 and assigned primary responsibility for American signals intelligence. Eventually, NSA capabilities would dwarf those of the FBI and CIA. The NSA had a number of predecessor agencies, including the World War II–era US Army Signals Intelligence Service (SIS). Under the leadership of William Friedman, America's foremost cryptanalyst, and, indeed, the individual who coined the term *cryptanalysis*, the SIS had broken many German and Japanese codes and developed America's unbreakable SIGABA cipher machine. The NSA was established within the Department of Defense and, like its predecessors, charged with intercepting and, if necessary, decoding communications that had potential military or diplomatic significance. In essence, the NSA was to spy electronically on foreign powers while detecting their efforts to spy on the United States.

Over the next several years, the NSA developed a variety of systems designed to intercept satellite-based communications throughout the world. One of these systems, code-named ECHELON, was deployed by NSA in cooperation with several American allies, including the United Kingdom, Canada, New Zealand, and Australia, though the American role was primary. By the 1990s, through ground-based listening stations and its own satellites, NSA had the potential to intercept much of the world's telephone and fax traffic.[21] In the late 1990s, however, the com-munication industry's shift from satellites to buried fiber-optic cables rendered ECHELON's systems obsolete. In cooperation with industry scientists, the NSA was able to develop mechanisms for intercepting and reading communications sent through fiber-optic systems. These devices were called PacketScopes and allowed the NSA to tap into fiber-optic networks and record the contents of messages, including emails, which could then be stored and analyzed. By 2001, NSA had secured the cooperation of much of the telecommunications industry for the installation of its PacketScopes and had the capacity to intercept and examine all the data flowing through their world-wide systems.

NSA was nominally tasked with collecting information that might be relevant to national security concerns. Inevitably, however, other security agencies as well as the White House became interested in making use of NSA capabilities for their own purposes. One early example of this phenomenon concerned data produced by NSA's Project SHAMROCK and Project MINARET. SHAMROCK was the code name for a project that involved the examination of telegrams coming into or leaving the United Sates. As in the case of Herbert Yardley's Black Chamber decades earlier, NSA and its predecessor agencies forged agreements with America's major telephone, telegraph, and cable companies that allowed it to intercept and transcribe virtually every telegram sent or received in the United States and to listen to any telephone calls in which it had an interest. Over 150,000 telegrams per month were viewed by NSA personnel, and results deemed interesting or suspicious were shared with the FBI, CIA, and other agencies.

In a related NSA program, Project MINARET, the agency checked intercepted communications against a "watch list" of American citizens and organizations with which it had been provided by federal law enforcement agencies and the White House. Between 1967 and 1973, the watch list grew to include thousands of individuals and organizations, including many involved in anti–Vietnam War and civil rights protests. Reports on these groups had initially been requested by President Lyndon Johnson and continued to be received by President Nixon.

The Church Committee and FISA

In 1974, in the aftermath of the Watergate affair, the various surveillance activities conducted by the FBI, CIA, NSA, and other federal agencies came under scrutiny by a number of congressional committees. Perhaps the most important of these was the Senate's Select Committee to Study Governmental Operations with Respect to Intelligence Activities, chaired by the late Senator Frank Church of Idaho. The Church committee identified a number of abuses associated with COINTELPRO, Operation CHAOS, Project MINARET, and the various federal surveillance programs and noted that every president from Franklin Roosevelt to Richard Nixon had used illegal surveillance to secure information about their political opponents.

In its report, the committee found that numerous individuals had been subjected to surveillance and subsequent action based solely upon their political beliefs. The report declared, "Too many people have been spied upon by too many government agencies and too much information has been collected. The government has often undertaken the secret surveillance of citizens on the basis of their political beliefs even when those beliefs posed no threat of violence or illegal acts on behalf of a hostile or foreign power.[22] Senator Church added:

> "The [National Security Agency's] capability at any time could be turned around on the American people, and *no American would have any privacy left, such is the capability to monitor everything:* telephone conversations, telegrams, it doesn't matter. There would be no place to hide. [If a dictator ever took over, the NSA] *could enable it to impose total tyranny, and there would be no way to fight back.*"[23]

It is worth noting that when Senator Church expressed these fears in 1975, the NSA could read telegrams and listen to phone calls. Along with other security agencies, it might also open mail, but in practice only a tiny fraction of the hundreds of millions of letters sent each year could be examined. Thus, Church's remarks embodied a bit of exaggeration at the time. The advent of email and social media, however, greatly enhanced the volume of information available to federal agencies and made the senator's comments more prescient.

In response to the findings of the Church Committee and other congressional inquiries, Congress in 1978 enacted the Foreign Intelligence Surveillance Act (FISA) designed to place limits on electronic surveillance by government agencies. Of course, these selfsame agencies, as well as successive presidents, had ignored or circumvented previous legal restrictions on electronic surveillance, such as those embodied in the 1968 Crime Control Act. Nevertheless, members of Congress hoped that by mandating stricter judicial supervision and stiff penalties for violators, government surveillance of American citizens might be curtailed and controlled.

FISA stipulated that in order to undertake electronic surveillance of Americans, the government would be required to apply for a warrant from a special court created by the statute. This was called the Foreign Intelligence Surveillance Court and initially consisted of seven federal district court judges appointed for seven-year terms by the chief justice of the Supreme Court. In 2001, the FISA Court was expanded to eleven judges. A second court created by the act, the Court of Review, consisted of a three-judge panel empowered to hear appeals by the government from negative decisions by the FISA Court. In practice, the Review Court has been relatively quiescent since the government has had reason to appeal only a handful of the FISA Court's decisions. Both the FISA Court and Court of Review deliberate in secret and the content of their decisions is not made public.

FISA stipulated that the court would issue a warrant only if it found probable cause to believe that the target of the surveillance was acting in concert with a foreign power or agent. The 1978 act defined *foreign power* as a nation-state, but this was subsequently amended to include non-state actors such as terrorist groups. The act also allowed the president to authorize warrantless surveillance within the United States if the attorney general certified to the FISA Court that the target was a foreign intelligence agent, and there was little chance that the privacy of any American citizen would be violated.

The effectiveness of the FISA process has been debated. On the one hand, between 1979 and 2012, only eleven of the nearly 34,000 requests for warrants made by government agencies, primarily the NSA and FBI, were turned down by the FISA Court.[24] This datum might suggest that the court was lax in its procedures. However, it may be that the FISA process forced the government to exercise at least some measure of caution in its surveillance activities, knowing that requests would need to withstand judicial scrutiny. Support for this latter view might be derived from the fact that in the aftermath of the 9/11 terror attacks, in its determination to expand electronic data collection, the Bush administration deemed it necessary to ignore the FISA process and launch a large-scale program of warrantless wiretapping.

What would later be called the President's Surveillance Program (PSP), launched in 2001, involved warrantless monitoring of virtually all telephone calls and email messages between the United States and foreign countries. As in previous major surveillance efforts, the NSA, in collaboration with several other federal agencies, was able to secure secret cooperation from the major telecommunications companies for this purpose. The result was that millions of telephone and email conversations were monitored. In some instances, voice intercept operators actually listened to the calls. More often, the information was stored, subjected to keyword searches, and, with the advent of the Defense Advanced Research Projects Agency (DARPA) Total Information Awareness project in 2002, the NSA began analyzing intercepted communications in conjunction with other data such as credit card usage, social network posts, traffic camera photos, and even medical records to search for suspicious patterns of activity.

Information not available electronically could be obtained by the FBI, which via secret National Security Letters (NSL) authorized by the 2001 Patriot Act, has compelled a variety of institutions ranging from universities to gambling casinos to turn over student or customer information without informing the subject. Congress ended DARPA funding for the Total Information Awareness program in 2004, but by then the methodology had become well developed. In addition, tens of thousands of NSLs have been issued annually since 2001, providing data that—particularly in conjunction with communications intercepts—allow federal authorities to learn an enormous amount about the activities of any individual or group.

In response to *New York Times* articles published in 2005 revealing the existence of PSP, several members of Congress expressed outrage at what they saw as violations of FISA and vowed to fully investigate the matter. The Bush administration, however, was able to convince Congress that its actions had been necessary if not entirely legal means of thwarting terrorism. After some deliberation, Congress enacted the Protect America Act of 2007, which amended FISA to loosen restrictions on electronic surveillance and, in effect, retroactively codified the legally questionable actions of previous years.[25] Thus, under the amended act, the government was empowered to intercept communications that began or ended outside the United States without any supervision by the FISA Court. Moreover, telecommunications companies, whose cooperation had previously been voluntary, were directed to lend assistance to federal agencies engaged in electronic surveillance if ordered to do so by the government and were immunized against any civil suits that might arise from providing such assistance.

The 2007 act contained a sunset provision requiring Congress to reconsider the surveillance issue in 2008. The resulting Amendments Act of 2008 was similar to the 2007 act, but it did place restrictions on the power of the NSA and other intelligence agencies to target Americans. At President Obama's behest, the act was renewed in 2012 for another five years. Between 2008 and 2013, the government insisted that it was not engaged in spying on Americans either at home or abroad. In March, 2013, for example, James Clapper, the director of national intelligence, testifying before the Senate, indignantly denied reports that the government was collecting data in millions of Americans. Similarly, NSA Director General Keith Alexander denied charges by a former NSA official that the agency was secretly obtaining warrantless access to billions of records of Americans' phone calls and storing the information in its data centers. General Alexander piously declared that doing such a thing would be against the law.[26]

In June 2013, however, an NSA contractor named Edward Snowden leaked classified documents describing the NSA's theretofore top-secret PRISM surveillance program, which had operated since 2007. Snowden's disclosures were published in the *Guardian* and the

Washington Post and revealed that through PRISM and several other programs, including BLARNEY, FAIRVIEW, LITHIUM, and the UPSTREAM surveillance of fiber-optic cables, the NSA had been collecting data on its own as well as collaborating with virtually all major telecommunications companies to intercept, examine, and store the electronic communications of millions of Americans. These included email, social network posts, Internet searches, and even local telephone calls. In essence, NSA appeared to have the capacity to monitor all forms of electronic communication. The agency was storing monitored communications and was, indeed, in the process of constructing a huge new storage center in Utah in anticipation of a growing need for much greater storage capability.

While the NSA's goal is said to be monitoring communications between the United States and foreign countries, officials acknowledge that some purely domestic communications have been accidentally accessed but said they did not keep records of the number. Communications among Americans nominally cannot be viewed without a warrant from the FISA Court but, in practice, this rule is frequently violated, said one official who did not wish to be named. The NSA essentially is responsible for policing itself, and, according to one telecommunications executive formerly involved in the NSA program, whatever the nominal legal restrictions, "There's technically and physically nothing preventing a much broader surveillance."[27] A lawsuit that brought about the declassification in 2013 of a 2011 FISA Court opinion revealed that the NSA had been accessing as many as 56,000 "wholly domestic" communications each year without warrants. In an angry opinion, the then-chief judge of the FISA Court, Judge John D. Bates, wrote, "For the first time, the government has now advised the court that the volume and nature of the information it has been collecting is fundamentally different from what the court had been led to believe."[28]

Most of the data collected by the NSA apparently consisted of the so-called *metadata*; that is, the times, senders, and recipients, but not the actual content of the communication. The NSA asserts that metadata are not covered by FISA. However, through the successors to the Total Information Awareness program, the NSA and other federal agencies have the ability to use even these metadata in conjunction with other data sources to obtain a very good picture of the friends, activities, and proclivities of any American. Moreover, whether purposefully or accidentally, the NSA has examined the actual contents of many tens of thousands of calls made by Americans within the United States without obtaining authorization from the FISA Court. According to some sources, NSA training manuals explain to data collectors and analysts how to record intercepts without providing "extraneous information" that might suggest that the actions were illegal if they happened ever to be audited.[29] As to the FISA Court, nominally charged with ensuring that the government does not violate laws governing surveillance activities, its chief judge, Reggie B. Walton, said in a written statement to the *Washington Post* that the court had no investigative powers and relied on the government, itself, to report any improper actions by its agents.[30]

In an August 2013 speech, President Obama addressed public concerns about the government's surveillance programs. The president pointed to the importance of interdicting terrorist attacks, declared himself to be confident that Americans' rights had not been abused, and said he hoped ways could be found to make the public more "comfortable" with government surveillance activities. Unfortunately, given the history of government surveillance, there is little reason for Americans to feel a sense of comfort. Using methods that seem so primitive today, J. Edgar Hoover's FBI collected information that made and broke political careers, disrupted dissident groups, and interfered with ordinary partisan politics. And, much of what Hoover did was undertaken at the behest of the various presidents whom he served. From Franklin Roosevelt to Richard Nixon, presidents could not resist the chance to collect information to be used against their political foes as well as dissident political forces.

Should we believe that no possible future president would be willing to use today's surveillance capabilities against his or her opponents? To believe this idea is comparable to believing in Santa Claus and the Easter Bunny. The framers of the Constitution certainly understood this point. James Madison wrote, "If angels were to govern men neither external nor internal controls on government would be necessary. In framing a government which is to be administered by men over men . . . experience has taught mankind the necessity of auxiliary precautions."[31]

And, as to the terrorist threat against which massive electronic surveillance is nominally directed, one former federal prosecutor commented that, "upon scrutiny," traditional surveillance of particular phone numbers of email addresses for which warrants could easily have been obtained, were far more important tools than massive data collection programs.[32] It appears that security, alone, may not require surrendering citizens' privacy and power to Big Brother.

SECRECY

Popular government requires a measure of government transparency as well as citizen privacy. Yet, every government seeks to shield parts of its actions from public view. In many instances, the major instrument used for this purpose is official censorship. In the United States, however, the First Amendment has made it difficult for the government to restrict press coverage except in wartime. Thus, while the courts did not interfere with official censorship during World War I or with the actions of the Office of Censorship during World War II, most government efforts to block press reports of sensitive material have been struck down on constitutional grounds. In the 1971 "Pentagon Papers," case, for example, the Supreme Court refused to condone the government's efforts to block publication of classified information leaked by a whistle blower.[33] Of course, in a small number of other cases such as those involving former CIA agents Victor Marchetti and Frank W. Snepp, the judiciary did grant government requests to suppress publication of at least some facts the authors wished to disclose.[34]

The US government does not have much power to censor press publication of material that comes into reporters' or publishers' possession. It lacks the equivalent of Britain's Official Secrets Act, which allows prior restraint of publications. However, an enormous quantity of allegedly sensitive information is classified so that anyone who makes it public or reveals it to the media is subject to criminal penalties. In 2013, for example, a US Army private, Chelsea Manning, was found guilty of publicly disclosing classified information and sentenced to a possible thirty-five years in prison. Another individual, Edward Snowden, was accused in 2013 of leaking information on illegal NSA surveillance practices to the *Washington Post*. While the government could not prevent the *Post* from publishing the material, it did indicate that Snowden would be prosecuted for leaking classified material. In order to avoid such prosecution and the likelihood of a stiff prison term, Snowden fled the country and sought asylum in Russia, a state that for its own reasons was willing to ignore American demands for his return. Thus, while the American press in not subject to much in the way of official censorship, those who provide it with information the US government deems confidential can be severely punished. This is little more than censorship by another name.

Governmental secrecy in the United States takes two main forms. The first is the official classification system, established by presidential order, and nominally designed to protect national security information. The classification system creates three "classes" of sensitive information. These are *confidential*, *secret*, and *top secret*, each governed by its own set of rules. Once information is classified, it can be viewed only by those with the requisite level of security clearance. Access to information classified as top secret—defined as potentially causing "grave damage" to the United States—is limited to a small number of individuals, and even then on a need-to-know basis. That is, even those with top secret security clearances are only allowed access to top secret information relevant to their own work. Information is classified as secret when its disclosure might threaten "serious damage" to the United States and information is classified as confidential when its disclosure might threaten "damage" to the United States.

A number of federal defense and security agencies are authorized, by presidential order, to classify information. Within those agencies, several thousand officials are designated "original classifiers" with the authority to classify material. The number of individuals possessing such authority is linked to the level of classification. Reportedly, only several hundred officials, including the president and vice president, can order a *top secret* classification. Perhaps as many as 2,500 are authorized to order lower levels of classification.[35] Information is usually classified for a specified period of time, usually ten, twenty-five, or fifty years depending upon its sensitivity, and then subject to declassification or a downgrade of its classification.

In addition to the formal secrecy system, information that one or another agency does not wish to release is shielded by the general opacity of government bureaucracies that have many procedures designed to impede public scrutiny of their actions. In recent years, indeed, several federal agencies have, without any statutory or presidential authorization, adopted their own classification schemes, labeling information "sensitive but unclassified," or "sensitive security information," or "critical program information," and restricting access to it.

Since George Washington, presidents have claimed the power to block Congress and the public from securing access to government information. In 1792, Washington hesitated before providing Congress with access to documents relating to a disastrous military expedition, commanded by General Arthur St. Clair, against a Native American tribe. According to notes of a cabinet meeting kept by Secretary of State Thomas Jefferson, Washington said he, "could readily conceive there might be papers of so secret a nature, as that they ought not to be given up." The cabinet agreed that, "the Executive ought to communicate such papers as the public good would permit, and ought to refuse those, the disclosure of which would injure the public."[36] Washington eventually decided to release the documents pertaining to the St. Clair expedition, but two years later refused a congressional request to provide papers relating to the treaty with England negotiated by John Jay.

The Classification System

The beginnings of formal document classification in the United States can be traced to an 1857 law concerning the management of American diplomatic and consular offices in which the president is authorized to "prescribe such regulations, and make and issue such orders and instructions . . . in relation to . . . the communication of information . . . as he may think conducive to the public interest."[37] Not until after the Civil War did the US Army issue formal regulations governing the protection of information. Regulations issued in 1869 and revised in subsequent years prohibited anyone from photographing or sketching military fortifications. In 1898, Congress enacted legislation attaching penalties to violations of these regulations.[38]

Since 1898, Congress's role in restricting access to information has been limited. The 1917 Espionage Act made it a crime to obtain and disclose defense information to a foreign power with the intent of injuring the United States. The 1946 Atomic Energy Act declared that information pertaining to the design and manufacture of atomic weapons was restricted. The 1947 National Security Act made the director of central intelligence responsible for protecting intelligence sources and methods from unauthorized disclosure. And, the 1999 Kyl–Lott Amendment established procedures slowing the declassification of classified material that might contain information about nuclear weapons. With the exception of these and a small number of other pieces of legislation, restrictions on information have been executive in origin and have often been aimed at preventing Congress itself from obtaining access to information.

In 1912, the US War Department issued a series of rules for the protection of defense information, declaring the militarily sensitive information was to be labeled "confidential," assigned serial numbers, and kept under lock and key. This system was expanded during the First World War into a tripartite classification system not too different from the one used today. The highest category, *secret*, referred to information deemed likely to threaten the nation's defense. *Confidential* was the label assigned to information that, while not endangering the nation's security, might be prejudicial to its interests. Information deemed to be such that its disclosure might somehow undermine "administrative privacy" was declared *restricted* and access denied to the general public. Because the military does not operate in a vacuum and has numerous dealings with civilian agencies, this classification system also came to affect the operations of numerous government agencies that had dealings with the War or Navy departments.[39]

In 1940, the White House took control of the existing document classification system. President Roosevelt issued Executive Order 8381, declaring that the existing tripartite classification system would apply to all military and naval documents. Roosevelt cited national defense as the justification for protecting information, and, for the most part, only the Army and Navy departments were given authority to classify information. Subsequent presidents have issued their own executive orders refining and expanding the classification system. The most sweeping change was instituted by President Truman, who, in place of the term "national defense," declared that the broader concept of "national security" was the underlying justification for the classification system. Consistent with this change in terminology, Truman's order expanded the number of federal agencies authorized to classify documents. Not only defense agencies but also several dozen agencies with some security responsibilities would be permitted to classify information. Truman also added a fourth classification category, *top secret* for information deemed especially sensitive.

The five presidents who followed Truman restored the national defense justification for restricting access to information, reduced the number of agencies authorized to classify information, and eliminated the lowest level of secrecy—*restricted*—creating today's tripartite system. Eisenhower, Kennedy, and Johnson generally narrowed the grounds on which information could be classified. President Ronald Reagan, however, expanded the range of information that could be classified, ended the automatic declassification of material after a set period of time, reclassified previously declassified material, and told agencies that when in doubt they should err on the side of classification.[40] President Clinton reversed the direction of Reagan's policies and ordered that information not be classified if there was significant doubt about the need for secrecy. Clinton also prohibited the reclassification of already-declassified documents. The Bush administration then reversed Clinton's policies, expanding the range of information that could be classified, slowed the declassification of older documents, and restored Reagan's order directing agencies to err on the side of classification. Upon taking office in 2009, President Obama asserted his support for government transparency but issued executive orders instituting only one major change in classification policy. Obama established the National Declassification Center (NDC) within the National Archives to speed the declassification of older documents deemed to be of historic interest but posing no security risks.

The precise number of documents currently classified by federal agencies is not known. It is clear, however, that the number is enormous. During each of the past several decades alone, some 200,000 documents per year, totaling tens of billions of pages, have been newly classified by various federal agencies.[41] Since 2009, pursuant to Obama's executive order, the NDC has hastened the declassification of several million pages of older documents.[42] During the same period, though, tens of millions of pages of new documents were classified. Thus, the rate of new classification far outpaces the rate of declassification. Critics have accused the NDC of working at a "languid pace," but of course the NDC must constantly deal with objections from agencies whose documents are being reviewed as well as the cumbersome and time-consuming Kyl–Lott procedure for reviewing documents that may contain information pertaining to nuclear weapons.[43] Several agencies, particularly the CIA, have resisted declassification of documents and have, indeed, sought to reclassify documents that had already been declassified. In recent years, the CIA has reclassified thousands of documents—mainly those related to American diplomatic history and originally belonging to the State Department or other agencies. The CIA declared that it had not been properly consulted when the declassification decisions were made.[44]

Leaked Information

Of course, there are legitimate and proper reasons for classifying information. America's security *is* threatened by foreign foes, terrorists, and even criminal enterprises. However, much that is declared secret or even top secret seems to pose less of a threat to the nation's security than to the security of various politicians and bureaucrats. This is one of the lessons of the various leaks of information that have so troubled officials in Washington in recent years. The issue here is not the propriety of individuals deciding on their own what information should or should not be in the public domain. Such individual decisions can threaten the nation's security. The question at hand is, rather, what the leaks tell us about the government's classification policies. What we find is that agencies classify information that might embarrass the government whether or not it poses a risk to national security. More than anything else, the classification system seems designed to prevent members of the public from becoming fully aware of the misconduct, duplicity, and errors of those who govern them.

Take, for example, the top secret Pentagon Papers, whose release was labeled by President Nixon's national security adviser, General Alexander Haig, as "a devastating security breach of the greatest magnitude."[45] Published in 1971, the documents leaked by Daniel Ellsberg represented a history of America's involvement in Vietnam from 1945 to 1967. The history and supporting documents had been developed by a Defense Department study group created by Secretary of Defense Robert McNamara and tasked with writing a detailed history of the Vietnam War. Ellsberg had briefly worked as a staffer for the study and was able to photocopy most of the information contained in the study's forty-seven volumes.

The Pentagon Papers provided a fascinating look at an important episode in American history, but all their information was historical and the only secrets they revealed concerned lies, evasions, and cover-ups by successive presidents and other government officials. Presidents Eisenhower, Truman, Kennedy, Johnson, and the various senior officials working for the White House had deceived the press, Congress, and the electorate while pursuing what turned out to be a disastrous policy in Southeast Asia. While President Kennedy was pretending to consult with South Vietnamese President Diem he was already planning to overthrow Diem and sanctioned the coup that led to Diem's death. While President Johnson was declaring, "We want no wider war," in his 1964 reelection campaign, he had already decided to expand the war. It is little wonder that the Pentagon Papers were classified top secret. An unauthorized individual reading them might have come away with the impression that America's leaders and government could not be trusted.

Former Solicitor General Erwin Griswold argued before the Supreme Court in 1971 that publication of the papers would cause great and irreparable harm to the nation's security. Writing in the *Washington Post* some fifteen years later, Griswold conceded that, "I have never seen any trace of a threat to the national security from the publication."[46] One might say that the threat was to the reputations of political leaders and the credibility of the government, not the security of the nation.

For another example, take the WikiLeaks case. In 2010, a US Army private named Chelsea Manning downloaded more than 700,000 classified documents from military servers and sent them to WikiLeaks, which shared the documents with a number of newspapers.[47] Some of the material raised genuine security concerns. The documents include videos that seem to depict instances of misconduct by American troops in Iraq and Afghanistan and documents suggesting that American authorities had failed to investigate cases of misconduct by Iraqi police and soldiers under their indirect command. Other documents included classified cables from US embassies assessing the competence—usually *incompetence*—of foreign leaders. Russia's Vladimir Putin is depicted as little more than a gangster; England's Prince Andrew is shown as rude and boorish; the former president of Tunisia and his daughter are revealed to have their favorite ice cream flown in from Saint Tropez at a time when many Tunisians could barely scratch out a living. Still other documents revealed corruption on the part of US allies, including Afghanistan, the Vatican, and Pakistan.[48] Some of the leaked documents arguably deserve to be classified if only to protect American intelligence sources. Others seem to have been classified to hide evidence of wrongdoing by the United States and its allies, or to avoid embarrassing one or another governmental entity. As in the case of the Pentagon Papers, many documents were classified less to protect the nation's security than to prevent the public from glimpsing the truth behind official facades. Perhaps the American people might have benefitted from knowing some of these facts.

For their part, the 2013 NSA eavesdropping revelations discussed above paint a picture of an agency that might charitably be said to skirt the boundaries of legality. Without any evidence that this activity actually serves the national interest, the telephone and email records of tens of millions of Americans are collected and, without the necessary court orders, some unknown number of these are "inadvertently" thoroughly examined. Presumably, America's foreign foes already suspected that their electronic communications just might be monitored. Government secrecy merely prevented the American public from knowing that its calls and emails were being watched.

Support for an unflattering view of the classification program can also be gleaned from the ongoing tug-of-war over the declassification of documents. In 2005, for example, the CIA reclassified a dozen documents that had been declassified and were publicly available in the National Archives. For the most part, these documents reveal foolish agency projects or missteps sometimes going back a half century. One document detailed an abortive CIA effort to drop propaganda leaflets into Eastern Europe by hot air balloon. Other documents described the intelligence community's faulty analysis of the Soviet nuclear weapons program in 1949. Still another document shows that the CIA was terribly wrong in its analysis of whether or not China would intervene in the Korean War in the fall of 1950.[49] Why were these now-ancient documents reclassified? Perhaps because they caused the agency some embarrassment and this, sometimes more than national security, is

deemed by the government to be an adequate reason to keep information from the public.

Congressional Access to Information

The Constitution assigns Congress the power to make the law. Presidents, however, have sought to limit congressional access to information. To begin with, every president since Franklin Roosevelt has
taken the position that the presidentially established system of security
classification applies to members of Congress and their staffs as well
as to the general public. In the Intelligence Oversight Act of 1980,
however, Congress explicitly required the president to keep congressional intelligence committees fully and currently informed of all
intelligence activities. The act also requires the director of national
intelligence to provide any information required by these committees
"consistent with the protection of sources and methods." Congress has
taken this phrase to mean that classified information will be given only
to members of the intelligence committees and that staff members of
those committees must possess requisite security clearances to receive
classified information.[50]

Since 1980, intelligence agencies have briefed congressional committees on many of their undertakings. There is, however, reason to
be concerned about the accuracy of the information given to Congress. For example, in March 2013, while testifying before the Senate
Intelligence Committee, National Intelligence Director James Clapper
responded to a question by saying that the NSA had not "wittingly"
collecting information on millions of Americans. Subsequent revelations revealed that Clapper's testimony was disingenuous. Leaving
aside the question of veracity, some members of Congress have com-
plained that intelligence briefings are usually filled with jargon and
designed to be confusing. Because of security restrictions, moreover,
members are usually barred from consulting expert advisers who might
challenge or at least more fully explain the programs being discussed.
And, by failing to disclose significant information in the first place,

intelligence agencies make it difficult for members of Congress to ask questions or request briefings. President Obama, for example, averred that any member of Congress could have asked for a briefing on the PRISM program. This claim, however, seems a bit dubious. "How can you ask when you don't know the program exists?" asked Representative Susan Collins of Maine, speaking on National Public Radio.[51]

Executive Privilege

On a number of occasions, presidents have explicitly refused to provide Congress with documents requested by lawmakers. In some instances there may be valid reasons for this refusal, but in most cases the aim seems to be to hide evidence of foolish or illegal action. When refusing, presidents generally claim "executive privilege." A related claim, used when the executive refuses to turn over documents to the courts, is called the "state secrets privilege," and was recently cited by the Obama administration in seeking to block a suit involving the targeted killing of a US citizen suspected of terrorist activities in Yemen.[52]

The actual term, *executive privilege*, was coined by President Eisenhower, who frequently refused to provide information to Congress when to do so, in his view, would violate the confidentiality of deliberations in the executive branch.[53] But, long before Eisenhower introduced the phrase, presidents claimed the power to withhold materials from Congress and from the courts.[54] George Washington, as noted above, was reluctant to accede to congressional requests for information about a disastrous campaign against the Indians and refused to provide Congress with documents about the circumstances surrounding the negotiation of the Jay Treaty between the United States and Britain. In the course of presiding over the criminal case against Aaron Burr, Chief Justice John Marshall gave some standing to such claims. Marshall indicated that in criminal cases the president could not be treated like an ordinary individual and might only be compelled to produce evidence if it was clearly shown by affidavit to be essential to the conduct of the case.[55] Because of the Watergate affair, the term *executive privilege* has developed a bad odor, and subsequent presidents have sometimes used other phrases to deny congressional or judicial requests for information. For example, in refusing to allow the director of Homeland Security to testify before Congress in March, 2002, President Bush asserted a claim of "executive prerogative."[56]

In *United States v. Nixon* the court, for the first time, explicitly recognized executive privilege as a valid presidential claim to be balanced against competing claims. The court indicated that where important issues were at stake, especially foreign policy questions as well as military and state secrets, presidential claims of privilege should be given great deference by the courts. Finding no such issues in the case at hand, though, the court ruled against Nixon. In a subsequent case, *Nixon v. Administrator of General Services*, the Court held that the former president's records were not privileged communications and could be transferred to the General Services Administration.[57] Once again, though, the court recognized the existence of executive privilege and said it could be used to protect the president's communications, "in performance of [his] responsibilities . . . and made in the process of shaping policy and making decisions." Thus, in both *Nixon* cases, precedents were established for claims of privilege, and in subsequent years the federal courts have upheld several such claims made by the president and other executive branch officials acting at the president's behest. For example, in *United States v. American Telephone & Telegraph*, in response to a presidential claim of privilege, the district court enjoined AT&T from providing a congressional subcommittee with the contents of a number of wiretaps conducted by the FBI.[58] Similarly, in *United States v. House of Representatives*, the district court refused to compel EPA Administrator Anne Gorsuch to hand over what she claimed were privilege documents to a House subcommittee.[59]

In their more recent decisions, federal courts have continued to rule in favor of executive privilege in national security cases and others as well.[60] Both presidential deliberations and those of presidential advisers and their staffs have been held to be privileged.[61] In a recent case, the vice president claimed privilege. This is the case of *United States v.*

District Court of the District of Columbia.[62] In this case, a coalition of public interest groups, including Judicial Watch and the Sierra Club, sought to obtain the records of an energy task force led by Vice President Dick Cheney in 2001. The public interest groups brought the suit after a similar suit brought by the director of the General Accounting Office (GAO) was dismissed for want of standing. The Cheney energy task force had been formed to make recommendations to the administration regarding federal energy policy. The public interest coalition charged that the task force gave inordinate influence to energy producers at the expense of consumer and environmental interests. A federal district court ordered Cheney to turn over his records. In a 7–2 opinion, however, the Supreme Court ruled that the vice president was entitled to the protection of executive privilege in order "to protect the executive branch from vexatious litigation that might distract it from the energetic performance of its constitutional duties."

In 2001, President Bush also invoked executive privilege to delay the release of presidential records from the Reagan administration to the Reagan presidential library. Bush issued an executive order declaring that executive privilege covered records that reflect, "military, diplomatic, or national security secrets; communications of the president or his advisors," and other matters. Similar privileges were asserted for the vice president.[63] As we will see below, President Obama has also found reason to invoke executive privilege.

Delay and Obfuscation

Though hundreds of thousands of pieces of information are classified every year, this represents only a tiny fraction of the information developed by federal agencies. The fact, however, that most information is not classified does not mean that it is made available to the public or even to the Congress. Most secrets are easily kept by federal agencies because they are hidden in an ocean of information, and no outsider even knows of their presence. Occasionally, however, a whistle blower, a clever reporter, or sheer accident will offer a glimpse of the existence of knowledge the agency would prefer to hide. If this happens, agencies will almost invariably seek to avoid fuller disclosure of information that does not present their actions in the most positive light. Agencies will vigorously resist efforts by the media or the Congress to pry loose their secrets, which sometimes turn out to include fraud, waste, abuse, illegal conduct, and poorly conceived plans. Whistle blowers, nominally protected by law, are almost certain to face agency retaliation to serve as a warning to others.[64] There are many recent example of agency efforts to hide embarrassing secrets.

In 2009, for example, agency whistle blowers revealed that the Arizona field office of the US Bureau of Alcohol, Tobacco, Firearms, and Explosives (ATF) had managed a poorly conceived "sting" operation code named "Fast and Furious," which allowed licensed firearms dealers in the United States to sell weapons to illegal buyers. The ATF apparently planned to trace the weapons back to Mexican drug cartel leaders. Unfortunately, most of the 2,000 weapons involved in the case were not recovered, though several were linked to subsequent crimes and murders, including the killing of a US Border Patrol Agent. In response to the revelations, ATF executives refused to provide documents pertaining to the operation and, instead, sought to retaliate against the agents who revealed its existence. Similarly, in 2013, the Environmental Protection Agency (EPA) granted one gasoline refinery (out of hundreds in the nation) an exception to the rule requiring a certain amount of ethanol to be blended into gasoline. This exception is worth millions to the refinery and, after it was noted by a *Wall Street Journal* reporter, the agency refused to explain why it had been granted. Some in Congress and the media suggested that perhaps some political motivation had been involved. Also in 2013, when conservative groups voiced suspicions that they had been subjected to extra scrutiny by the Internal Revenue Service (IRS), the agency refused to provide relevant documents.

Two of the main tools that can be used to force government agencies to make documents public are the congressional subpoena power and a public request under the Freedom of Information Act (FOIA).

As to the first of these tools, congressional committees have the power to order federal officials to produce desired documents. An official who refuses may be cited for contempt of Congress, which may, in principle, result in a prison term. In recent years, a number of officials have been held in contempt for refusing to provide Congress with information. During the Bush administration, the president's counsel, Harriet Miers, and chief of staff, Joshua Bolten, were cited for contempt when they refused to comply with congressional subpoenas for documents. During the Nixon administration, Interior Secretary James Watt, Energy Secretary James Edwards, and EPA officials Anne Gorsuch and Rita Lavelle were held in contempt for refusing to turn over documents. In all these cases, the named officials eventually agreed to comply with the subpoenas.

President Obama's Attorney General, Eric Holder, was cited for contempt of Congress in 2012 for failing to comply with a congressional subpoena for documents related to the ATF's Fast and Furious operation. Though Holder eventually submitted some 7,000 pages of documents, he refuse to turn over another 1,300 pages demanded by Congress, and President Obama invoked executive privilege to shield these documents. Representative Darrell Issa (R-CA), chairman of the House Oversight and Government Reform Committee, contended that the Justice Department was hiding some 140,000 additional pages of documents. Since Fast and Furious had been launched under the Bush administration, it is unclear why President Obama's Justice Department is making such a determined effort to keep pertinent documents from Congress. The House of Representatives has asked the federal courts to enforce its subpoena, and the matter is currently being litigated.

Generally speaking, efforts by congressional committees to secure information from executive do not reach the point of confrontation produced by the Fast and Furious case. Typically, agencies go through the motions of cooperating with Congress while delaying, providing only limited responses to congressional demands, and hiding facts that would enable Congress to focus on, or even learn of the existence of, the most pertinent pieces of information. As one critic noted, an agency may provide tens of thousands of pieces of information, assert that it has complied with congressional demands and fail to find other pieces of information or, in the event that Congress learns of their existence, take the position that these were not covered by the subpoena.[65]

Similar problems can blunt the impact of a second tool of governmental transparency, FOIA.

FOIA was enacted in 1966 and represented a potentially important mechanism for reducing agency discretion to withhold records from the public. With the advent of FOIA, agencies could no longer arbitrarily declare that a release of documents would not be in the public interest, as had been their typical practice. FOIA requires that all federal agencies must make their records available to any person upon request within twenty days, unless the documents fall within one or more of nine exemptions, which include classified documents, trade secrets, sensitive law enforcement records, and personal or medical records. If a requested document contains some information that falls under one of the exemptions, FOIA requires that the non-exempt portions of the record must still be released with an indication of the location of the deleted portion of the document. Requestors who believe that their FOIA requests have been improperly denied may ask a federal court to order the relevant agency to comply.

Since its enactment, FOIA has allowed individuals, news agencies, and public interest groups some limited measure of access to government documents and has provided many examples of government mismanagement. In 2012, for example, several US Secret Service agents were interrupted by Columbian police when they were engaged in an altercation with prostitutes. The agents were assigned to protect President Obama during an international conference. Secret Service executives described the incident as an isolated case, but FOIA requests filed by news agencies compelled the Secret Service to produce documents that appeared to show a long-standing pattern of problematic behavior on the part of its agents. This included sexual assaults, involvement with prostitutes, improper use of weapons, and public intoxication.[66]

Federal agencies, however, have learned to undercut FOIA in a variety of ways. To begin with, FOIA requires that only documents that qualify as "agency records" can be requested. Agencies tend to construe the term "records" narrowly and take the position that records of meetings that took place somewhere other than agency property are not agency records, that emails sent via officials' personal email accounts are not agency records, and that records maintained by non-agency personnel are not agency records. Agencies, moreover, may delay responding to requests, delete much of the requested information, provide information in dribs and drabs necessitating multiple FOIA requests, assert that the requested information does not exist or cannot be found and so forth. FOIA also exempts those records that are " necessarily withheld to encourage the deliberative process." In other words, records of deliberations leading to a final decision do not have to be produced in response to a FOIA request. Agencies are inclined to classify their most important records as "deliberative" and to refuse access to them.

During the Bush administration, Attorney General John Ashcroft advised agencies to "carefully consider" possible exemptions before releasing documents in response to a FOIA request. The attorney general promised that the Justice Department would defend the withholding of documents unless there was no legal basis for so doing. Reporters found that agency responses to FOIA requests were slow and incomplete and judicial review of agency decisions unhelpful.[67]

After taking office in 2009, President Obama promised a more transparent government. In an experiment, however, *Bloomberg News* recently sent rather mundane FOIA requests to fifty-seven federal agencies. The requests asked for a list of trips taken by agency heads and a breakdown of their travel expenses. Twenty-seven agencies ignored the requests altogether, and only eight complied within the twenty-day period specified by the FOIA statute.[68] Reporters or individuals seeking more sensitive information than travel schedules typically find that turning the FOIA spigot will produce a few droplets from the vast and ever-growing federal sea of information.

Information and Popular Government

Without information, popular government is an impossibility. Citizens would have little choice but to believe what they were told and the unfortunate fact of the matter is that politicians and public officials tend to be practiced liars, viewing what is useful or convenient as far more important than the truth. "I have previously stated and I repeat now that the United States plans no military intervention in Cuba," said President John F. Kennedy in 1961 as he planned military action in Cuba. "As president, it is my duty to the American people to report that renewed hostile actions against United States ships on the high seas in the Gulf of Tonkin have today required me to order the military forces of the United States to take action in reply," said President Lyndon Johnson in 1964 as he fabricated an incident to justify expansion of American involvement in Vietnam. "We did not, I repeat, did not—trade weapons or anything else [to Iran] for hostages, nor will we." said President Ronald Reagan in November, 1986, four months before admitting that US arms had been traded to Iran in exchange for Americans being held hostage there. "Simply stated, there is no doubt that Saddam Hussein now has weapons of mass destruction," said Vice President Dick Cheney in 2002. When it turned out that these weapons did not exist, Assistant Defense Secretary Paul Wolfowitz explained, "For bureaucratic reasons, we settled on one issue, weapons of mass destruction (as justification for invading Iraq) because it was the one reason everyone could agree on." After leaks showed that his 2013 congressional testimony denying the existence of NSA's surveillance program was false, Director of National Intelligence James Clapper declared, "I responded in what I thought was the most truthful or least untruthful manner by saying, 'No.'"

The Athenians subjected their officials to the *euthyna* because, without a public audit of their actions in office, how would anyone know whether they deserved praise or censure. Surely officials could not be trusted to judge their own performance and give an accurate account of their activities. This seems quite reasonable, but the gov-

ernment of the United States, while practicing secrecy and conceal-
ment, exhorts its citizens to show trust.

SURVEILLANCE, SECRECY
AND POPULAR GOVERNMENT

Popular government requires transparency on the part of the government and privacy for the citizenry. Citizens can hardly exercise influence
over a government whose actions are hidden from them. And, as the
authors of the Fourth Amendment knew, citizens are inhibited from crit-
icizing or working against officials who monitor their political activities.
Unfortunately, the government of the United States has reversed this
democratic formula of governance in favor of secrecy for itself and transparency for its citizens. How appropriate that the government currently
views as the worst of all possible traitors an individual whose actions
had the effect of exposing this new formula of governance in action.
By revealing the government's secret program of surveillance, Edward
Snowden's leaks to the media illustrated the manner in which secrecy
and surveillance, two of the chief antitheses of popular government, are
closely intertwined in the current American state. In so doing, Snowden
has also shown the extent to which America has turned its wars inward,
eroding political freedom. It is difficulty to miss the irony of Snowden's
subsequent flight to freedom—to Russia.

CONCLUSION

THE TRUTHS OF WAR

War is terrible, but it has also been a major engine of human progress. War has contributed to technology, economic development, more humane governance, and, perhaps most important, has helped humans learn to think rationally. As I observed at the outset, societies dominated by irrational modes of thought have seldom survived the rather harsh audit of war. The Lakota "Ghost Shirt" of the 1880s turned out not to stop bullets. Similarly, Nazi "Aryan Science" of the 1930s was shown to be rather inferior to what might be called the applied *Judenphysik* of the Manhattan Project.

The modern-day equivalent of the ghost shirt is the idea that war can somehow be organized or legislated out of existence—that philosophy and rhetoric can stop bullets and that enlightened individuals will study war no more. As I have argued elsewhere, these contemporary ghost dancers adhere to two main schools of thought, the Hobbesian and the Kantian. For Hobbes, the solution to the problem of war was the creation of a powerful sovereign authority that would put an end to strife and violent conflict.[1] For Kant, the solution was an increase in the number of republican governments, a type of regime that, in his view, was extremely reluctant to engage in acts of armed aggression.[2] Modern-day neo-Hobbesians like political scientist Joshua Goldstein favor the construction and empowerment of supranational organizations.[3] Modern-day neo-Kantians like Bruce Russett count upon the spread of liberal democracy to bring about a "democratic peace."[4] Each of these solutions is questionable. Let us first consider the Hobbesian case.

Hobbes famously wrote that in the state of nature, the life of man was "solitary, poor, nasty, brutish and short," and constantly afflicted by insecurity and violence. The solution was submission to a government with absolute power. Hobbes wrote, "The only way to erect such a common power, as may be able to defend them from the invasion of foreigners and the injuries of one another . . . is to confer all their power and strength upon one man, or assembly of men, that may reduce all their wills, by plurality of voices, unto one will."[5] In the Hobbesian Commonwealth, war and violence were to be eliminated by the complete subordination of the wills of members of the populace to the will of the sovereign. The possibility of strife was then foreclosed by the sovereign's absolute authority.[6] This sovereign must, indeed, be absolute according to Hobbes, since any limitations upon its power would open the way to disputes which might, in turn, lead to violence. Thus, the Hobbesian solution to the problem of violence was, in effect, acceptance of tyranny. For Hobbes, tyranny was to be preferred to anarchy and violence. "Sovereign power is not so hurtful as the want of it," he averred.[7]

The Hobbesian solution to the problem of war and violence is problematic in at least two ways. To begin with, it is not clear that tyranny is to be preferred to violence and disorder. The prevalence of popular revolution in the contemporary world might suggest that large numbers of individuals prefer violence to tyranny. In recent years, thousands of Libyans, Syrians. Tunisians, Egyptians, and so forth seemed to choose the former over the latter, even in the face of tanks and machine guns. In a similar vein, the former German Democratic Republic (DDR) was a very orderly place but during its four decades as a nation, hundreds of thousands of its citizens risked their lives leaving the DDR for the disorder and uncertainty of life in the West.

Second, the Hobbesian solution to the problem of violence would seem to require a great deal of violence for its implementation. Hobbes indicates that men might "agree amongst themselves to submit" to the sovereign. If not, however, they must be compelled to submit "by natural force" or "by war." And, once a Hobbesian Commonwealth is established, considerable violence is likely to be required to maintain its power. The DDR kept the peace by a program of surveillance, intimidation, and punishment that enrolled nearly a quarter of the populace in the regime's various security forces or as informers. Behind an orderly facade was a very violent place.

Perhaps there are cases where a Hobbesian "agreement" might be reached peacefully, but these would seem most likely to be instances in which states or other entities already have few or relatively manageable antagonisms toward one another and see submission to a single authority as a means of advancing their mutual interests. The thirteen American states in 1789 or the economically advanced Western European states today are examples. The imposition of some sort of sovereign authority over mutually antagonistic states and political forces would seem likely to require considerable violence and a continuing regime of coercion. In other words, it would entail an imperial project that seems more a recipe than a cure for violence.

Now, as to the neo-Kantians, there is some support for the idea that democracies are less likely than other sorts of states to go to war, especially with one another. The statistical evidence, however, is far from conclusive.[8] Moreover, the world's premier liberal democracy, the United States of America, is among the most bellicose nations on the face of the earth. Since the Civil War, American forces have been deployed abroad on hundreds of occasions for major conflicts as well as minor skirmishes. And, of course, America's military arsenal and defense budget dwarfs those of the other nations of the world. Ironically, America has justified many of its wars, including the 2002 Iraq War, by the claim that its goal was to transform its adversary into a peaceful liberal democracy. This might cause some concern that Kant's democratic peace might require a good deal of bloodshed to compel unwilling states to become liberal democracies.

There is, of course, a diffuse but hopeful school of thought that views war and violence as moral problems that can be addressed through proper moral education and example. No doubt, moral education can be effective and, certainly, if all could be persuaded of the desirability of converting their swords into plowshares, peace would prevail. However, even those who would like to reject violence should be wary of others not as enlightened as themselves. The Moriori of the Chatham Islands remained true to their pacifist principles when attacked by the Taranaki Maori. The result, though, was that most of the Moriori were enslaved or killed, even eaten, by the Maori invaders.

We might also remember that most groups and nations that avow strong commitments to peace are somewhat less principled than the unfortunate Moriori. Indeed, several forms of pacifism are less peaceful than might meet the eye. Though professing a commitment to peace, some practitioners of nonviolent protest count upon the violence of their opponents to bring intervention by even more powerful, and potentially more violent forces. Hence, nonviolence might be seen as a tactic of fomenting, rather than engaging in, violence. Also quite common is what might be called "contingent pacifism." Often, political actors denounce the use of force by some groups or nations while casting a tolerant eye at the use of violence by others. Politically progressive elements typically denounce military actions by the United States while accepting the need for third-world regimes to resort to violence. Politically conservative groups generally take the opposite view. Finally worth noting is what might be called liberal pacifism. Tolerant, politically liberal individuals shrink from using violence under almost any circumstance. Most, however, accept the protection of the government and its military and police forces, paying taxes to support the systemic violence that preserves their often-comfortable lives. And, in the international realm, by opposing war and violence they are effectively condemning many peoples to live under tyranny.

For those who find these considerations insufficiently depressing, let me conclude with one more dispiriting thought. War reveals truths—and one of these is an unpleasant truth about America. When the United States is not fighting others, it often turns on itself. As I observed above, the late historical sociologist Charles Tilly—one of the world's most perceptive analysts of the growth and evolution of government—famously characterized the state as an entity built for the purpose of warfare. He said, "war makes states and states make war," and went on to characterize the warlike state as a "protection racket," offering its citizens protection from foreign foes in exchange for their taxes and service.[9] There is a good deal of truth to Tilly's quip and his characterization. Everywhere we look, ruling groups working to guard or expand their territorial domains seek to build governments with sufficient administrative, extractive, and coercive capabilities to ward off internal and external rivals. Today's states are the survivors of millennia of culling in which their weaker rivals were defeated or absorbed. Many of these states added to their power by persuading most if not all of their ordinary subjects that they were citizens with some stake in the state's welfare and, moreover, that only the state could protect them from the hostile foreigners across the border.

While derived from the European experience, this account seems, in some ways, especially relevant to the United States. Americans are divided, not united, by race, religion, and ethnicity; their history as a nation is brief; and their dominant political ideology questions the need for government. Tens of millions of Americans, even today, believe in individual self-help and the minimalist state. How does a state establish itself in such an unpromising setting? How does it sink its taproots into such a barren soil? Part of the answer is that it emphasizes protection. It becomes, as historian Geoffrey Perret observed, "a country made by war."[10] That is, America is a country whose citizens are connected to one another and to their government less by the blood in their veins than the blood they have shed—their own and that of others. Americans have, at various times, responded to pleas to remember the Alamo, the day of infamy, the events of 9/11, and other days when the nation came under attack and looked to the protection of the state.

So far, so good. But, what happens if a state is, like the United States, so adept at its chosen task of war making that it periodically defeats, however temporarily, its various rivals? What happens to a state built around war making if there is no war to fight? How does such a state convince its citizens that they still need its protection? The danger, at least hypothetically, is that such a state may turn its power inward, using what might be called excess administrative capacity for domestic purposes and using now-superfluous coercive capacity against its own citizens. Lacking external enemies, moreover, such a state may seek internal threats to persuade its citizens that they still need its protection. As we saw, both these phenomena are apparent in American history and contemporary American politics. The US government's electronic surveillance programs were products of multiple wars and were honed to perfection during the war on terror. Interestingly, most of the external expressions of this particular war have ground to a halt. American combat forces have been withdrawn from Iraq. Most American forces have been withdrawn from Afghanistan. America's program of targeted killings employing drone strikes has been stepped back. Consistent, however, with the historic pattern, government agencies seem loathe to surrender wartime powers and, possessing now-superfluous capabilities, they seem inclined to turn them inward in search of new foes.

PROTECTION

Tilly, as noted above, characterized the state as a large-scale "protection racket," extracting resources and services from the citizenry in exchange for the promise of protection from foreign threats. In actual times of war, states are often able to build a considerable amount of heartfelt popular support and solidarity among their citizens. The idea of shared danger and shared sacrifice in wartime can build a sense of national community and purpose. During World War II, as journalist Tom Brokaw shows in his well-known book *The Greatest Generation*, most Americans came to believe that they had a common goal and purpose toward which they needed to work as a nation.[11]

Americans willingly undertook their assigned military duties, and those too old to fight volunteered to serve in such organizations as the Civil Air Patrol and the Coast Guard Auxiliary. Women volunteered to work for the Red Cross, the USO, and other agencies aimed at bolstering soldiers' morale. Millions of Americans participated in scrap collection and recycling. Similarly, In Britain, according to historian Robert Mackay, most citizens "became actively committed to the project their leaders put before them, who cooperated with the drastic reordering of daily life this entailed and who, on the whole, did so in a spirit of stoical endurance that did not exclude good humour."[12]

For better or worse, foreign threats are usually plentiful but, here too, the absence of overt external dangers generally does not lead states to declare that their citizens no longer need protection. Instead, states may identify internal enemies to substitute for the temporarily absent foreign foes. In the 1950s, the United States made war on domestic "subversives." Today, the government conducts wars on crime, on drugs, and on corporate malefactors, as well as the domestication of the war on terror. As law professor Jonathan Simon has forcefully argued, these wars have redefined Americans as victims or potential victims, a terminology made explicit in the 1994 Violent Crime Control Act.[13] This terminology is very significant.

When Americans are characterized as "citizens," the term implies individuals with rights, liberties, and personal autonomy. Citizens, indeed, have some power *vis-à-vis* the government. And, since the state needs popular cooperation against external foes, it continues to promote a sense of citizenship even when extending its protection. Victims, on the other hand, are weak persons in need to the government's protection. Victimhood represents a significant demotion for citizens. Rather than exercise power, victims cower in their homes hoping to be kept safe. And yet, as Simon points out, political discourse and legislation seem intent on describing Americans as crime victims, the loved ones of crime victims, and potential victims of crime rather than citizens. Protecting citizens from crime becomes the state's business instead of and in addition to protecting them from foreign threats. And, under the rubric of increasing such protection, the US government, in its domestic wars on crime, drugs, corporate crime, and the internal terrorist threat, has, in recent years, greatly expanded the reach and power of its coercive and administrative machinery. As in the case of any other protection racket, the protector becomes as much or more of a threat than the putative attacker.

In recent years, thousands of new federal criminal statutes have been written to protect the public and safeguard the potential victims of crime. There are currently some 4,500 federal criminal laws on the books, nearly half enacted since 1970.[14] It should be recalled that the Constitution, itself, listed only three federal crimes: treason, piracy, and counterfeiting. Most of these statutes deal with environmental protection, securities regulation, corporate governance, product and workplace safety, terrorism, and the myriad of other matters related to the expansion of the national government's authority and responsibility. Not surprisingly, given the growing number of federal laws that it is now possible to violate, the number of federal prosecutions has increased as well—by nearly 150% since 1980.[15]

Accompanying this expansion of federal criminal law has been a determined effort by the executive branch to circumvent the limitations that traditional procedural safeguards impose upon the ability of the government to incarcerate those it deems blameworthy. Under pressure from the Justice Department and afraid of appearing soft on crime, Congress has enacted statutes that federal prosecutors have been able to use to remove one after another impediment to the prosecution and conviction of the targets of their investigations. For example, a number of federal criminal statutes, such as the Clean Water Act, weaken the traditional *mens rea* requirement, allowing criminal prosecution of individuals who were, at most, negligent. In one recent case, a construction supervisor was sentenced to six months in prison and a $5,000 fine for Clean Water Act violations when a backhoe operator on his crew accidentally pierced an oil pipeline discharging oil into a nearby river.[16] The Supreme Court has said that overlooking questions of intent may be necessary to protect complex regulatory arrangements.[17]

In a similar vein, Congress has enacted statutes that have been used by the Justice Department to criminalize efforts by individuals to defend themselves or even to assert their innocence. For example, in a well-known recent case, Martha Stewart was prosecuted for violating the federal fraud statute, as well as the statute that prohibits making false statements to federal investigators, in her response to the government's allegations that she engaged in insider trading. The government was never able to muster the evidence needed to actually charge Stewart with insider trading. This inconvenient fact, however, did not stop Justice Department prosecutors from charging that she made false statements to federal investigators and committed securities fraud by frequently and publicly asserting her innocence. The government claimed that Stewart's assertions of innocence were actually efforts to halt the slide in value of her company's stock and, thus, constituted a form of fraud.[18]

In addition, acting without a clear statutory mandate, the Justice Department has worked to develop new techniques to circumvent limits on prosecutorial discretion. One of many important prosecutorial strategies that have evolved in recent years is the tactic of discouraging white collar and—especially—corporate defendants from fully availing themselves of the legal advice to which their resources would normally give them access. At least since 1999, the Justice Department has told defendants that they would be more likely to face criminal charges if they "lawyered up." This policy was formalized in the often-cited "Thompson Memorandum," drafted in 2003 by then–Deputy Attorney General Larry Thompson.[19] The Thompson Memorandum states that in deciding whether to charge a corporation with a crime, federal prosecutors should consider, "the corporation's timely and voluntary disclosure of wrongdoing and its willingness to cooperate in the investigation of its agents, including, if necessary, the waiver of corporate attorney–client and work product protection." The memorandum goes on to say that the prosecutor should consider "whether the corporation appears to be protecting its culpable employees and agents," and may consider "the advancing of attorneys' fees" and sharing of information pursuant to a joint defense agreement. In other words, corporate officers are to be discouraged from retaining counsel, refusing to disclose privileged information, or developing complex defense strategies, by the threat that the government will treat these as indications of likely guilt. Some of these policies were modified but not ended by the Justice Department in 2006.[20]

Lest it be thought that the erosion of legal safeguards affects only greedy corporate chieftains or dangerous terrorists, it is worth taking note of some contemporary federal cases. In recent years, a Michigan landowner was convicted of a criminal violation of the Clean Water Act for moving sand onto his property without a federal permit. A minor union leader was convicted of making false statements for replying "no" to federal investigators who asked him if he had accepted a bribe. A college teacher was convicted of mail fraud for granting degrees to students whose work had been plagiarized.[21] Perhaps these cases remain the exceptions rather than the norm, but they illustrate the possibilities. As sovereignty is boundlessly strengthened, the influence and the security of the citizenry are reduced and the chance that ordinary citizens will be subjected to arbitrary treatment is increased.

Of course, all this is sugarcoated by government agencies that claim to be acting only for the benefit of the public. Security services need to spy on millions of Americans to protect us from foreign terrorists. Schoolchildren need to be subjected to urine tests to battle drug abuse. We need a federal agency protecting us from the most important threat facing the nation today—the use of performance-enhancing steroids by professional athletes. And, of course, this discussion sheds a different light on the issue of gun control. Armed citizens are far less likely than their unarmed fellows to need and seek the protection of the state.

In these, and many other ways, the aftermath of war can change the character of the state's protection racket without bringing it to an end. Absent war abroad, the state seeks enemies at home against whom to protect its people. In so doing, it transforms citizens into victims who will fearfully pay for protection from one another.

NOTES

INTRODUCTION

1. Henry George, "The Law of Human Progress," in *Progress and Poverty* (New York: Classics Club Library, 1942).

2. John U. Neff, *War and Human Progress* (Cambridge: Harvard University Press, 1950), 19.

3. Geoffrey Perret, *A Country Made by War* (New York: Vintage, 1990).

4. William H. McNeill, *Plagues and Peoples* (New York: Anchor, 1977).

5. Johan Galtung, *Peace by Peaceful Means: Peace, Conflict, Development and Civilization* (New York: Sage, 1996).

6. Philip Kitcher, "The Taint of Social Darwinism," *New York Times*, April 8, 2012, http://opinionator.blogs.nytimes.com/2012/04/08/the-taint-of-social-darwinism/.

7. See Richard Nelson's review of Geoffrey Hodgson and Thorbjørn Knudson, "The Limits of Lamarckism Revisited," *Evolutionary Theories in the Social Science*, May 18, 2004, http://www.etss.net/index.php/weblog/booksandreviews full/189/. See also Geoffrey Hodgson and Thorbjørn Knudson, "Evolutionary Theorizing beyond Lamarckism: A Reply to Richard Nelson," *Journal of Evolutionary Economics*, 17:353–359 (April 13, 2007), http://www.geoffrey-hodgson .info/user/image/rejoindernelsonjee.pdf. For a useful review of the various issues surrounding efforts to apply evolutionary theories to societies, see John Laurent and John Nightingale, eds., *Darwinism and Evolutionary Economics* (Northampton, MA: Edward Elgar Publishers, 2001).

CHAPTER 1: WAR AS AN AGENT OF RATIONALITY

1. Azar Gat, *War in Human Civilization* (Oxford, UK: Oxford University Press, 2006). Also, Philip Bobbitt, *The Shield of Achilles: War Peace and the Course of History* (New York: Knopf, 2003).

2. Angus Campbell et al., *The American Voter* (New York: John Wiley & Sons, 1960), ch.7.

3. Norman Podhoretz, *Why Are Jews Liberals* (New York: Doubleday, 2009).

4. See Michael Shermer, *The Believing Brain: From Ghosts and Gods to Politics and Conspiracies* (New York: Times Books, 2011). Also, Ariel Gluklich, *The End of Magic* (New York: Oxford University Press, 1977).

5. David Kuo, *Tempting Faith* (New York: Free Press, 2006).

6. Geoffrey Conrad and Arthur Demarest, "The Aztec Imperial Expansion," in *Religion and Empire: The Dynamics of Aztec and Inca Expansionism* (New York: Cambridge University Press, 1984).

7. "The Inca Imperial Expansion," in ibid.

8. Christopher Tyerman, *God's War: A History of the Crusades* (Cambridge, MA: Belknap Press, 2006).

9. Edward Peters, *Inquisition* (Berkeley: University of California Press, 1989), 84.

10. Conrad and Demarest, *Religion and Empire*, 126.

11. Ibid., 41.

12. Benjamin Ginsberg, *The Fatal Embrace: Jews and the State* (Chicago: University of Chicago Press, 1993), 42–43.

13. Peter Pulzer, *The Rise of Political Anti-Semitism in Germany and Austria*, rev. ed. (Cambridge, MA: Harvard University Press, 1988), 315–16.

14. Raul Hilberg, "The Bureaucracy of Annihilation," in Francois Furet, ed., *Nazi Germany and the Genocide of the Jews* (New York: Schocken, 1989), 120–30.

15. Detlev J. K. Peukert, *Inside Nazi Germany: Conformity, Opposition and Racism in Everyday Life* (New Haven: Yale University Press, 1987). Also Michael Geyer, "The Nazi State Reconsidered," in Richard Bessel, ed., *Life in the Third Reich* (New York: Oxford, 1987), 57–68.

16. Daniel Goldhagen, *Hitler's Willing Executioners: Ordinary Germans and the Holocaust* (New York: Vintage, 1997), 166.

17. Martin Van Creveld, "An Army Marches on Its Stomach!" in *Supplying War: Logistics from Wallenstein to Patton* (New York: Cambridge University Press, 2004).

18. Kenneth Slepyan, *Stalin's Guerrillas: Soviet Partisans in World War II* (Lawrence: University Press of Kansas, 2006), 39.

19. Richard Overy, *Russia's War: A History of the Soviet Effort, 1941–1945* (New York: Penguin, 1988), 133.

20. Van Creveld, *Supplying War*, 175–80.

21. Gordon Fraser, *The Quantum Exodus* (New York: Oxford University Press, 2012), 118.

22. Ibid., 111.

23. Ibid., appendix.

24. Ibid., 119.

25. Ibid., 125.

26. Richard Rhodes, *The Making of the Atomic Bomb* (New York: Simon & Schuster, 1986), 415.

27. Ibid., 445.

28. Fraser, *Quantum Exodus*, 78–83.

29. Jean M. Hungerford, "The Exploitation of Superstitions for Purposes of Psychological Warfare," *The Rand Corporation*, ASTIA Document No. ATI 210673, April 14, 1950.

30. Thucydides, *History of the Peloponnesian Wars*, vol. 5.

31. Sun Tzu, *The Art of War* (New York: Amazon Digital Services, 2014).

32. Ernest Volkman, *Science Goes to War* (New York: Wiley, 2002).

33. Niccolò Machiavelli, "Of New Dominions Which Have Been Acquired by One's Own Arms and Powers," in *The Prince* (New York: Mentor, 1952).

34. Carl von Clausewitz, *On War* (Princeton: Princeton University Press, 1989).

35. B. H. Liddel Hart, *Strategy* (New York: Meridian, 1991).

36. Arthur Ferrill, *The Fall of the Roman Empire* (London: Thames & Hudson, 1988).

37. Peter Heather, *The Fall of the Roman Empire* (New York: Oxford University Press, 2006). See also Edward Luttwak, *The Grand Strategy of the Roman Empire* (Baltimore: Johns Hopkins University Press, 1979), and Edward Luttwak, *The Grand Strategy of the Byzantine Empire* (Cambridge, MA: Belknap, 2011).

38. Sun Tzu, "Waging War" in *Art of War*.

39. Niccolò Machiavelli, *The Art of War* (New York: Da Capo, 1965), 13.

40. Machiavelli, *Prince*, 82.

41. Kautilya, *The Arthashastra* (New York: Penguin Books, 1987), part 5.

42. Michael Bweckley, "Economic Development and Military Effectiveness," *Journal of Strategic Studies* 22, no. 1 (2010).

43. Walter S. Dunn Jr., *Hitler's Nemesis: The Red Army, 1930–1945* (Westport, CT: Praeger, 1994), 4.

44. Heather, *Fall of the Roman Empire*, part 1.

45. Martin Van Creveld, *Fighting Power: German and US Army Performance, 1939–1945* (Westport, CT: Greenwood, 1982).

46. Gat, *War in Human Civilization*, part 1.

47. Kautilya, *Arthashastra*, part 11.

48. Publius Flavius Vegetius Renatus, *De Re Militari*, book 1, http://www.pvv.ntnu.no/~madsb/home/war/vegetius/dere03.php.

49. Machiavelli, *Art of War*, 58.

50. Ibid., 162.

51. Kautilya, *Arthashastra*, part 11.

52. Randall Collins, *Violence: A Micro-Sociological Theory* (Princeton: Princeton University Press, 2008).

53. Karl Marlantes, *What It Is Like to Go to War* (New York: Atlantic Monthly, 2011).

54. The exception involves what Collins calls "forward panic," most often associated with military confrontations when armies in retreat are slaughtered by their advancing foes. Collins, "Forward Panic," in *Violence*.

55. David Grossman, *On Killing: The Psychological Cost of Learning to Kill in War and Society* (Boston: Back Bay Books, 2009).

56. S. L. A. Marshall, *Men against Fire: The Problem of Battle Command* (Norman: University of Oklahoma Press, 1947).

57. Grossman, *On Killing*, 177.

58. Ibid., 258.

59. Henry Guerlac, "Vauban: The Impact of Science on War," in Peter Paret, ed., *Makers of Modern Strategy* (Princeton: Princeton University Press, 1986), 64–90.

60. Ibid., 70–71.

61. Ibid., 71.

62. Paul Kennedy, *Engineers of Victory: The Problem Solvers Who Turned the Tide in the Second World War* (New York: Random House, 2013).

63. Sun Tzu, *Art of War.*

64. Ibid.

65. Donald W. Engels, *Alexander the Great and the Logistics of the Macedonian Army* (Berkeley: University of California Press, 1990).

66. Timothy May, *The Mongol Art of War* (Yardley, PA: Westholme Publishing, 2007).

67. Victor Davis Hanson, *Carnage and Culture* (New York: Doubleday, 2001), 77.

68. Van Creveld, *Supplying War*, 82.

69. Ibid., 97.

70. Geoffrey Perret, *A Country Made by War* (New York: Random House, 1989), 230.

71. Russell F. Weigley, *The American Way of War* (Bloomington: Indiana University Press, 1973), 131.

72. Ibid.

73. Perret, *Country Made by War*, 322.

74. Joanne E. Johnson, "The Army Industrial College and Mobilization Planning between the Wars," monograph prepared for the Industrial College of the Armed Forces, National Defense University, Fort McNair, District of Columbia, 1993, http://handle.dtic.mil/100.2/ADA276612.

75. Sun Tzu, *Art of War.*

76. Machiavelli, *Art of War*, 17.

77. Ibid., 176.

78. Machiavelli, "In What Way Princes Must Keep Faith," in *Prince.*

79. Von Clausewitz, *On War*, 1:50.

80. Max Weber, *Economy and Society*, ed. Guenther Roth and Claus Wittich (Berkeley: University of California Press, 1978), 2:1,151.

81. Charles Tilly, ed., *The Formation of National States in Western Europe* (Princeton: Princeton University Press, 1975).

82. Samuel Finer, "State and Nation Building in Europe: The Role of the Military," in ibid., 84–163.

83. Bhavya Lal, "Knowledge Domains in Engineering Systems: Systems Analysis," (MIT, 2001), https://docs.google.com/viewer?a=v&q=cache :QzF6sYI4CjoJ:web.mit.edu/esd.83/www/notebook/Systems%2520Analysis.doc +&hl=en&gl=us&pid=bl&srcid=ADGEESh7EN0V5R8o9riakMCiqg-Ma8 i81tlo0ELxuapqphzvwsSBwuuaHnBSNX7bJbc8yFwfjano1YAKFgbd-CDDqX

UlMX1-2KlYbOvOgM4X-ZK8zPrzIt-nLrP9SLHQ-n3_a432nOv1&sig=AHIEt
bQ47SzlYePjRyYBShlsKrwiQ-rEBA.

84. Weber, *Economy and Society*, 1,155.

85. Ibid., 1,156.

86. Marcus Vitruvius Pollio, *The Ten Books on Architecture* (New York: Dover Publications, 1960).

87. David Williams, "Mass-Produced Chinese Pre-Han Bronze Crossbow Triggers: Unparalleled Manufacturing Technology in the Ancient World," *Arms & Armor* 5, no. 2 (October 2008): 142–53.

CHAPTER 2: WAR AND TECHNOLOGICAL PROGRESS

1. William H. McNeill, *The Pursuit of Power* (Chicago: University of Chicago Press, 1982), 44–45.

2. Ibid., 45.

3. Jared Diamond, *Guns, Germs and Steel: The Fates of Human Societies* (New York: Norton, 1999), 75.

4. McNeill, *Pursuit of Power*, 81.

5. Samuel E. Finer, "State and Nation-Building in Europe: The Role of the Military," in Charles Tilly, ed., *The Formation of National States in Western Europe* (Princeton: Princeton University Press, 1975), 105.

6. Douglas E. Streusand, *Islamic Gunpowder Empires: Ottomans, Safavids and Mughals* (Boulder, CO: Westview Press, 2010).

7. Finer, "State and Nation Building," 107.

8. David Arnold, *Science, Technology and Medicine in Colonial India* (Cambridge: Cambridge University Press, 2000), 106.

9. Ibid., 108.

10. Ibid., 110.

11. Clive Dewey, "Some Consequences of Military Expenditure in British India: The Case of the Upper Sind Sugar Doab, 1849–1947," in Clive Dewey, ed., *Arrested Development in India: The Historical Dimension* (Riverdale, MD: Manohar Publishers, 1988), 143.

12. Alexander Werth, *Russia at War: 1941–1945* (New York: E. P. Dutton, 1964), 426.

13. *Reuters*, "Illicit Israeli Military Technology Transfers Continued amidst US State Department Infighting-Audit," November 23, 2011, http://www.reuters.com/article/2011/11/23/idUS142969+23-Nov-2011+PRN20111123.

14. Dan Senor and Saul Singer, *Start-Up Nation* (New York: Hachette Books, 2009).

15. Michael Birnbaum and Joby Warrick, "German Factory Yields an Iran Mystery," *Washington Post*, April 16, 2013.

16. McNeill, *Pursuit of Power*, 241.

17. Michael C. Horowitz, *The Diffusion of Military Power* (Princeton: Princeton University Press, 2010), 134.

18. McNeill, *Pursuit of Power*, 241.

19. Horowitz, *Diffusion of Military Power*, 151.

20. Ibid., 162.

21. Mary Habeck, *Storm of Steel* (Ithaca, NY: Cornell University Press, 2003).

22. Sari Horwitz, "United Technologies Acknowledges Coverup of Sale of Military Software to China," *Washington Post*, June 28, 2012, http://articles.washingtonpost.com/2012-06-28/world/35461534_1_pratt-whitney-canada-z-10-z10.

23. *Defense News*, April 23, 2012, http://www.defensenews.com/article/20120423/DEFREG02/304230009/Brazil-Wants-U-S-Military-Technology-Transfer-Restrictions-Lifted.

24. *UPI*, March 26, 2013, http://www.upi.com/Science_News/Technology/2013/03/26/US-is-leading-espionage-target/UPI-95491364298755/.

25. Walter Hickey, "14 Brazen Examples of Iranian Agents Stealing Technology from the US," *Business Insider*, July 16, 2012, http://www.businessinsider.com/14-brazen-examples-of-iranian-agents-stealing-technology-from-america-2012-7.

26. Ariana Eunjung Cha and Ellen Nakashima, "Google China Cyberattack Part of Vast Espionage Campaign, Experts Say," *Washington Post*, January14, 2010, http://www.washingtonpost.com/wp-dyn/content/article/2010/01/13/AR2010011300359.html?sid=ST2010011300360.

27. Gordon Fraser, *The Quantum Exodus* (New York: Oxford University Press, 2012).

28. P. W. Singer, *Wired for War* (New York: Penguin, 2009).

CHAPTER 3: WHY WAR MITIGATES GOVERNMENTAL BRUTALITY

1. Mao Zedong, "On Contradiction," http://www.marxists.org/reference/archive/mao/selected-works/volume-1/mswv1_17.htm.

2. Pieter Spierenburg, "The Body and the State," in Norval Morris and David J. Rothman, *The Oxford History of the Prison: The Practice of Punishment in Western Society* (New York: Oxford University Press, 1995), 48.

3. Benjamin Ginsberg, "Force and Governance," in *The Value of Violence* (Amherst, NY: Prometheus Books, 2013).

4. Khaled Fahmy, "The Nation and Its Deserters: Conscription in Mehmed Ali's Egypt," in Erik J. Zurcher, ed., *Arming the State: Military Conscription in the Middle East and Central Asia 1775–1925* (London: I. B. Tauris, 1999), 59–78.

5. Nicoletta F. Gullace, *The Blood of Our Sons: Men, Women and the*

Renegotiation of British Citizenship during the Great War (New York: Palgrave Macmillan, 2002).

6. Martin van Creveld, *Supplying War*, 2nd ed. (New York: Cambridge University Press, 2004).

7. Samuel Finer, "State and Nation-Building in Europe: The Role of the Military," in Charles Tilly, ed., *The Formation of National States in Western Europe* (Princeton: Princeton University Press, 1975), 84–163.

8. Ruth O'Brien, "Taking the Conservative State Seriously: Statebuilding and Restrictive Labor Practices in Postwar America," *Journal of Labor Studies* 21 (Winter, 1997): 61.

9. Richard Bensel, *Yankee Leviathan: The Origins of Central State Authority in America, 1859–1877* (New York: Cambridge University Press, 1990), 248.

10. Ellis Paxson Oberholtzer, *Jay Cooke: Financier of the Civil War* (Philadelphia: Jacobs, 1907).

11. Eric L. McKitrick, "Party Politics and the Union and Confederate War Efforts," in *The American Party Systems: Stages of Political Development*, ed. William N. Chambers and Walter Dean Burnham, 2nd ed. (New York: Oxford University Press, 1975), 147.

12. Donald R. Stabile and Jeffrey A. Cantor, *The Public Debt of the United States: An Historical Perspective, 1775–1990* (New York: Praeger, 1990), 79.

13. Richard Overy, *Russia's War: A History of the Soviet Effort, 1941–1945* (New York: Penguin, 1998), 155.

14. Theda Skocpol, Ziad Munson, Andrew Karch, and Bayliss Camp, "Patriotic Partnerships: Why Great Wars Nourish American Civic Voluntarism," in *Shaped by War and Trade: International Influences on American Political Development*, ed. Ira Katznelson and Martin Shefter (Princeton: Princeton University Press, 2002), 134.

15. Philip M. Taylor, *Munitions of the Mind: A History of Propaganda from the Ancient World to the Present Day*, 3rd ed. (Manchester, UK: Manchester University Press, 2003), 31.

16. Kautilya, *The Arthashastra*, ed. and trans. L. N. Rangarajan (New York: Penguin, 1997), 13.1:7–10.

17. Taylor, *Munitions of the Mind*, 115.

18. Ibid.

19. Thomas Paine, *The Crisis*, December 23, 1776, http://www.ushistory.org/paine/crisis/c-01.htm.

20. Taylor, *Munitions of the Mind*, 150.

21. Ibid., 154.

22. Quoted in ibid., 155.

23. George Creel, *How We Advertised America* (New York: Harper & Brothers, 1920). Quoted in Frederick Irion, *Public Opinion and Propaganda* (New York: Crowell, 1952), 414.

24. Chester Bowles, *Promises to Keep* (New York: Harper & Row, 1971), 93.

25. Taylor, *Munitions of the Mind*, 216.

26. Susan A. Brewer, *Why America Fights: Patriotism and War Propaganda from the Philippines to Iraq* (New York: Oxford University Press, 2009), 92.

27. Ibid., 113.

28. Clayton R. Koppes and Gregory D. Black, *Hollywood Goes to War: How Politics, Profits and Propaganda Shaped World War II Movies* (Berkeley: University of California Press, 1990), 103.

29. Ibid., 59.

30. Allan M. Winkler, *The Politics of Propaganda: The Office of War Information, 1942–1945* (New Haven, CT: Yale University Press, 1978), 56.

31. Ibid., 61.

32. Koppes and Black, *Hollywood*, 66.

33. Bosley Crowther, "The World at War (1942)," *New York Times*, September 4, 1942, http://movies.nytimes.com/movie/review?res=9900E3D91E3CE33BBC4C53DFBF668389659EDE.

34. Steven A. Bank, Kirk J. Stark, and Joseph J Thorndike, *War and Taxes* (Washington, DC: Urban Institute, 2008), 98.

35. Carolyn Jones, "Mass-Based Income Taxation: Creating a Taxpaying Culture, 1940–1952," in *Funding the Modern American State, 1941–1995: The Rise and Fall of the Era of Easy Finance*, ed. W. Elliott Brownlee (New York: Cambridge University Press, 1996), 107–8.

36. Ibid.

37. John Bush Jones, *The Songs That Fought the War: Popular Music and the Home Front, 1939–1945* (Waltham, MA: Brandeis University Press), 2006.

38. Quoted in Lawrence R. Samuel, *Pledging Allegiance: American Identity and the Bond Drive of World War II* (Washington, DC: Smithsonian Institution, 1997), 16.

39. Adam J. Berinsky, *In Time of War: Understanding American Public Opinion from World War II to Iraq* (Chicago: University of Chicago Press, 2009).

40. Overy, *Russia's War*, 161.

41. Roger R. Reese, *Why Stalin's Soldiers Fought: The Red Army's Military Effectiveness in World War II* (Lawrence: University Press of Kansas, 2011), 177.

42. Alexander Werth, *Russia at War* (New York: Discus, 1970), 410–12.

43. Amnon Sella, *The Value of Human Life in Soviet Warfare* (New York: Routledge, 1992), 153.

44. Roger Reese, *The Soviet Military Experience: A History of the Soviet Army, 1917–1991* (New York: Routledge, 2000).

45. Overy, *Russia's War*, 162.

46. Jay Leyda, *Kino: A History of the Russian and Soviet Film*, 3rd ed. (Princeton: Princeton University Press, 1983), 379.

47. Ibid., 377.

48. Peter Kenez, *Cinema and Soviet Society: From the Revolution to the Death of Stalin* (London: I. B. Tauris, 2009), 177.

49. Quoted in Catherine Merridale, *Ivan's War: Life and Death in the Red Army, 1939–1945* (New York: Metropolitan Books, 2006), 183.

50. Ben Fritz, Bryan Keefer, and Brendan Nyhan, *All the President's Spin* (New York: Touchstone, 2004), 252–53.

51. Ibid., 357.

52. Bruce D. Porter, *War and the Rise of the State* (New York: Free Press, 1994), 180.

53. Ibid., 183.

54. Ibid., 184.

55. Gregory J. Kasza, "War and Welfare Policy in Japan," *Journal of Asian Studies* 2 (May 2002): 417–35.

56. Goran Therborn, "The Rule of Capitalism and the Rise of Democracy," *New Left Review* 103 (May 1977): 3–41.

57. Catherine Lyle Cleverdon, *The Woman Suffrage Movement in Canada* (Toronto: University of Toronto Press, 1950).

58. Chilton Williamson, *American Suffrage from Property to Democracy, 1760–1860* (Princeton: Princeton University Press, 1960).

59. *The Hornet* 1, no. 6 (1802).

60. *Continental Journal*, January 9, 1777.

61. Williamson, *American Suffrage*, 133.

62. Ibid., 141.

63. Christian G. Samito, *Becoming American under Fire* (Ithaca, NY: Cornell University Press, 2009).

CHAPTER 4: WAR AND ECONOMIC PROGRESS

1. Michael Beckley, "Economic Development and Military Effectiveness," *Journal of Strategic Studies* 33, no. 1 (2010): 43–79.

2. Daron Acemoglu and James A. Robinson, "Who's Afraid of Economic Development?" *Reuters*, March 15, 2012, http://blogs.reuters.com/why-nations-fail/2012/03/15/whos-afraid-of-economic-development/.

3. Paul Kennedy, *The Rise and Fall of the Great Powers* (New York: Random House, 1987), 77.

4. Scott B. MacDonald and Albert Gastmann, *A History of Credit and Power in the Western World* (New Brunswick, NJ: Transaction Publishers, 2001), 131.

5. Mark Kishlansky, *A Monarchy Transformed: Britain, 1603–1714* (New York: Penguin Books, 1977), 340.

6. Carl Wennerlind, *Casualties of Credit: The English Financial Revolution, 1620–1720* (Cambridge, MA: Harvard University Press, 2011), 109.

7. Douglass C. North and Robert Paul Thomas, *The Rise of the Western World* (Cambridge: Cambridge University Press, 1973), 155.

8. Wennerlind, *Casualties of Credit*, 110.

9. John Brewer, *The Sinews of Power: War, Money and the English State, 1688–1783* (New York: Knopf, 1989), 88.

10. Ibid., 94.

11. William H. McNeill, *The Pursuit of Power* (Chicago: University of Chicago Press, 1982),178.

12. Franklin Allen et al., "How Important Historically Were Financial Systems for Growth in the UK, US, Germany, and Japan?" *World Bank Project on Financial Structure*, October 25, 2010, http://fic.wharton.upenn.edu/fic/papers/10/10-27.PDF.

13. McNeill, *Pursuit of Power*, 181.

14. Ibid., 211.

15. Ibid., 175.

16. Ibid., 176.

17. Ibid., 183.

18. Richard Bonney, "The Rise of the Fiscal State in France, 1500–1914," in Bartolomé Yun-Casalilla and Patrick K. O'Brien, *The Rise of Fiscal States: A Global History 1500–1814* (New York: Cambridge University Press, 2012), 98.

19. MacDonald and Gastmann, *History of Credit*, 160.

20. McNeill, *Pursuit of Power*, 227.

21. Allen et al., "How Important," 33.

22. Kennedy, *Rise and Fall*, 212.

23. Ibid., 211.

24. Richard Franklin Bensel, *Yankee Leviathan: The Origins of Central State Authority in America, 1859–1877* (New York: Cambridge University Press, 1990), 248.

25. John F. Witte, "The Income Tax through World War I," in *The Politics and Development of the Federal Income Tax* (Madison: University of Wisconsin Press, 1985).

26. Margaret Myers, *A Financial History of the United States* (New York: Columbia University Press, 1970), 160–62.

27. Ellis Paxson Oberholtzer, *Jay Cooke: Financier of the Civil War* (Philadelphia: Jacobs, 1907).

28. Eric L. McKitrick, "Party Politics and the Union and Confederate War Efforts," in *The American Party Systems*, ed. William Nisbett Chambers and Walter Dean Burnham, 2nd ed. (New York: Oxford University Press, 1975), 147.

29. Irwin Unger, *The Greenback Era: A Social and Political History of American Finance, 1865–1879* (Princeton: Princeton University Press, 1964). Also, Robert Sharkey, *Money, Class and Party: An Economic History of Civil War and Reconstruction* (Baltimore: Johns Hopkins University Press, 1959).

30. Bensel, *Yankee Leviathan*, 252–53.

31. Bensel, "Legislation, the Republican Party, and Finance Capital during Reconstruction," in ibid. Also, Unger, *Greenback Era*, and Sharkey, *Money, Class and Party*.

32. Allen et al., "How Important," 34.

33. Beckley, "Economic Development," 1.

34. Ibid., 7.

35. Kennedy, *Rise and Fall*, 51.

36. A. G. Hopkins, "The Victorians and Africa: A Reconsideration of the Occupation of Egypt, 1882," *Journal of African History* 27, no. 2 (1986): 372.

37. Correlli Barnett, *The Audit of War* (London: Macmillan, 1986).

38. Kennedy, *Rise and Fall*, xvi.

39. Benjamin Ginsberg, "America: A Tough Nation," in *The Value of Violence* (Amherst, NY: Prometheus Books, 2013).

40. Alexander Hamilton and James Madison, *Letters of Pacificus and Helvidius* (New York: Scholars Facsimiles and Reprints, 1999).

41. Ira Katznelson, "Flexible Capacity: The Military and Early American Statebuilding," in *Shaped by War and Trade: International Influences on American Political Development*, ed. Ira Katznelson and Martin Shefter (Princeton: Princeton University Press, 2002), 82–110.

42. Theda Skocpol et al., "Patriotic Partnerships: Why Great Wars Nourished American Civic Voluntarism," in ibid., 143–80.

43. Michael D. Pearlman, *Warmaking and American Democracy* (Lawrence: University Press of Kansas, 1999), 57.

44. Chilton Williamson, *American Suffrage from Property to Democracy, 1760–1860* (Princeton: Princeton University Press, 1960).

45. Benjamin Ginsberg, *The Consequences of Consent* (New York: Random House, 1982).

46. Eric Foner, *Free Soil, Free Labor, Free Men: The Ideology of the Republican Party before the Civil War* (New York: Oxford University Press, 1970).

47. Iver Bernstein, *The New York City Draft Riots* (New York: Oxford University Press, 1997).

48. Jack F. Leach, *Conscription in the United States* (Rutland, VT: Charles E. Tuttle, 1952), 296.

49. David M. Kennedy, *Over Here: The First World War and American Society* (New York: Oxford University Press, 1986), 144–67.

50. Stephen Kohn, *Jailed for Peace* (Westport, CT: Greenwood, 1986).

51. Kennedy, *Over Here*, 144–67.

52. Martin Shefter, *Political Parties and the State* (Princeton: Princeton University Press, 1994), 88–91.

53. For a discussion of *postmaterial* politics, see Jeffrey M. Berry, *The New Liberalism* (Washington, DC: Brookings, 1999).

54. Herbert D. A. Donovan, *The Barnburners* (New York: New York University Press, 1925).

55. George L. Mayer, *The Republican Party, 1854–1966* (New York: Oxford University Press, 1967), 71.

56. Ibid., 161.

57. Howard Jones, *Crucible of Power* (Wilmington, DE: SR Books, 2001), 103–5.

58. Senator Hiram Johnson, quoted in Mayer, *Republican Party*, 354.

59. Mayer, *Republican Party*, 353.

60. Ellen Schrecker, *Many Are the Crimes* (Boston: Little, Brown, 1998).

61. Herbert Shapiro, "The Vietnam War and the American Civil Rights Movement," in *The Vietnam Antiwar Movement*, ed. Walter Hixson (New York: Garland, 2000), 71–95.

62. Benjamin Ginsberg and Martin Shefter, *Politics by Other Means*, 3rd ed. (New York: Norton, 2002), 91.

63. Robert D. Johnson, "The Origins of Dissent: Senate Liberals and Vietnam," in Hixson, *Vietnam Antiwar*, 151–275.

64. Scott Gartner, Gary Segura, and Michael Wilkening, "Local Losses and Individual Attitudes toward the Vietnam War," in ibid., 193–218.

65. Bartholomew Sparrow, "Limited Wars and the Attenuation of the State," in Katznelson and Shefter, *Shaped by War*, 277–78.

66. Allan R. Millett and Peter Maslowski, "American Defense Policy for Extended Deterrence and Containment: 1953–1965," in *For the Common Defense* (New York: Free Press, 1964).

67. Allan R. Millett, *Semper Fidelis: The History of the United States Marine Corps* (New York: Free Press, 1991), 292–96.

68. Millett and Maslowski, "American Defense Policy," 366.

69. John P. Burke, *The Institutional Presidency*, 2nd ed. (Baltimore: Johns Hopkins University Press, 2000), 37–40.

70. Joel R. Paul, "The Geopolitical Constitution: Executive Expediency and Executive Agreements," *University of California Law Review* 86 (July 1998): 713–14.

71. Ibid., 720–21.

72. Ibid. Also, Louis Fisher, *The Politics of Shared Power: Congress and the Executive* (College Station: Texas A&M University Press), 190–91.

73. Harold W. Stanley and Richard Niemi, *Vital Statistics on American Politics, 2001–2002* (Washington, DC: Congressional Quarterly, 2001), 334.

74. John C. Yoo, "Laws as Treaties? The Constitutionality of Congressional-Executive Agreements," *University of Michigan Law Review* 99 (February 2001): 757.

75. Judith Goldstein, "International Forces and Domestic Politics: Trade Policy and Institution Building in the United States," in Katznelson and Shefter, *Shaped by War*, 214–21.

76. Phillip J. Cooper, *By Order of the President: The Use and Abuse of Executive Direct Action* (Lawrence: University of Kansas Press), 144.

77. Ibid., 158.

78. Rhodri Jeffreys-Jones, *The CIA and American Democracy*, 3rd ed. (Yale University Press, 2003) 55–56.

79. Arthur M. Schlesinger Jr., *The Imperial Presidency* (New York: Houghton-Mifflin, 1973), 167.

80. Keith Whittington and Daniel P. Carpenter, "Executive Power in Amer-

ican Institutional Development," *Perspectives on Politics* 1, no. 3 (September, 2003): 495–513.

81. Ibid., 505–6.

82. Robert J. Donovan, *Conflict and Crisis: The Presidency of Harry S. Truman, 1945–1948* (New York: W. W. Norton, 1977), 296–97.

83. Athan Theoharis, ed., *The Truman Presidency: The Origins of the Imperial Presidency and the National Security State* (Stanfordville, NY: E. M. Coleman, 1979), 257–61.

84. Schlesinger, "The Secrecy System," in *Imperial Presidency.*

85. George Q. Flynn, *The Draft, 1940–1973* (Lawrence: University Press of Kansas, 1993), 265.

86. Douglas Bandow, "Fixing What Ain't Broke: The Renewed Call for Conscription," *Policy Analysis* 351 (August 31, 1999): 2.

87. Charles B. Rangel, "Bring Back the Draft," *New York Times*, December 31, 2002, A21.

88. Thomas E. Ricks, "Ready," in *Making the Corps* (New York: Simon & Schuster, 1997).

89. Ole R. Holsti, "Of Chasms and Convergences: Attitudes and Beliefs of Civilians and Military Elites at the Start of a New Millennium," in Peter D. Feaver and Richard H. Kohn, *Soldiers and Civilians* (Cambridge, MA: MIT Press, 2001), 15–100.

90. Jonathan Turley, "The Military Pocket Republic," *Northwestern University Law Review* 97 (Fall 2002): 1.

91. David M. Halbfinger and Steven A. Holmes, "Military Mirrors a Working-Class America," *New York Times*, March 30, 2003, 1. Also, David Shiflett, "An Army That Drawls: Johnny Reb Goes to Iraq and Everywhere Else," *National Review*, May 5, 2003, 29–30.

92. Vernon Loeb, "In Iraq, Pace of US Casualties Has Accelerated," *Washington Post*, December 28, 2003, 1.

93. Lawrence F. Kaplan, "Willpower: Why the Public Can Stomach Casualties in Iraq," *New Republic*, September 8, 2003, 19–22.

94. Dana Priest, "Private Guards Repel Attack on US Headquarters," *New York Times*, April 6, 2004, 1.

95. James Dao, "Private Guards Take Big Risks, for Right Price," *New York Times*, April 2, 2004, 1.

96. Dana Priest and Mary Pat Flaherty, "Under Fire, Security Firms Form an Alliance," *Washington Post*, April 8, 2004, 1.

97. P. W. Singer, *Corporate Warriors: The Rise of the Privatized Military Industry* (Ithaca, NY: Cornell University Press, 1977), 207.

98. Ibid., 208.

99. Ibid., 210–11.

100. Geoffrey Perret, *A Country Made by War* (New York: Random House, 1989), 305–8.

101. George Friedman and Meredith Friedman, *The Future of War: Power,*

Technology, and American World Dominance in the 21st Century (New York: St. Martin's, 1996).

102. Matthew Brzezinski, "The Unmanned Army," *New York Times Magazine*, April 20, 2003, 38–80.

103. MacGregor Knox and Williamson Murray, eds., *The Dynamics of Military Revolution, 1300–2050* (New York: Cambridge University Press, 2001), 188–92.

104. Christopher Palmeri, "A Predator That Preys on Hawks?" *Business Week*, February 17, 2003, 78.

CHAPTER 5: BEATING SWORDS INTO MALIGN PLOWSHARES

1. Charles Tilly, "Reflections on the History of European State Building," in *The Formation of National States in Western Europe*, ed. Charles Tilly (Princeton: Princeton University Press, 1975), 3–83.

2. Robert Higgs, *Crisis and Leviathan: Critical Episodes in the Growth of American Government* (New York: Oxford University Press, 1987).

3. Herbert O. Yardley, *The American Black Chamber* (Indianapolis, IN: Bobbs-Merrill, 1931).

4. James Bamford, "They Know Much More Than You Think," *New York Review*, August 15, 2013, 4–8.

5. Jennifer Bachner, Katherine Wagner Hill, and Benjamin Ginsberg, eds., *Analytics, Policy and Governance* (Baltimore: Johns Hopkins University Press, 2014).

6. Ellen Nakashima, "Skepticism Deepens about NSA Program," *Washington Post*, August1, 2013, 1.

7. Daniel J. Solove, *Nothing to Hide: The False Tradeoff between Privacy and Security* (New Haven: Yale University Press, 2011).

8. Ibid.

9. Jean Hampton, *Hobbes and the Social Contract Tradition* (New York: Cambridge University Press, 1988), 46. Hampton indicates that this quote is 'after Bacon,' whom Hobbes served as a secretary.

10. Matthew Dillon and Lynda Garland, eds., *Ancient Greece: Social and Historical Documents from Archaic Times to the Death of Alexander* (New York: Rutledge, 2010), 18.

11. Thomas P. Crocker, "The Political Fourth Amendment," *Washington University Law Review* 88, no. 2 (2010): 347.

12. 367 US 717 (1961).

13. Herring v. United States, 555 US 135 (2009).

14. Curt Gentry, "The Man Who Came to Dinner," in *J. Edgar Hoover: The Man and the Secrets* (New York: W. W. Norton, 2001).

15. Ibid., 782.

16. Ronald Kessler, *The Bureau* (New York: St. Martin's, 2003), 137.

17. Gentry, "Listen," in *J. Edgar Hoover*.

18. Ibid., 725.

19. Quoted in Kessler, *Bureau*, 157.

20. Seymour Hersh, "Huge CIA Operation Reported in US against Antiwar Forces, Other Dissidents in Nixon Years," *New York Times*, December 22, 1974, 1.

21. James Bamford, *The Shadow Factory* (New York: Anchor, 2009).

22. Quoted in Solove, *Nothing to Hide*, 10.

23. James Bamford, "The Agency That Could Be Big Brother," *New York Times*, December 25, 2005, http://www.nytimes.com/2005/12/25/weekin review/25bamford.html?pagewanted=all&_r=0.

24. "Foreign Intelligence Surveillance Act Court Orders 1979–2012," Electronic Privacy Information Center, http://epic.org/privacy/wiretap/stats/fisa_stats .html.

25. Bamford, "They Know Much More," 4.

26. Ibid.

27. Siobhan Gorman and Jennifer Valentino DeVries, "HSA Reaches Deep into US to Spy on Net: Fresh Details Show Programs Cover 75% of Nation's Traffic, Can Snare Emails," *Wall Street Journal*, August 21, 2013, A8.

28. Ellen Nakashima, "NSA Collected Thousands of Domestic E-mails," *Washington Post*, August 22, 2013, 1.

29. Barton Gellman, "Audit: NSA Repeatedly Broke Privacy Rules," *Washington Post*, August 16, 2013, 1.

30. Carol D. Leonnig, "Surveillance Judge Says Court Relies on Government to Report Its Own Actions," *Washington Post* August 16, 2013, 1.

31. James Madison, *The Federalist*, No. 51.

32. Bamford, "They Know Much More," 6.

33. New York Times v. United States, 403 US (1971).

34. Gabriel Schoenfeld, "Black-Letter Law," in *Necessary Secrets: National Security, The Media and the Rule of Law* (New York: Norton, 2010).

35. Kenneth Jost, "Government Secrecy," *CQResearcher*, December 2, 2005, 1009.

36. Harold C. Relyea, "Government Secrecy: Policy Depths and Dimensions," *Government Information Quarterly* 20 (2003): 395–418.

37. 11 Stat. 60 (1857).

38. Relyea, *Government Secrecy*, 397.

39. Ibid., 398.

40. Ibid., 400.

41. "2011 Secrecy Report," OpenTheGovernment.org, 2012.

42. National Archives and Records Administration, "Bi-annual Report on Operations of the National Declassification Center. Reporting Period: July 1, 2012–December 31, 2012," http://www.archives.gov/declassification/ndc/reports/ 2012-biannual-july-december.pdf.

43. Nate Jones, "Declassification-as-Usual Mindset Responsible for the National Declassification Center's Languid Pace," National Security Archive, February 1, 2012, http://nsarchive.wordpress.com/2012/02/01/declassification-as-usual-mindset-responsible-for-the-national-declassifcation-centers-lanugid-pace/.

44. Matthew M. Aid, "Declassification in Reverse: The US Intelligence Community's Secret Historical Document Reclassification Program," National Security Archive, February 21, 2006, http://www2.gwu.edu/~nsarchiv/NSAEBB/NSAEBB179/.

45. Schoenfeld, *Necessary Secrets*, 175.

46. Ibid., 185.

47. Peter Walker, "Bradley Manning Trial: What We Know from the Leaked WikiLeaks Documents," *Guardian*, July 30, 2013, http://www.theguardian.com/world/2013/jul/30/bradley-manning-wikileaks-revelations.

48. Greg Mitchell, "A Long List of What We Know Thanks to Private Manning," *Nation*, August 23, 2013, http://www.thenation.com/blog/175879/long-list-what-we-know-thanks-private-manning#axzz2cvltDsQm.

49. Aid, "Declassification in Reverse."

50. Kate Martin, "Congressional Access to Classified National Security Information," *Center for National Security Studies*, March 2007.

51. Dan Nosowitz, "Congress Was Not Really Briefed on PRISM," *Popular Science*, June 12, 2013, http://www.popsci.com/technology/article/2013-06/obama-said-all-congress-was-briefed-prism-nonsense.

52. Ryan Devereaux, "Is Obama's Use of State Secrets Privilege the New Normal?" *Nation*, September, 2010, http://www.thenation.com/article/155080/obamas-use-state-secrets-privilege-new-normal#axzz2cWH5ZitX.

53. Archibald Cox, "Executive Privilege," *University of Pennsylvania Law Review* 122 (1974): 1383.

54. Raoul Berger, *Executive Privilege* (Cambridge: Harvard University Press, 1974).

55. US v. Burr, 25 F. Cas. 187 (1807).

56. Jeffrey P. Carlin, "Walker v. Cheney: Politics, Posturing and Executive Privilege," *Southern California Law Review* 76, no. 235 (November 2002): 245.

57. 433 US 425 (1977).

58. The appeals court, however, developed a procedure that gave the subcommittee limited access to documents under court supervision. 551 F.2nd 384 (DC Cir. 1976).

59. 556 F. Supp. 150 (DDC 1983). As in the AT&T case, the court developed a procedure providing limited access to the contested documents.

60. See, for example, Bareford v. General Dynamics Corp., 973 F.2nd 1138 (5th Cir. 1992).

61. See, *In re Sealed Case*, 121 F.3rd 729 (D.C. Cir. 1997).

62. 124 S.Ct.1391 (2004).

63. Relyea, "Government Secrecy," 402.

64. Dana Milbank, "The Price of Whistleblowing," *Washington Post*, August 21, 2013, A17.

65. Christopher C. Horner, *The Liberal War on Transparency: Confessions of a Freedom of Information Criminal* (New York: Threshold Editions, 2012).

66. "US Secret Service Agents' Alleged Scandals since 2004 Revealed," *Guardian*, June 15, 2012, http://www.theguardian.com/world/2012/jun/15/us -secret-service-scandals-revealed.

67. Jost, "Government Secrecy," 1011.

68. *Bloomberg News*, "Testing Obama's Promise of Government Transparency," September 27, 2012, http://go.bloomberg.com/multimedia/bloomberg -checks-obama-transparency/.

CONCLUSION

1. Thomas Hobbes, *Leviathan*, ed. Ian Shapiro (New Haven: Yale University Press, 2010).

2. Immanuel Kant, "Perpetual Peace: A Philosophical Sketch," http://www.mtholyoke.edu/acad/intrel/kant/kant1.htm.

3. Joshua S. Goldstein, *Winning the War on War* (New York: Penguin, 2012).

4. Bruce Russett, *Grasping the Democratic Peace* (Princeton: Princeton University Press, 1994).

5. Thomas Hobbes, *Leviathan*, ed. Michael Oakeshott (New York: Collier, 1962), 132.

6. Charles D. Tarleton, "The Despotical Doctrine of Hobbes, Part II: Aspects of the Textual Substructure of Tyranny in Leviathan," *History of Political Thought* 23, no.1 (Spring 2002): 82.

7. Hobbes, *Leviathan*, 141.

8. James Lee Ray: "Wars between Democracies: Rare, or Nonexistent?" *International Interactions* 18, no. 3 (February 1993). Also, Joanne Gowa, *Ballots and Bullets: The Elusive Democratic Peace* (Princeton: Princeton University Press, 1999), and Sebastian Rosato, "The Flawed Logic of Democratic Peace Theory," *American Political Science Review* 97 (2003): 585–602.

9. Charles Tilly, "War Making and State Making as Organized Crime," in *Bringing the State Back In*, ed. Peter Evans, Dietrich Rueschmeyer, and Theda Skocpol (Cambridge: Harvard University Press, 1985), 169–86.

10. Geoffrey Perret, *A Country Made by War* (New York: Vintage, 1990).

11. Tom Brokaw, *The Greatest Generation* (New York: Random House, 2004).

12. Robert MacKay, *Half the Battle: Civilian Morale in Britain during the Second World War* (Manchester: Manchester University Press, 2002), 248.

13. Jonathan Simon, *Governing through Crime: How the War on Crime Transformed American Democracy and Created a Culture of Fear* (New York: Oxford University Press, 2007), 106–10.

14. John S. Baker, "Jurisdictional and Separation of Powers Strategies to Limit the Expansion of Federal Crimes," *American University Law Review* 54 (February 2005): 548.

15. Sara Sun Beale, "From Morals and Mattress Tags to Overfederalization," *American University Law Review* 54 (February 2005): 747.

16. US v. Hanousek, 176 F. 3rd 116 (9th Cir. 1999).

17. Morisette v. US, 342 US 246 (1952).

18. John Hasnas, "Ethics and the Problem of White Collar Crime" (February 2005): 606.

19. Memorandum by Larry Thompson, Deputy Attorney General, to Heads of Departments and US Attorneys, available at http://www.usdoj.gov/dag/cftf/corporate_guidelines.htm.

20. "The McNulty Memorandum," *Wall Street Journal*, December 13, 2006, A18.

21. Eric Luna, "The Overcriminalization Phenomenon," *American University Law Review* 54 (February 2005).

INDEX